STUDIES IN WELSH HISTORY

Editors

RALPH A. GRIFFITHS   CHRIS WILLIAMS
ERYN M. WHITE

18

NORTH WALES MINERS

A FRAGILE UNITY, 1945–1996

NORTH WALES MINERS

A FRAGILE UNITY, 1945–1996

by

KEITH GILDART

Published on behalf of the
History and Law Committee
of the Board of Celtic Studies

UNIVERSITY OF WALES PRESS
CARDIFF
2001

© Keith Gildart, 2001

British Library Cataloguing-in-Publication Data
A catalogue record for this book is available from the British Library.

ISBN 0-7083-1706-5

Cover design by Jane Parry
Typeset at the University of Wales Press
Printed in Great Britain by Dinefwr Press, Llandybïe, Dyfed

EDITORS' FOREWORD

Since the Second World War, Welsh history has attracted considerable scholarly attention and enjoyed a vigorous popularity. Not only have the approaches, both traditional and new, to the study of history in general been successfully applied to Wales's past, but the number of scholars engaged in this enterprise has multiplied during these years. These advances have been especially marked in the University of Wales.

In order to make more widely available the conclusions of recent research, much of it of limited accessibility in postgraduate dissertations and theses, in 1977 the History and Law Committee of the Board of Celtic Studies inaugurated a new series of monographs, *Studies in Welsh History*. It was anticipated that many of the volumes would originate in research conducted in the University of Wales or under the auspices of the Board of Celtic Studies. But the series does not exclude significant contributions made by researchers in other universities and elsewhere. Its primary aim is to serve historical scholarship and to encourage the study of Welsh history. Each volume so far published has fulfilled that aim in ample measure, and it is a pleasure to welcome the most recent addition to the list.

CONTENTS

LIST OF ILLUSTRATIONS

PREFACE

This book is based on many years of thinking about working-class communities, their culture, and the politics that emerged from them in the twentieth century. Growing up on a council estate in north Wales, I was acutely aware of the importance of class divisions in Britain. A sense of 'them and us' pervaded every aspect of community life. This was most apparent in terms of education, the law and employment prospects. Large family gatherings, holidays in Blackpool, and a world that revolved around the pit, the pub and the betting shop, gave me a sense of a collective identity that I shared with other children. I soon realized that this identity was underpinned by class. To my family and others on the council estate, class was an uncomplicated term related to money and culture. It was a simple fact to all of us that the working class, 'us', had little money, while the middle and upper classes, 'them', had lavish amounts. Culturally we enjoyed popular music, action films, pubs, football and *Coronation Street*, while 'they' enjoyed opera, theatre, classical music and ballet.

There may have been divisions between and within families, but all shared similar patterns of consumption and a fear of poverty. Class was used to make sense of political events and the Labour Party was viewed as the vehicle that could transform the apparent inequalities that existed in society. In everyday discourse, there was a keen sense of who was for and against you. The Tories were clearly the enemy. Along with other children, I quickly concluded that there were things that were 'not for the likes of us', a mindset that was reinforced by the education system.

After I had been branded a failure by the local comprehensive school, a much more significant process of education began when I entered the mining industry at the age of seventeen in 1985. I had always been aware of coal, pits, miners and the link that they had to the Labour Party, but was unaware of the processes of such a history. My earliest memory is of visiting the sandpit on the yard of Parsonage colliery in Lancashire with my grandfather. I remember his tales of the General Strike and the betrayal of the miners by Jimmy Thomas. Many years later, working with Albert Davies and Walter Evans, two elderly Wrexham colliers, I was given a further insight into the psyche of the average miner and the culture of the mining community. The meal break during the shift became my unofficial classroom. The politics of the union I discovered later through three very different individuals, Les Kelly, Vic Roberts and Keith Hett. All these people along with my mother and father, who had come from a generation of coal miners, encouraged me to pursue my thirst for knowledge.

After five years underground, I had my first taste of formal higher education as a student at Northern College, Barnsley. This experience strengthened my belief in the importance of working-class education and the central role that this had played in the labour movement. After a short return to the pit, I entered the University of Manchester to study for a degree in Politics and Modern History. At Manchester, David Howell and others encouraged me to question my preconceived beliefs concerning politics in general and labour history in particular. After graduating, the University of York gave me the opportunity to pursue the doctoral research on which this book is based. The outcome of my personal journey through the village, the coal mine and the lecture hall is contained in the following pages. The book should give the reader an insight into the politics and culture of the North Wales Coalfield. I hope that it adequately illustrates the importance of labour institutions in attempting to protect workers in an increasingly hostile economic environment.

ACKNOWLEDGEMENTS

I am indebted to many individuals and institutions for assistance in enabling me to complete this book on the coal miners of north Wales. Four educational institutions have been central in providing me with the ability to undertake a serious study such as this. Firstly, the National Union of Mineworkers (North Wales Area) provided me with a second chance to pursue education by encouraging me to attend courses organized by the TUC and the national union. Secondly, Northern College in Barnsley provided me with a broad social science education that allowed me to pursue further study towards a degree. Bob Fryer, Ed Ellis and Salim Essop were instrumental in giving me confidence to make my way in the university sector. Thirdly, the University of Manchester, through my degree in Politics and Modern History, enabled me to concentrate on labour history. Professor David Howell gave me unlimited support and encouraged me to convert my interest in mining politics into study towards a doctorate. He continues to be a source of encouragement. Over the years, he has made critical suggestions concerning my work and without his guidance, the book would be a lot poorer. I should like to thank him for his help and friendship and the discussions that we continue to have regarding working-class history. Fourthly, the University of York made the research possible by providing me with a studentship and the opportunity to teach a number of courses. I should also like to thank Professor R. Merfyn Jones who examined the thesis and provided me with ideas on improving it for future publication.

This book would not exist but for the work of the Miners' Offices in Wrexham and the Flintshire County Record Office in Hawarden in preserving the records of the north Wales miners. My thanks go to Les Kelly and Rosemarie Williams at the union office in Wrexham for their interest and providing me with access to all materials. Paul Mason and Fiona Skett at the

Record Office have walked many miles in order to supply me with documents and I shall be ever grateful for their patience. I should also like to thank the staff of the following institutions: the Public Record Office, Denbighshire Record Office, National Museum of Labour History, Wrexham Library, Rhos Library, Rhyl Library, National Library of Wales, Aberystwyth, and the South Wales Miners' Archive in Swansea.

I am particularly grateful to the editors of the Studies in Welsh History series. Professor Chris Williams and Professor Ralph Griffiths provided me with insightful suggestions on improving the manuscript and had to spend many hours reading the initial drafts. I should also like to thank the University of Wales Press for giving me the opportunity to publish the book. Duncan Campbell, Ceinwen Jones and Liz Powell have provided a great service in preparing the book for publication.

The material that makes up the following pages would not have been possible without the north Wales miners. Over the last six years, I have interviewed a whole range of individuals who worked in or were associated with all the nationalized pits in the coalfield and I am grateful to everyone who has shared their memories with me. In particular, Jack Read, Colin Newell (Sailor), John Alan Jones, Jimmy Williams (Yanto), Keith Hett, Ann Hett, Sylvia Jones, Paul Parry, Heather Parry, Jack Gough, Tony Bellis, Albert Davies, Norman Jones, Eddie Lloyd, Patrick Heesom, Kieth Jones, Hugh Jones and the 'secret six'. My thanks also go to individuals involved in the north Wales Labour Party branches and miners' support groups, along with activists from the wider trade union movement. A special appreciation is also due to all my former workmates at Point of Ayr Colliery, especially Mike Green, who was my dump-truck partner and fellow radical. The people of Mostyn have been of great help through the years, especially the pint-pot philosophers in the Glan-y-Don Inn, although some will almost certainly disagree with my interpretations.

A number of individuals have protected my sanity throughout the period of the research for this book. Kirsten Windfuhr, who by now must be sick of hearing stories from the mines, has been a great source of support. I thank her for love and encouragement and for putting up with my obsession with labour history and rock music. Kevin Jones, Jason McClellan, Ed Amman, John Sanby, and Gidon Cohen have all provided me with friendship and the chance to get away from the archives. My gratitude goes out to all of them for showing an interest in my work and putting up with my occasional rants.

Lastly and most importantly I should like to make special reference to my family for being a constant source of support. My sisters Bev, Lorraine and Gill along with the wider Gildart family, have always been there when needed. My parents Brian and Sheila Gildart have encouraged me at every stage to pursue my education and research interests; without them this book would not exist and I would now probably be just another unemployed coal miner. I dedicate this book to both of them.

ABBREVIATIONS

AEC	Area Executive Committee
ASLEF	Associated Society of Locomotive Engineers and Firemen
BACM	British Association of Colliery Management
BICC	British Insulated Calendar's Cables
CLP	Constituency Labour Party
CND	Campaign for Nuclear Disarmament
COSA	Colliery Officials and Staffs Association
CP	Communist Party
CRO	Clwyd Record Office
DCLP	Delyn Constituency Labour Party
ERM	Exchange Rate Mechanism
ERS	Electoral Reform Society
GLC	Greater London Council
ILP	Independent Labour Party
IMO	International Miners' Organization
ISTC	Iron and Steel Trades Federation
LRC	Labour Representation Committee
MFGB	Mineworkers' Federation of Great Britain
MSG	Miners' Support Group
NACODS	National Association of Colliery Overmen, Deputies and Shotfirers
NALGO	National and Local Government Officers' Association
NCB	National Coal Board
NEC	National Executive Committee
NPLA	National Power Loading Agreement
NUM	National Union of Mineworkers
NUPE	National Union of Public Employees
NUR	National Union of Railwaymen
NWBCMA	North Wales and Border Counties Mineworkers Association
NWCOA	North Wales Coal Owners Association
NWMA	North Wales Miners Association
PLP	Parliamentary Labour Party
POAIU	Point of Ayr Industrial Union
RMT	Rail, Maritime and Transport Union
SDF	Social Democratic Federation
SDP	Social Democratic Party

SLP	Socialist Labour Party
SWMF	South Wales Miners' Federation
T&GWU	Transport and General Workers' Union
TUC	Trades Union Congress
UCATT	Union of Construction, Allied Trades and Technicians
UDM	Union of Democratic Mineworkers
USDAW	Union of Shop, Distributive and Allied Workers
WAPC	Women Against Pit Closures
WRP	Workers Revolutionary Party

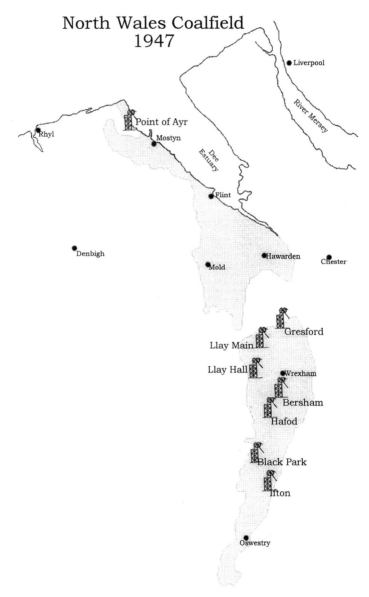

The North Wales Coalfield at the time of the nationalization of the coal industry in 1947. Note the separation of Point of Ayr from collieries in the Denbighshire coalfield, and the proximity of the coalfield to the English border.

INTRODUCTION

The complex relationship between coal, community and politics is central to the history of Wales in the nineteenth and twentieth centuries. The modern history of the country has been marked by the importance of coal as a vital energy source and this, in turn, has had an impact on British politics. In the popular consciousness of the British people, Wales is an industrial society with radical traditions. But recent decades of industrial decline have fragmented the material foundations of a society based on both collective action and the forging of a Labourist identity. As a nation, Wales has been constructed in part around the Welsh language but also by means of a collective identity, forged in coalfield communities. In terms of labour history, the chapel, the community, radical politics and a distinct industrial identity have played central roles, reverberating through the speeches of Aneurin Bevan and the songs of the male voice choirs. Images of a mining past are constructed through a lens of romantic iconography: intransigent employers, closed villages and the collective action of the workers, epitomized by the formation of the South Wales Miners' Federation (SWMF) in 1898 and the industrial conflicts of 1921 and 1926.[1]

Industrial Wales provides a rich history of mining disasters, heroic strikes and the emergence of a class of labour leaders who remained as much at home with the collier as with wealthy employers and grandees in the corridors of Parliament. Luminaries such as William Abraham (Mabon), Frank Hodges, James Griffiths and Aneurin Bevan epitomized the diverse nature of the Welsh labour leadership and its ability to transcend the barriers of class deprivation and English cultural élitism.[2] A

[1] The best book on the south Wales miners is still one that uses a popular iconography to construct a dramatic history of the coalfield and the place of the working class in it. See Hywel Francis and David Smith, *The Fed: The South Wales Miners in the Twentieth Century* (London, 1980).

[2] E. W. Evans, *Mabon (William Abraham, 1842–1922): A Study in Trade Union Leadership* (Cardiff, 1959); Frank Hodges, *My Adventures as a Labour Leader* (London, 1925); James Griffiths, *Pages from Memory* (London, 1969); Michael Foot, *Aneurin Bevan, 1897–1945* (London, 1982).

chronological account of labour in Wales is littered with such cultural and political references to coal, with the centrality of the workplace a theme running throughout the narrative. Nonetheless, the politics of the Welsh working class, and specifically of the miners, was, from the outset, contested, generating different responses to the problems of industrial society. Mabon symbolized a Liberal route to emancipation, an attempt to involve the state at specific levels in the advancement of the working class through limited social reforms. Conversely, the authors of *The Miners' Next Step*,[3] along with Arthur Cook, provided a radical critique of Lib-Labism, gradualist Labour politics and the perceived timidity of the union establishment.[4] A less celebrated tradition within south Wales colliery politics was represented by the pragmatism of Arthur Jenkins and James Griffiths.

The Tonypandy riots and the solidarity of the lockouts of 1921 and 1926 are deeply ingrained in Welsh labour historiography, leading to the construction of powerful images.[5] The role of communists such as Arthur Horner and Will Paynter and the eventual state ownership of the mines in 1947 have reinforced this teleological image of workers' struggle. These images were recreated within and beyond mining communities in the strike of 1984–5 and in the subsequent pit closure programme that reached its peak in 1992–3.[6] Little remains apart from industrial museums illustrating the importance of a mining past. Tower colliery stands as a reminder of an industrial history, producing coal for an increasingly shrinking market. In the south Wales valleys miners' institutes remain symbols that perhaps seem alien to the unemployed youths who inhabit former mining localities.

---

[3] *The Miners' Next Step* was published by a group of militant miners in the south Wales coalfield in 1912. It is widely regarded as a statement of British syndicalism and a powerful critique of the leaders of the SWMF. For an account of the development of syndicalism in south Wales, see David Egan, 'The unofficial reform committee and *The Miners' Next Step*', *Llafur: Journal of Welsh Labour History*, 2, 3 (1978), 64–80.

[4] For a detailed account of Cook and his involvement with syndicalism, see Paul Davies, *A. J. Cook* (Manchester, 1987).

[5] This is most apparent in the four-volume study of the MFGB by R. P. Arnot, *The Miners: A History of the Miners' Federation of Great Britain, 1889–1910* (London, 1949), and subsequent volumes.

[6] Ironically, a number of south Wales leaders in 1984 attempted to deconstruct these images of a militant past in order to stifle the claims of Arthur Scargill. The South Wales Area started to talk of a progressive radicalism rather than the more destructive variant espoused by the militants of Yorkshire. Hywel Francis raises this issue in his obituary of Emlyn Williams, the south Wales leader, in *Llafur: Journal of Welsh Labour History*, 7, 1 (1996), 5–7.

Coal represents a rich Welsh history that has left its mark on the national consciousness, and mining, along with rugby, choirs and a perceived social solidarity based on a notion of nationhood, still provides an image of Wales that sets the country apart from other regions of the United Kingdom. This image of Wales is a romanticized notion of the past that has been enforced by the historiography. In recent years, however, reflecting general shifts in the study of industrial workers, myths and traditions have been challenged. In labour history, studies of the working class have moved away from the straitjacket of the institutional focus. Contemporary revisions have painted a more complex picture of coal society.[7] More importantly, in Wales the dominant image has been geographically specific, leading to the development of an iconography that has been, at best, partial. The south Wales valleys have imposed a stereotypical view of the miner, the pit and the wider society. A focus on the North Wales Coalfield therefore, contributes to a more balanced picture of the Welsh working class.

Assumptions relating to the habits and political culture of the British miners can be strongly contested by moving beyond accepted images of the past. The miners of north Wales offer one means whereby the world of industrial Wales, and the complex relationships between occupation, identity, politicization, class, community and the nation state, may be re-examined.[8]

This book draws on various strands of labour historiography to emphasize the importance of both structure and agency in shaping the politics of the north Wales miners. In many ways, it is unashamedly traditional, concentrating on the trade union and the Labour Party as an expression and vehicle of working-class consciousness. Nonetheless, it breaks from the purely institutional by moving the focus beyond the workplace and into the

[7] The leading exponent of this revisionism has been Ina Zweiniger-Bargielowska, 'South Wales miners' attitudes towards nationalisation: an essay in oral history', *Llafur: Journal of Welsh Labour History*, 6, 3 (1994), 70–84.
[8] The literature on the north Wales coalfield is limited. See Emlyn Rogers, 'The development of trade unionism in the north Wales coalfield to 1914', serialized in *Transactions of the Denbighshire Historical Society*, 12–23 (1963–74); Sally Venn, 'Labour politics in north-east Wales: a study of the North Wales Miners' Association, 1898–1947' (unpublished MA thesis, University of Wales, 1994); R. Merfyn Jones, 'A note on 1926 in north Wales', *Llafur: Journal of Welsh Labour History*, 2, 2 (1977), 59–64; David Howell, 'The miners' strike of 1984–85 in north Wales', *Contemporary Wales*, 4 (1991), 67–98; G. G. Lerry, *The Collieries of Denbighshire* (Wrexham, 1968).

community and the wider society of the north Wales coalfield. Methodologically, the approach owes much to the Marxist tradition and stresses the place of economic and class relations in shaping the tensions between capital and labour. Yet, by using archival sources and oral testimony, the picture of coal society presented here alerts us to the nuances and ambiguities within working-class politics.

Central to the narrative is the relationship that developed between the miners of north Wales and Labour politics, epitomized by the ideals of the party regarding the public ownership of industry and the redistribution of wealth. For many years within British labour history, the politics of Labourism as both a political ideal and a parliamentary practice received only critical appraisal. Raphael Samuel and Gareth Stedman Jones in their perceptive piece on the subject typify the Marxist view: 'Labourism is thought of . . . not so much as an ideal type but as a deformed variant of an ideal type – that of the revolutionary party of the working class.'[9] To some Marxists, the party was a barrier to socialist politics, diluting working-class radicalism.[10] Revisionist writers have painted a more negative picture of such radicalism, regarding the party as more advanced in terms of socialism than its conservative followers in its core constituencies.[11] It is contended here that both Marxist and revisionist approaches to the Labour Party and the working class suffer from a tendency to overgeneralize that only micro-level analysis can deconstruct.

In the North Wales Coalfield, Labourism was clearly a mobilizing force for working-class advance. The Labour governments of 1945–51 provide a defining episode, ushering in the nationalization of coal and welfare reforms. The party was easily able to defeat challenges to its mining constituency from left and right, and formed a basis of unity across coalfields reaching beyond the sectional political identities of the area unions which formed the

[9] Raphael Samuel and Gareth Stedman Jones, 'The Labour Party and social democracy', in R. Samuel and G. S. Jones (eds.), *Culture, Ideology, Politics: Essays for Eric Hobsbawm* (London, 1982), p.325.

[10] This view can be found in a number of books, but the degree of scepticism with the party differs. Ralph Miliband, *Parliamentary Socialism: A Study in the Politics of Labour* (London, 1973); John Saville, *The Labour Movement in Britain* (London, 1998); Gregory Eliot, *Labourism and the English Genius: The Strange Death of Labour England* (London, 1993).

[11] Steve Fielding, Peter Thompson, and Nick Tiratsoo, *England Arise: The Labour Party and Popular Politics in 1940s Britain* (Manchester, 1995).

National Union of Mineworkers (NUM). Nonetheless, the basis of such unity had fragile foundations, exhibiting little beyond a general commitment of the miners to nationalization and the welfare state. Labourism was unable to provide forms of solidarity beyond electoral support for the party. The events of 1984–5 were to shatter any illusions of a greater working-class unity, able to transcend local identities and sectional interests.

Along with rescuing the concept of Labourism from the clutches of Marxists and revisionists, this work adds to the recent literature that has aimed to resurrect the study of labour in its broadest form. Reflecting the shifting parameters of working-class history, it explores issues of ethnicity, identity and gender, and how these patterned responses to economic and political change. In each chapter, the tensions between the national and the local are apparent. Labour history has attempted for too long to construct a cohesive canvas of a national working-class experience and consciousness. This history of the north Wales miners, it is contended, forces labour historians to be more attentive to the perils of such a project.[12]

The structure of the book is both chronological and thematic. Chapter 1 looks at developments in the coal industry and the wider north Wales labour movement in response to public ownership and electoral success after 1945. Chapter 2 examines the nature and impact of pit closures and the experience of the group of English miners who settled in the coalfield in the late 1960s. Chapter 3 surveys the dramatic strikes of 1972 and 1974 and the construction of the north Wales miners as an important faction within national union politics. Chapter 4 is dominated by the divisive strike of 1984–5 and how the drama of the dispute unfolded in the two remaining north Wales collieries. Chapter 5 charts the closure of the last mine in Wales and the political struggle that kept the national union factionalized while the British coal miner became an increasingly endangered species.

---

[12] The methodological basis and theoretical goal of labour history have been debated on both sides of the Atlantic in the pages of *Labour History Review* and *Labor History*. Nonetheless, although many academics have talked 'a good fight' about extending the boundaries of the discipline, many have retained their entrenched positions as to what they believe 'labour history' to be. See David Howell, 'Editorial', *Labour History Review*, 60, 1 (1995), 2; 'Comments' by M. Chase, S. Fielding, K. Flett and J. Halstead and D. Martin, *Labour History Review*, 60, 3 (1995), 46–53; J. Saville, 'The crisis in labour history: a further comment', *Labour History Review*, 61, 3 (1996), 322–8.

Throughout the book, previously neglected groups, individuals and traditions are uncovered, in order to reveal the complex nature of work, community and politics in the British coal industry.

Coal deposits in north Wales were extensively mined from the Middle Ages to the last decade of the twentieth century, though the coalfield was always peripheral to the major coal-producing regions such as south Wales, Lancashire, Durham and Yorkshire. North Wales had much in common with Cumberland, the Forest of Dean and Leicestershire in terms of the size of its coal deposits and its consequential representation within the Mineworkers' Federation of Great Britain (MFGB) and later the NUM. For much of the nineteenth century, colliery development was small-scale, as was the pattern of ownership. At the turn of the century, production began to increase but the number of pits declined. The last pit to be sunk in the coalfield was Llay Main, situated between Mold and Wrexham, in 1923. Before the 1921 lockout, the number of miners peaked at around 18,000, a tiny workforce when compared with that of larger producing regions.[13]

The proximity of the coalfield to England had implications for the industry economically and culturally. Coal owners in north Wales found themselves increasingly in competition with nearby English coalfields which encroached on local markets. Cultural-ly, the proximity to England had both diluted and reinforced a sense of separation. Struggles in the coalfield in the nineteenth century often focused on anti-English hostility towards colliery ownership. Nonetheless, this did not represent nationalist aspira-tion as the miners of north Wales had little contact with their counterparts in the south and retained closer links with mining unions in England.[14] Even within the coalfield, a degree of

[13] In 1910, the membership of the MFGB in Durham stood at 121,805; south Wales at 137,553; Yorkshire 88,271. In north Wales, the membership was around 10,000. From these figures, one can see the peripheral nature of north Wales in terms of both production and union membership.

[14] The miners in north Wales were primarily divided geographically, but also culturally and politically. Many miners in the north would not have visited the south. Culturally, industrialization remained less of a phenomenon in places like west Flintshire, posing less of a threat to political elites. In this way, left political initiatives in terms of unionization and party affiliation were often imported from nearby Lancashire rather than from the south Wales coalfield. Merfyn Jones explores the issue of the uneven political development of north and south Wales in 'Notes from the margin: class and society in nineteenth century Gwynedd' in D. Smith (ed.), *A People and a Proletariat* (London, 1980), p.205.

separation was apparent, as colliery development based itself in two counties, Denbigh and Flint. This posed geographical and cultural problems that inhibited attempts at unionization and centralized collective bargaining. At the end of the nineteenth century, Denbighshire provided the nucleus of the coalfield. Wrexham was central to the industry, providing labour for a number of collieries on the outskirts of the town in Brymbo, Gwersyllt and the Rhos. A little further towards the Flintshire border, the village of Llay consisted of two major pits, which also drew miners from Mold who had been displaced due to earlier colliery closures. To the south of Wrexham, on the English border, collieries were situated around a number of villages close to Chirk. The character of the Denbighshire coalfield contrasted sharply with the south Wales district. Colliery settlements were geographically separated and diverse identities persisted in a number of villages that were not wholly dependent on coal. The village of Rhosllannerchrugog was perhaps the only archetypal pit village in the coalfield and was the centre of union activity in the major strikes of the twentieth century.[15] Denbighshire and Flintshire were not major coal producers; their deposits and collieries were regarded as separate districts, though the miners were combined in one labour organization.

Flintshire had been a district in economic decline throughout the nineteenth century. The coalfield stretched from Hawarden, close to Chester, along the River Dee and west to the Point of Ayr colliery. There was also a small pit at Neston on the Wirral that contributed to the funds of the North Wales Miners Association (NWMA). By the early 1900s, the Flintshire coalfield remained concentrated in a small area between the towns of Flint and Prestatyn. The most important collieries were Bettisfield, Englefield and Point of Ayr. A feature of the county was the separation of labour from the immediate environs of the pit. As

---

[15] For reminiscences of life at Hafod colliery, see Colin Gibbs, *Clatter of Clogs* (Bersham, 1990).

early as the 1890s, Point of Ayr was drawing its labour from a number of villages where pits had previously closed.[16]

The geography of the coalfield is crucial to an understanding of the politics of the north Wales miners. Within the district, there was a clear division between Denbighshire and Flintshire, culturally, economically and politically. In contrast to the south Wales coalfield, the collieries of Denbighshire and Flintshire concentrated on production for local markets, and the amount of coal exported was negligible. Once central to the local economy of Flintshire, by the late nineteenth century, coal mining along the Dee estuary rapidly declined. In Wrexham, however, coal remained important until the 1930s, providing employment and local energy supplies for industry and the domestic market.

The peripheral position of coal thus affected the relationship between coal capitalists and miners in both counties. Tensions between capitalists and workers did not impact on the local economy in the same way as in the south, for both protagonists made up small competing interests in a polity that contained other institutions unconcerned with the economy of coal. Further, the process of combination in the south in the latter years of the nineteenth century was absent from the north through to the period of public ownership in the 1940s. Colliery ownership remained generally local, parochial and resistant to change. In 1854, an Inspector of Mines report indicated that there were twenty-six collieries in Denbighshire, each owned by a different company.[17] The trend against amalgamation continued and, as late as 1934, the north Wales coalfield contained twenty-five pits under twenty-three different owners. Point of Ayr Colliery Company remained a one-pit organization up to

[16] The playwright Emlyn Williams recalls growing up in Glanrafon, and described the mix of agricultural workers and miners who inhabited the district before the First World War. See Emlyn Williams, *George: An Early Autobiography* (London, 1961), pp.3–18. Details of the collieries of Mostyn, brief accounts of accidents and explosions can be found in Robert Galloway, *Annals of Coal Mining and the Coal Trade, Vol.2* (London, 1971), pp.125–7. Mostyn also had a radical tradition throughout the nineteenth century. A number of strikes in mining were complemented by the politics of Evan Pan Jones, who was the Congregationalist minister for the village and a popularizer of land nationalization. See P. Jones-Evans, 'Evan Pan Jones – Land Reformer', *Welsh History Review*, 4, 2 (1968), 143–59. The mining population of Mostyn was diluted in 1884 after a disaster at the Mostyn Quay Colliery. Miners moved to Lancashire and south Yorkshire. For details of the development of the Mostyn miners in Yorkshire, see Melvyn Jones, 'Long-distance migrants and cultural identity: the example of a Welsh colony in South Yorkshire', *The Local Historian*, 26, 4 (1996), 223–36.
[17] Lerry, *Collieries of Denbighshire*, p.25.

the eve of public ownership in 1947 and proved as intransigent in its relations with other coal capitalists as it did in its dealings with the NWMA. Brynkinallt and Ifton collieries, on the English border, were owned by William Craig & Sons, paternalist employers who advised the workers not to strike in 1912 and gained a favourable response, much to the discomfort of the union leadership in Wrexham.[18] A similar climate of consensual industrial relations was apparent at Black Park under the ownership of James Darlington. He became director of the company in 1895, taking an interest in public affairs. He served on many local government bodies, was chair of the North Wales Coal Owners Association (NWCOA) and was influential in the building of the parish hall and cottage hospital at Chirk.[19] Although north Wales had its owners' association, the climate between the various companies was one of cautious hostility.[20] What appears in the 1930s is a rapidly decreasing complement of local owners who were united in their pursuit of profitability, but divided over pay rates, industrial relations and recognition of the NWMA.

The economic pressures forcing the owners into combination in other coalfields were resisted in north Wales as small companies worked to consolidate their independence. At the same time, this prevented a similar response from organized labour in its attempts at streamlining collective bargaining procedures. The diversity of ownership impeded the efforts of local union leaders in strengthening the position of the NWMA across the coalfield.[21] The union still had a problem with the incidence of non-unionism, victimization and a counter-organization at Point of Ayr supported by the company. Since the coalfield was in decline and a depression in the coal trade continued to affect prices, the union was cross-pressured by factors acting against

---

[18] Ibid., pp.51–3.

[19] Ibid., p.49.

[20] Records of the NWCOA are incomplete and I have only been able to make assumptions from individual company attitudes to amalgamation and the recognition of the MFGB at particular pits. NWCOA papers and correspondence, 1929: CRO, Denbighshire, DD/LH/272.

[21] During the lockout of 1926, the union agent, Hugh Hughes, had most difficulty with members at pits that were not owned by members of the NWCOA. But even in the pits outside, attitudes to union representation differed. In the 1930s Brynkinallt colliery advised membership of the MFGB when recruiting miners and remained critical of the stance taken by the owners of Point of Ayr who refused to recognize the union.

the consolidation of its bargaining position. Between 1913 and 1934 production fell, as did employment, from a peak of 18,881 to 10,582.[22] The most damaging years were between 1927 and 1938 as local markets began shrinking and the union had still not recovered from the defeat of the 1926 lockout.[23]

During the 1930s, when depression rocked the British coal trade, more collieries in north Wales closed and the geographical distance between those that remained became greater. This reinforced local identities, consolidated the hegemony of the owners and hindered the pursuit of the collective aims of the union. The effects of the defeat of 1926 left the leadership of the NWMA in a precarious position. While industrial relations developed into mutual recognition in Denbighshire, the owners of Point of Ayr exploited their advantage by refusing to recognize the MFGB and withdrawing from the NWCOA. The division between the miners of Denbighshire and Flintshire was now more firmly entrenched both geographically and culturally. The north Wales miners in the twentieth century represented an industrial proletariat in decline and one pressured by disparate factors informing their political and cultural affiliations. The role that they played in the MFGB/NUM was as much shaped by local experiences as it was by the organization of a national body bringing miners together to pursue common interests through collective action. Flintshire had no metropolitan centre where the miners could gather. Rhyl, Holywell, Prestatyn, Flint and Mold all competed for custom from the various villages containing miners. Reinforcing this, each settlement retained a sense of history and culture that was not dependent on mining as a source of local identity. In his autobiography, the actor and playwright Emlyn Williams recalls that travel to one of the towns prior to the First World War was rare: 'Holywell I knew vaguely by name.' Williams was educated in the town and immediately experienced the clannishness of the villages that fed it.[24] Williams also recalls the mix of occupational identities in Glanrafon, close

[22] Political and Economic Planning Group, *Report on the British Coal Industry: A Survey of the Current Problems of the British Coal Industry and the Distribution of Coal, with Proposals for Reorganisation* (London, 1936).
[23] The coalfield was almost decimated during this period, witnessing the closure of Englefield, Bettisfield, Gatewen, Brynmally, Vron, Vauxhall, Wynnstay and Plas Power collieries.
[24] Emlyn Williams, *George*, p. 107.

to Point of Ayr: 'it was inhabited by farm-hands, colliers and workers on the estate.'[25] The prominence of a landed aristocracy in Mostyn also led to a fragmented political culture that resonated through the various villages and impeded the development of Labour politics.

In Denbighshire, Wrexham was the sole focus for cultural amenities and a place where the miners of the county could gather at various times to protest at levels of relief during disputes. Here we have a clear metropolitan influence in a major town situated in the heart of the coalfield. In contrast to Flintshire, a specifically Labourist political culture had been emerging from the early years of the century, becoming consolidated in the late 1920s. By this time, the miners had firmly committed themselves to the Labour Party both locally and nationally. The identity of the various villages had also been transformed by demographic changes as mines closed. With miners moving from pit to pit around Wrexham, they left behind fragments of their local particularities, yet maintained their identity as miners.[26]

Hafod colliery in Denbighshire and Point of Ayr in Flintshire illustrate this diversity of experience. Hafod, with its proximity to the village of Rhosllannerchrugog, was the closest that the coalfield came to representing an archetypal image of the miner, the pit and the community. The village was effectively dependent on local coal production and formed the nucleus of support for early initiatives in terms of unionization. Yet, even here, the link between the lodge and the leadership of the union in Wrexham was a tenuous one. Autonomy had been expressed at various junctures in the past as Rhos miners had withdrawn from the union in protest at the way funds were managed.[27] In the disputes of 1912, 1921 and 1926, miners from the village remained the most committed in north Wales to the policies of the MFGB. The support systems that evolved during these events

[25] Ibid., p. 24.
[26] The collective consciousness of the Wrexham miners was also reinforced by the Gresford disaster of 1934 in which 266 perished as result of an explosion. See Roger Laidlaw, 'The Gresford disaster in popular memory', *Llafur: Journal of Welsh Labour History*, 6, 4 (1995), 123–46.
[27] For details of the disputes between the miners of the Rhos and the district leadership, see Emlyn Rogers, 'The Union Society of the Miners of Rhosllanerchrugog and its neighbourhood, 1876–1901', *Transactions of the Denbighshire Historical Society*, 22 (1973), 236–46.

paralleled developments in some of the larger coalfields. The union was able to work with the growing Labour Party in order to dilute the debilitating hardships suffered by miners and utilize a range of initiatives that were absent in Flintshire when similar circumstances emerged. In Flintshire, the depression in the industry in the 1920s and earlier had swept away the archetypal colliery village. Both Bagillt and Mostyn contained no pits by the late 1930s. As the remaining colliery in Flintshire, Point of Ayr became detached from any specific village as labour was drawn from up to a dozen settlements within a ten-mile radius. The union was left to contend with divergent patterns of industrial relations and a geographical separation across two counties that did not bode well for future unity amongst its members.

Colliery ownership dictated the nature of industrial relations in north Wales, with strong local identities impeding the efforts of union organization. The pits south of Wrexham had experienced long periods of paternalist ownership, though this often fell short of the construction of model villages and the consequential pervasiveness of the company on the scale experienced from the 1920s by the miners of the Dukeries in Nottinghamshire.[28] At Brynkinallt and Ifton collieries in the 1930s, union membership was encouraged and the Labour Party started to make inroads into the non-mining sector of the Wrexham working class. A lively local press also seemed more receptive to Labour, providing significant space for union representatives as opposed to its counterpart in Flintshire. All the elements of a developing working-class culture could be found in Wrexham by the 1920s: sport, popular entertainment, trade unionism and social organizations such as miners' institutes.

West Flintshire between Holywell and Prestatyn, where Point of Ayr was located, remained largely agricultural and lacking in labour institutions that could develop and sustain a working-class consciousness beyond the point of production. The miners of Flintshire were a minority in decline, finding it difficult to inject their politics into the local structures of power that were split between a landed aristocracy and a Liberal presence exhibiting little radicalism. The uneven development of the coalfield thus

---

[28] For the development of the Nottinghamshire coalfield, see Robert Waller, *The Dukeries Transformed: The Social and Political Development of a Twentieth Century Coalfield* (Oxford, 1983).

led to a complex problem for miners' leaders in forging unity across county boundaries against intransigent employers and local power structures. The problems facing the north Wales miners culturally, politically and economically were far greater than those faced by the MFGB in the larger coalfields such as south Wales and Yorkshire. Consequently, it was difficult to construct a working-class identity that was related to occupation and common experiences. The imbalance of political development in the coalfield continued to plague the actions of the NWMA, with Flintshire constantly posing a threat to the ascendancy of Labourism in Denbighshire.

Miners in both counties expressed their political and cultural identity in a number of ways, though each county was different in terms of its political development in the first decades of the twentieth century. The Welsh language was stronger in Flintshire than in the pits around Wrexham, but a sense of nationality remained a cultural force.[29] As with the quarrymen of Gwynedd, 'nationalist consciousness' never became a clearly defined movement. Welshness remained part of a communal identity but did not pose an overtly political challenge to the main British parties.[30] In former mining localities, this identity was still apparent in the 1990s in terms of sport and a loosely defined claim to nationhood, although support for Welsh devolution remained weak in both Denbighshire and Flintshire.

Politically, both counties were strong Liberal bases in the nineteenth century. In Flintshire, the Mostyn family dominated the political scene until the Conservatives took the seat in 1924, lost it in 1929 and regained it in 1935. In 1950 the constituency was divided, with Flint West a Conservative stronghold until 1992. In Denbighshire, there were several contests in the nineteenth century dominated by a number of influential families. With the onset of industrialization, the old rural élites became pressurized both culturally and politically. In 1918, the Labour

---

[29] For the decline of the Welsh language in Denbighshire and Flintshire, see W.T.R. Pryce, 'Language areas in north-east Wales c. 1800–1911', in Geraint H. Jenkins (ed.), *A Social History of the Welsh Language: Language and Community in the Nineteenth Century* (Cardiff, 1998), pp. 21–61.

[30] For details of the quarrymen of Gwynedd, see R. Merfyn Jones, *The North Wales Quarrymen, 1874–1922* (Cardiff, 1982).

Party started its challenge for the new seat of Wrexham, taking it
in 1922.[31]

With the formation of the Labour Representation Committee
(LRC) in 1900, an independent working-class electoral strategy
was pursued by a number of unions. Socialism, however, re-
mained underdeveloped both electorally and in terms of its
impact on the unions affiliated to the MFGB.[32] The Social
Democratic Federation (SDF) and the Independent Labour
Party (ILP) made few inroads in Denbighshire and Flintshire.[33]
The NWMA opposed affiliation to the Labour Party in the 1906
and 1908 MFGB ballots and did not move as quickly as south
Wales in generating support for a clean break with Liberalism.
This does not suggest an absence of Labourist values: leaders in
north Wales were at this stage becoming increasingly aware of
the marginalization of the organized working class within Liberal
politics. In 1903, discussions took place at a number of district
council meetings stressing the desirability of running a Labour
candidate in Flintshire. The meaning of Labour representation
was contested, as were routes towards parliamentary power.
Some argued for representation through the Liberal Party with
others arguing for straight independence. A motion was eventually moved in support but this was to be initially attempted
through the local Liberal Association.[34] A Labourist commitment developed slowly and the miners themselves played an
influential role in proselytizing against the main parties of
capital. In the same year, the NWMA sent congratulations to
William Davies, the union representative of the Bettisfield
miners, who won election to the Holywell District Council,
representing the Bagillt West ward.[35]

In both Denbighshire and Flintshire, the politics of working-
class Liberalism were slow to disappear in electoral terms, but

---

[31] For details of the electoral history see A. J. James and J. E. Thomas, *Wales at Westminster: A History of the Parliamentary Representation of Wales, 1800–1979* (Llandysul, 1981).

[32] See Roy Gregory, *The Miners in British Politics, 1906–14* (Oxford, 1968).

[33] The Wrexham branch of the Independent Labour Party was slow to develop, but in 1907 its secretary, Tom Platt, formed two new branches in Rhosllannerchrugog and Flintshire and started to make inroads in rural Gwynedd. See Cyril Parry, *The Radical Tradition in Welsh Politics: A Study of Liberal and Labour Politics in Gwynedd, 1900–1920* (Hull, 1970).

[34] *North Wales Miners Magazine*, 1, 2 (1903), 25: NUM, Wrexham.

[35] Ibid., 66.

developments in the industry nationally and the impact of war were to transform the politics of the miners.[36] By 1909, MFGB affiliation to the Labour Party was constitutionally secure but was on tenuous electoral foundations as many miners in various coalfields retained their established allegiances. The relationship between the Labour Party and the miners' district unions was built on Liberal shortcomings, economic experiences and a developing class awareness that expressed itself in some coalfields more clearly than in others. The 1912 minimum wage strike fostered a bond of unity within the MFGB and alerted district leaders to the importance of the state in influencing owners and to its ability to intervene in industrial relations.[37] In the same year, the Labour dominance of the MFGB was symbolized by the accession of Robert Smillie to the presidency: a socialist and long-term member of the ILP who was committed to a formal break with Liberalism and the promotion of a clear socialist programme.[38] This view was reinforced by the impact of the war economy that caused some trade unionists to break finally with Liberalism. In 1922, Edward Hughes, the NWMA leader, welcomed the trade union acquisition of the *Daily Herald* to 'counteract the poison of the capitalist press'.[39] In speech after speech he castigated both the Conservative and Liberal parties. The work of the miners and others in the Wrexham coalfield proved successful with the election of Robert Richards as MP for the town in 1922.[40] Adult education had also played a role in the election as, after the war, the Workers' Educational Association set up courses locally, some taught by Richards himself.[41]

The affiliation of the miners to Labour represented a decisive indication of a commitment to Labourism, with the state

---

[36] The strength of Liberalism in both counties was slow to disappear and the affinity of Lloyd George with the workers of north Wales was important. During the 1926 lockout, at a meeting of the Welsh Liberal Federation in Rhyl, he donated £20 to the wives and children of miners. *Wrexham Leader*, 16 July 1926.

[37] Although a Liberal government was promoting state initiatives, the thrust of the support from the Welsh working class was increasingly radical, manifesting itself in increased support for the Labour Party after the war. See Ian McAllister, 'The Labour Party in Wales: the dynamics of one-partyism', *Llafur: Journal of Welsh Labour History*, 3, 2 (1981), 79–89.

[38] Gregory, *The Miners in British Politics*, p.49.

[39] North Wales Miners' Association Annual Report 1922: NUM, Wrexham.

[40] Kenneth O. Morgan, *Rebirth of a Nation: Wales, 1880–1980* (Oxford and Cardiff, 1981), pp.191–2.

[41] A. H. Dodd (ed.), *A History of Wrexham* (Wrexham, 1989), p.297.

providing a focus for solving the problems of the industry.
Although state intervention had been inherent in some aspects of
Liberalism, and embraced by some miners' leaders, the establishment of a new party signified a decisive break both organization-
ally and ideologically. The shift towards political independence
was now tempered with notions of the centrality of class. This
became particularly important by 1918, as the wartime experiences of the state and the increased number of miners' seats
affected the MFGB. The immediate post-war gains and, then,
their loss, crystallized the union agenda for the future. The ability
of the miners to press their claims collectively increased, ushering
in a period in all coalfields in which district unions were able to
influence policy developments in constituency parties.[42] Although
industrial militancy remained, it was tempered by the hope of
election victories, Labour governments and the goal of public
ownership.

  In both Denbighshire and Flintshire, leaders at the colliery
level were able to overcome established cultural and political
structures in order to press for support for Labour politics. In
Wrexham, this proved to be an easier task, as the main body of
miners was mobilized in conjunction with the small but growing
number of ILP activists and sympathetic intellectuals to forge a
Labourist identity. In Flintshire, the task was more difficult.
Conservative and Liberal allegiances held relatively firm as the
number of miners declined. Nonetheless, by 1918, the miners of
Bettisfield, Englefield and Point of Ayr were pursuing progressive
policies in the NWMA and working to secure local representation for the Labour Party. But owing to the NWMA's declining
membership throughout the 1920s and its inability to consolidate
its success in terms of unionization in both counties, the union
soon faced problems. Serious tensions emerged within the
coalfield: unofficial strikes, non-unionism and the formation of a
company union that drove the MFGB out of Flintshire. Because
of the increasingly peripheral role of coal in the local economy,
both the Conservatives and the Liberals maintained electoral
support up to the Second World War and beyond, as miners at
particular pits became isolated in Conservative constituencies.

---

[42] In 1910 miners accounted for 40–50 per cent of the electorate in east Denbighshire.
Gregory, *The Miners in British Politics*, p.13.

Between the 1921 lockout and the onset of public ownership in 1947, the north Wales coalfield entered a period of decline. Westminster, Rhosddu and Gwersyllt closed, as did most of the last Flintshire mines, and the NWMA continued to be plagued by the growth of non-unionism and by falling wages.[43] In the debates at national level, the north Wales delegation promoted a pragmatic response to the call for wage reductions. Hugh Hughes[44] spoke at a special wages conference in February 1925, claiming that 'we do not believe anymore in asking for the moon, we have been asking for the moon long enough'.[45] However, members in the coalfield were becoming increasingly radicalized during the year owing to economic hardship. In June 1925, a lengthy strike lasting five months began at Llay Main against the wishes of the district executive. A month earlier, the district had faced another strike at Gatewen colliery, with NWMA members refusing to work with non-unionists. Government intervention and the work of the Samuel Commission settled the crisis, but this only delayed the inevitable. In May 1926, the problems of the coal industry led to the General Strike and miners' lockout. From May 1926 to December, the north Wales coalfield became a storm centre of activity.[46] However, the unity of the miners was brittle and divisions within the workforce were to last into the post-war period.

The Wrexham Labour Party played an important role in promoting the miners' cause once they had been left by the TUC to fight alone. In May, A. J. Cook travelled to a number of pits in Denbighshire and Flintshire, and attracted large crowds.[47] The Wrexham Board of Guardians increased the amount of relief for wives and children under pressure from a series of union demonstrations. At the end of July, Hughes reported to the executive that almost all miners were standing firm in the coalfield.[48] In August, cracks began to appear in both counties as

[43] *Wrexham Leader*, 27 February 1925.
[44] Hughes became agent for the NWMA in 1925 after the death of his father, Edward Hughes. For a report of the funeral with speeches by A. J. Cook, see *Mold, Deeside and Buckley Leader*, 20 March 1925.
[45] MFGB minutes of special conference on wages, 26 February 1925: NUM, Wrexham.
[46] For an account of the 1926 lockout from a national perspective, see Gerard Noel, *The Great Lock-out of 1926* (London, 1976).
[47] *Wrexham Leader*, 14 May 1926.
[48] MFGB minutes of special conference, 30 July 1926: NUM, Wrexham.

miners became pressured by poverty and attractive offers from
particular owners. At Brynmally men were returning, and at
Llay Main miners were offered the maintenance of a seven-hour
day and no reduction in pay.[49] The district executive maintained
its support for MFGB policy but found that backing within the
union and wider social mechanisms of support were declining.[50]
The Wrexham Board of Guardians was increasingly proving
resistant to claims for more relief. In Flintshire, the Holywell
Board of Guardians had been less sympathetic from the outset.
By the end of September, most collieries in north Wales were
open.

The position of Labour in Denbighshire and Flintshire had
weakened the position of the district union in its pursuit of
solidarity. In Flintshire the Labourist culture was weaker and had
not been able to influence external social institutions, in contrast
to the situation at Wrexham. In Ffynnongroyw, close to Point of
Ayr, the fund for feeding children had been exhausted by
September. The local press in Prestatyn had also been less
sympathetic to the plight of the miners than had its counterpart
in Wrexham. The *Prestatyn Weekly* clearly represented the voice of
coal capitalism, while the *Wrexham Leader* retained a semblance of
impartiality. In October, the MFGB rejected the government's
proposals for a settlement, but each coalfield had significant
numbers back at work. Half of the miners of north Wales had
returned and the organization of a number of large-scale meetings in Wrexham could not stem the flow. For the next two
months, distress became more acute because some companies
had prohibited outcropping on their land, and union funds
began to dwindle. On 4 December, the NWMA declared an end
to the dispute in north Wales. Developments at Point of Ayr
presented a particular problem, with accusations of victimization. A company union soon emerged that was to trouble the
NWMA through to the advent of nationalization and beyond.

The district leadership mobilized its diminishing forces in the
late 1920s to counter the problem of non-unionism, company
unionism, poverty and declining membership as a result of pit

[49] *Wrexham Leader*, 13 August 1926.
[50] The NWMA voted in July in favour of the so-called 'Bishops' Proposals' as a means
of settlement but later rejected the government's terms in November. MFGB minutes of
special conferences, 29 July 1926, 19 November 1926: NUM, Wrexham.

closures.[51] In 1934, Hugh Hughes retired and was succeeded by Edward Jones, who later became vice-president of the NUM. From the outset, Jones made full unionization and the eradication of the Point of Ayr Industrial Union (POAIU) the central plank of his policy.[52] In the same year, the Gresford disaster sent the union and the coalfield into a state of shock, and compensating the families of the victims became the dominant concern. With the help of the company, POAIU membership grew steadily from only twenty-one in 1926 to 482 ten years later.[53] Once the district executive had tied up the loose ends concerning Gresford, it concentrated on gaining membership at Point of Ayr. Throughout the district, resolutions from various lodges were reaching the executive calling for strike action over non-unionism and representation in Flintshire.[54] In 1939, Jones submitted a list of proposals to the owners after months of attempting to settle the problem through negotiation. He wanted to avoid a strike and, instead, concentrated on increasing the proportion of NWMA men at the colliery. A period of lengthy negotiations had lasted for three years when, in 1942, the Ministry of Labour intervened to prevent a strike that could have encompassed all coalfields and damaged wartime production. A court of inquiry was held at Chester on 17 April 1942 and heard representations from the three parties. After two days of deliberations, an agreement was finally reached. Contributions for the MFGB were to be collected on the colliery premises and each union would be given its own notice board. The POAIU survived until 1944, retaining ninety members, the last breakaway union in the British coalfields.[55]

---

[51] The decline in the health of the working class in Wrexham during this period is charted by David Lee Williams, 'A healthy place to be? The Wrexham coalfield in the interwar period', *Llafur: Journal of Welsh Labour History*, 7, 1 (1996), 87–95. During the 1920s, several Welsh miners emigrated to the coalfields of the United States, a number of them from Denbighshire. An account of their experiences can be found in an edited collection of letters, though all seem to be from the south. Alan Conway (ed.), *The Welsh in America: Letters from Immigrants* (Cardiff, 1961), pp.164–210.

[52] For an account of the first three miners' leaders in north Wales see Keith Gildart, 'Men of coal: miners' leaders in north east Wales, 1890–1961, *Llafur: Journal of Welsh Labour History*, 8, 1 (2000), 111–29.

[53] POAIU report of tenth anniversary 1926–36: CRO Flintshire, D/NM/781.

[54] NWBCMA minutes of ordinary council meeting, 6 June 1936. At this meeting there were calls for strike action from Bersham, Black Park and Llay Hall Lodges: CRO Flintshire D/NM/34.

[55] Keith Gildart, 'Militancy, moderation, and the struggle against company unionism in the north Wales coalfield, *Welsh History Review*, 20, 3 (2001), 532–64.

On the eve of the nationalization of the coal industry, almost all miners in north Wales were members of the NUM, which seemed to be attaining one of its long-sought aims. The formation of the NWMA, the development of Labour politics, the struggle against company unionism and the retention of autonomy all helped to shape the post-war politics of the NUM in Denbighshire and Flintshire. The coalfield embodied distinctive characteristics that dictated the development of labour organization and the political consciousness of the miners it contained. The local union leadership pursued a delicate policy of negotiation and pragmatism in order to consolidate MFGB membership and Labour representation. Both structural and cultural factors thus affected the shape of union politics in the mines of Denbighshire and Flintshire. The uneven development of Labour representation in both counties was a problem for the union until 1945. Even after the election of Clement Attlee's Labour government and the advent of public ownership, Point of Ayr remained isolated in a Conservative enclave. Nonetheless, a culture of Labourism became the dominant creed amongst the miners, and determined future responses to the politics of coal, both impeding and promoting collective action within the North Wales Area of the NUM. The peculiarity of the coalfield and its society had produced a fragile unity that held for almost forty years. The strike of 1984–5 was to lead to its dissipation.

I

THE GOLDEN AGE OF LABOURISM, 1945–1963

So what can we do to put things straight?
Will the Red shouted, 'form a Socialist State'.
A Socialist State was then voted upon,
They were all in favour, Will's motion had won.[1]

The 1940s were a decade in which the British mainland was exposed to some of the horrors of war. This led to significant political shifts, with electoral success for left-wing independent candidates in a series of parliamentary by-elections.[2] The victory of the Labour Party in the 1945 general election is generally viewed as the culmination of the popular radicalism of the period, although recent revisionist accounts have painted a more complex picture. The policies adopted by Labour from 1945 to 1951 had a significant impact on the miners, going on to shape and confirm the politics of their trade union for decades to come. The period is also notable for its continuities as well as its ruptures. Within the British coalfields, the Labour Party was well established and, electorally, the relationship between the NUM and the party was maintained. Due to its commitment to the war during its 'popular front' period, even the Communist Party (CP) found itself working with officials of particular unions. However, this was soon challenged by the politics of the Cold War and developing factionalism within the trade union movement.

The north Wales coalfield played its part during the war in increasing coal production, aided by the state in securing full trade union membership at each pit. Unofficial strikes were criticized by the leadership: Arthur Horner, Will Paynter and others in the CP challenged the legitimacy of unofficial action in their own coalfields.[3] In essence, the war and the subsequent

---

[1] Extract from 'Red Red Robin' by Keith Hett, from *Bersham Pit Bottom and Other Poems* (private publication, 1986).

[2] The most significant development was the success of the left-wing Common Wealth party. Common Wealth candidates were successful in parliamentary by-elections in Eddisbury (April 1943), Skipton (January 1944), and Chelmsford (April 1945).

[3] Arthur Horner, *Incorrigible Rebel* (London, 1960), p.164.

success of the Labour Party in the general election neutralized the politics of the NUM. The commitment to the party electorally had been established earlier, but after 1947 there was a more clearly defined ideological support that remained secure through to the 1960s. Jack Read of Hafod colliery expresses such a view in his assessment of the situation: 'we thought that it would be a new horizon. The men would have more control, as would the union. Further, the Labour Party, our party, would take over the big industries and solve the problems of poverty and insecurity.'[4] A host of other interviewees also illustrate the appeal of the Labour government and subsequent nationalization, though this was always expressed as merely representing a 'better way' of organizing the industry and reducing the animosity between owners and miners. The party itself did not offer anything more. Stafford Cripps, speaking before a huge audience at the Rhos miners' institute in May 1945 promised nationalization of the mines, full employment and an enhanced role for the union in the development of the industry.[5] The 1945 government represented the zenith of the Labourist project to which the miners of north Wales and Britain remained committed for the next fifty years.

The radicalization of the wider working class clearly influenced the miners of Denbighshire and Flintshire. There were a number of stoppages during the war owing to unhappiness over payment rates and animosity towards new working practices. By 1947, the strength of the union was consolidated, as all miners in north Wales were now members.[6] The post-war period was to witness less unofficial strike activity, owing to the formulation of conciliation procedures favoured by left and right within the union. During the war, each lodge committee worked to maintain output, but still faced difficulties with the attitude of management. At Point of Ayr, the recently established lodge committee experienced problems of communication.[7] The union won a successful strike in 1943 over the dismissal of two canteen workers, the first dispute at the pit since 1926.

---

[4] Interview with Jack Read, January 1997.
[5] *Wrexham Leader*, 25 May 1945.
[6] Reports on disputes at Gresford and Point of Ayr collieries, 1940–4: NUM, Wrexham.
[7] NWMA Point of Ayr Lodge minutes, October 1943: CRO Flintshire D/NM/770.

As is evident, there were cracks in the notion of the 'people's war' as disputes also unsettled the coal industry in south Wales, but the union nationally maintained its ability to steady the ship.[8] Given the need to increase production, lodges were finding it easier to settle disputes. The relationship established in the war between the union, employees and the state provided a pointer to the future complexion of the industry. The route to national-ization of the industry and the reorganization of the union might have been a disjointed one marked by tensions between areas, but it came together in 1947 as a Labourist construct in which compromises were made and the politics of the centre of the union remained dominant. The miners themselves did not expect a socialist utopia, just an improvement in conditions and an enhanced role for their representatives. Further, the new management structure, whereby workers from the coalface could take advantage of training schemes and work their way up the promotional ladder, consolidated the consensus.[9]

The reorganization of the MFGB in the form of the NUM pre-dated the nationalization of the industry but changed little in terms of the status of each district. The debates that preceded the change were coloured by animosity between coalfields and by fear of a loss of local autonomy. By 1943, the complete dissolution of the district organizations had been ruled out. The foundation of the NUM was to be the 'centralization of the whole of the industrial activities of the several district associations immediately, though in view of the substantial divergence of practice and custom as between the different districts . . . there should be as little interference as possible.'[10] Thus, the union was reorganized, but local autonomy was maintained.

In 1946, the Labour government accepted the NUM's Miners' Charter which called for better youth training, welfare provision, the seven-hour day and the five-day week.[11] Ebby Edwards left

---

[8] After four years of war, strikes were still apparent in south Wales. Between September 1939 and October 1944, there were 514 stoppages. However, involvement in the pit production committees and Arthur Horner's arguments against strikes cemented radicals to the constitutional benefits of parliamentary activity. See Hywel Francis and David Smith, *The Fed: A History of the South Wales Miners in the Twentieth Century* (London, 1980), p.398.

[9] Norman Jones interview, 1997.

[10] MFGB Report of NEC, annual conference 1943, p.385: NUM, Wrexham.

[11] For further details, see W. R. Garside, *The Durham Miners, 1919–1966* (London, 1971), p.395.

his job as NUM general secretary to join the National Coal Board (NCB) in the labour relations department. His departure promoted a view of consensus and of the union's enhanced role in playing its part in the development of the industry. In north Wales, Albert Davies had worked in both private and national-ized mines in the late 1940s; the private mine paid higher wages but he longed for employment in an NCB pit owing to the nature of industrial relations at the nationalized collieries.[12]

In 1948, at the NUM annual conference, the platform sent a message of goodwill to the NCB and the president, Will Lawther, stressed the need for greater production to show gratitude to the government for the nationalization of the industry. Concerning unofficial stoppages, he declared that 'they are wrong, they are criminal; they cannot be tolerated'.[13] A year later an agreement was signed between the NCB and the NUM for deductions for union dues to be made by the NCB at each pit; this was followed by a further fall in disputes at each colliery.[14] Taylor is not far off the mark in arguing that the NUM had transformed itself into an 'adjunct of the Ministry of Power to secure nationalization and sustain a Labour government'.[15] The broader issue is of greater importance: what did the government/union partnership mean to the majority of the miners?

In north Wales, there was a clear view of nationalization: it was introduced by a Labour government and, as most miners in the region voted Labour, it was seen as an obvious response to their wishes. This view was complemented by a notion of 'power with responsibility'. Many miners were aware of the power that they could wield but thought that this would be unnecessary, owing to the capture of the state by a party representing the interests of working people.[16] This was reinforced at the national level by the presidency of Lawther, who stressed that:

> It is not playing the game to give expressions of approval to the great achievements of your Labour government and then to stop the pit on some paltry, trivial matter, when the greatest good you can do for yourselves and

[12] Interview with Albert Davies, February 1997.
[13] NUM Information Bulletin, 3, 8 (August 1948): CRO Flintshire D/NM/985–90.
[14] NUM Information Bulletin, 4, 2–3 (Feb.–March 1949): CRO Flintshire D/NM/985–90.
[15] Andrew Taylor, *The Politics of the Yorkshire Miners* (London, 1984), p.14.
[16] Interviews with Albert Davies, Jack Read and Ernest Edwards, 1997.

your fellows is to have the matter put right by ordinary negotiations and consultations.[17]

The problems of the coal industry finally seemed to be solved by the government's commitment to state intervention and a comprehensive industrial relations programme. To the miners, 1947 also represented, to union activists at least, the end of a particular period of struggle from the cataclysmic defeat of 1926, the depression of the 1930s and the divisiveness of company unionism. This is not to suggest that there was a definite progression up to 1947, or indeed that nationalization represented more than a limited reorganization of the industry and the union. But, in terms of its symbolism and its practical effects on the relationship between the NUM and the government, the event was of substantial significance. Mining communities had been supporters of the Labour Party since at least the 1920s, but until 1947 the actual practice of Labourism, except to a limited degree in local government, had not been realized. For better or for worse, the 1945 Labour government cemented the ideology of Labourism to its practice, at the same time consolidating the relationship between significant sections of the working class and the party.

With the advent of nationalization, the north Wales miners seemed finally to have established themselves as an important community within the national structure of the union and the politics of the region. There had been a number of disputes in the war, but the positive role of the state in working with the trade union movement had proved beneficial to the coalfield. Point of Ayr still posed a problem, with the company union retaining members until 1944. The lodge committee minutes show that, even in 1946, there were still thirty-five non-unionists.[18] The lodge had firmly established itself, partly due to individuals such as Jack Griffiths and Gwilym Hughes. Griffiths took the chair in 1942 when the union had not yet gained full recognition at the colliery, going on to become delegate, president of the area and NEC member.[19] He was a Labour

[17] NUM Information Bulletin, 4, 8 (1949), p.74: CRO Flintshire D/NM/985–90.
[18] NUM Point of Ayr Lodge minutes, 15 October 1946: CRO Flintshire D/NM/771.
[19] Jack Griffiths interview carried out by Val Lloyd, 28 July 1981, transcript in CRO Flintshire NT/789.

Party stalwart, a local councillor and active in community politics, characteristics that appeared to become common to the leadership qualities of a number of lodge officials.

The leadership of the union was still in the hands of Edward Jones, who had been elected in 1934 and commanded respect from each lodge. A range of interviews verify the fact that Jones had few enemies either locally or nationally.[20] When Jones was elected to the post, north Wales was second from the bottom in the district wage league; when nationalization came, it was sixth from the top. Like other miners, he had worked in a number of collieries, starting at Wynnstay, then moving to Gresford and Llay Main. As a Labour Party member, he won election to the Wrexham Borough Council. In 1954, he was elected vice-president of the NUM and subsequently became the longest serving member of the NEC.[21] Jones was totally committed to nationalization and wanted to make it work. Personal advancement was secondary for Jones, as shown when he refused Hugh Gaitskell's offer in 1949 to be a member of the NCB in London, a position that could possibly have led to him becoming chairman. Gaitskell, when minister of fuel and power, felt that Jones was one of the most able NUM leaders and he had a good relationship with him throughout his term of office.[22]

The structure of the area union was clearly built on seniority; there was respect for officialdom and the deference between lodge members and leaders was pronounced. This limited the development of factions within the coalfield, and leadership decisions were often secured through appeals to loyalty and experience. Jones personified the able negotiator and pragmatic politician who placed local interests above the wider claims of the national union.

Economically the industry had been significantly rationalized before nationalization. Many of the smaller pits in the Wrexham area had been closed in the twenties and thirties and the only remaining pit in Flintshire was Point of Ayr.[23] In 1947, eight were nationalized: Point of Ayr, Black Park, Hafod, Bersham,

---

[20]   Jack Read, Albert Davies, Eddie Lloyd, Norman Jones and Colin Newell interviews with author, 1997.

[21]   *Wrexham Leader*, 24 February 1961.

[22]   Philip M. Williams, *The Diary of Hugh Gaitskell, 1945–1956* (London, 1983), p.156.

[23]   For a short review of the history of each pit up to the onset of nationalization, see G. G. Lerry, *The Collieries of Denbighshire* (Wrexham, 1968).

Llay Hall, Gresford, Ifton and Llay Main. A number of smaller pits not given over to the NCB because of their size, including Black Lane and Smelt, retained their union membership, though eventually the men were absorbed into other NCB pits after closure.[24] The strength of localism remained an important factor in shaping the future identity of the union; within the area it was claimed that each pit had a distinctive character. Albert Davies recalls moving from Llay Main to Gresford and noticing that blasphemy and bad language were more commonplace in the latter.[25] The strength of community was probably strongest at Hafod, where most of the workforce came from the locality of Rhosllannerchrugog. Rhos also had a miners' club and library to parallel those of south Wales; though in contrast to the south it witnessed little Communist activity. Point of Ayr remained isolated from the Wrexham coalfield, signifying a potentially weak link in the union chain.

Overall, the localism of the coalfield was influenced by its Welsh identity. Disputes in the nineteenth century often centred on reactions to the appointment of an English manager. Even in the 1940s, there was debate over the organization of the industry under public ownership; the Gresford lodge passed a resolution objecting to NCB administration from Manchester.[26] In essence, the coalfield was characterized by its geographical fragmentation, with each colliery being socially isolated. Public ownership and the miners' commitment to it replaced the bonds of the colliery village, with Labourism providing the basis for a collective consciousness. Only Bersham and Hafod collieries retained the link to villages that were dependent on coal for employment.

Although there were celebrations across coalfield communities in 1947, mixed reactions to the nationalization process soon emerged. To celebrate Vesting Day, plans were made to include all retired miners and their families in a series of events at each pit. Letters appeared in the local newspapers praising the government for bringing the mines under state ownership, some

---

[24] The statement of lodge accounts for 1947 give an outline of the membership of the union at the time of nationalization: POA 472, Black Park 328, Hafod 1350, Bersham 700, Llay Hall 385, Gresford 1685, Ifton 856, and Llay Main 2165: CRO Flintshire D/NM/103.
[25] Albert Davies interview, January 1997.
[26] Resolutions from lodges for 1947, NUM North Wales Area annual delegate meeting: CRO Flintshire D/NM/103.

even acknowledging that this placed a degree of power in the hands of the workers. H. Y. Gilpin had worked at Bersham colliery for thirty-three years and saw himself as a Christian socialist, but he warned against complacency: 'It is imperative that we should understand fully the responsibility placed on us and not to abuse it in any way.'[27] Ernest Edwards, who had worked at Gwersyllt colliery since 1920, moving on to Llay Main, also reflected this view, and recalls greeting the under-manager with 'we are in charge now'; such was the level of expectation.[28]

A large crowd enjoyed the ceremony at Ifton colliery and Edward Jones stressed that the days of 'old practices' had now gone and the 'age of co-operation' was beginning. The lodge treasurer also emphaized the need for consensus at Bersham, where he advocated discipline amongst the workforce.[29] The response to nationalization highlights the pragmatism of the miners and their perception of the nature of the British state, now that the Labour Party appeared to control it. At Gresford, a large crowd assembled as Harold Lloyd hoisted up the NCB flag. Lloyd had worked in the industry for fifty years and welcomed public ownership emotionally.

> We are today commemorating the liberation of the mining community from the claws of capitalism, we are turning over a new leaf in the history of mining in Great Britain. In 1945 the working class were in agreement. We decided that conservatism and capitalism were to go, and we put in power our comrades . . . here you have a socialist government returned.[30]

Lloyd's sentiments show that Labourism now appeared to be a living entity to the miners of north Wales. Socialism was decoded as a nationalized coal industry and as welfare reforms that Labour introduced to improve the lifestyle of the working class. The impact of 1947 has been lost in retrospective Marxist debates and recent revisionist claims that public ownership meant little. It has been easy to marginalize the impact of nationalization, and although disillusionment was to emerge, this

---

[27] *Wrexham Leader*, 10 January 1947.
[28] Ernest Edwards, interview with author, 1997.
[29] *Wrexham Leader*, 10 January 1947.
[30] Ibid.

was not directed at the Labour Party. The union, both nationally and locally, remained a compliant power broker within union/party relationships, committing itself to public ownership.

At Point of Ayr, enthusiasm for the ceremony was not as strong. Jack Griffiths reflected on the day with some caution. To Griffiths, 'the men did not know what was coming to them', or what effect public ownership would have on the pattern of authority within the workplace.[31] The men at this pit were Labour voters but were not familiar with the ideology and policy developments of Labour in power. Many voted Labour because their mothers and fathers had, and the party was certainly weaker than in Denbighshire. Black Park colliery, known for its generational continuity in terms of the workforce, also celebrated Vesting Day. The manager congratulated the men for being in the tradition of mining stretching back four hundred years. The lodge treasurer, William Parrish, grandfather of the future Labour Party deputy leader John Prescott, had been a socialist for many years. Expressing the view of Chirk miners, he welcomed nationalization with the cry, 'we fought for this'.[32]

The consultative mechanism introduced by the NCB had initially been established during the war, and the benefits of negotiation were clear as the union gained representation at all levels. In 1946, officials met incoming NCB leaders in Wrexham, where Edward Jones agreed with the need for greater output and co-operation between management and men.[33] Hyndley and Citrine[34] were in attendance and the very symbolism of the meeting placed the area leaders on a higher social platform than had been enjoyed in the preceding decades. However, within a year of nationalization, the problems of the industry in north Wales were still apparent. Disputes arose over the introduction of new machinery, and lodges became sceptical of the pace of reform. The 1948 annual delegate meeting passed a resolution requesting the NEC to consult with the NCB in order to obtain a

---

[31] Lloyd, interview with Jack Griffiths.

[32] Colin Brown, *Fighting Talk: The Biography of John Prescott* (London, 1997), p.14.

[33] *Wrexham Leader*, 18 October 1946.

[34] Hyndley became the first chair of the NCB after a distinguished career with the Powell Duffryn Coal Company for a number of years. Lord Citrine, after years working in the trade union movement, also became a member of the NCB, emphasizing the consensual nature of the nationalization process. See Robin Page Arnot, *The Miners: One Union, One Industry* (London, 1979).

greater measure of workers' control in the industry.[35] The important point about this resolution was its emphasis on consultation with the NCB. Union officials had now accepted that significant change could be brought about through the existing structures and clearly defined channels of negotiation. It was generally agreed that the union now had an enhanced role but, in reality, little had changed in terms of the methods of production or the stratification of the labour process underground.

The year 1948 brought an increase in production in most pits in the area as miners began to settle into the new pattern of public ownership. Hafod started to break production records, as did Point of Ayr, though Llay Hall suffered from a fire and explosion which left ten men injured and the Brassy area of the pit sealed off.[36] The workforce now numbered 9,000, and the area was totally unionized, taking advantage of the check-off system and the enhanced role the union enjoyed in terms of national collective bargaining.[37] Public ownership was beneficial in that it introduced a codified, uniform system of industrial relations throughout the coalfield and allowed trade union involvement at all levels of negotiation. This, once more, was a powerful symbol for miners. The victory of the Labour Party in 1945 had delivered for the miners a range of limited benefits, but more importantly it was seen as a potent symbol of the effectiveness of a progressive administration. This had the effect of politicizing the miners, who campaigned more vigorously for the party in Wrexham and Flintshire.

PARTY POLITICS IN NORTH-EAST WALES

The activist strand within the NWMA had provided staunch Labour supporters since the early 1900s and was effective in mobilizing the workforce in electoral support for the party. Ernest Edwards, a rank and file member of the union who was born in 1906, could not remember a time when the miners were not Labour. Jack Read also stressed that the community of Rhos

---

[35] North Wales NUM minutes of annual delegate meeting, 20 March 1948: CRO Flintshire D/NM/1–4.
[36] *Wrexham Leader*, 17 January 1947.
[37] With the nationalization of the industry the NCB agreed to deduct union dues direct from miners' wages.

was an established stronghold from the days of his childhood.[38] Even in the more Conservative constituency of Flintshire, the collieries of Point of Ayr, Bettisfield and Englefield carried the torch of democratic socialism in unfavourable circumstances. Jack Griffiths of Point of Ayr became a Labour councillor and stressed that in the early days of party activity, around 99 per cent of miners identified with the ideals of the organization.[39] Nonetheless, in Flintshire, a strong Liberal tradition existed that continued to shape the voting behaviour of particular families. Eddie Lloyd, who started work at Point of Ayr soon after nationalization, recalled that his father was always Labour, as were most of the workers in the village of Ffynnongroyw. Yet, two miles away in the village of Mostyn, anti-Labour hostility remained a powerful force, no doubt due to the legacy of deference shown to Lord Mostyn, who had previously wielded significant influence amongst the local population.[40]

Women represented a minority in the north Wales labour movement during this period.[41] Eirene White, the future MP for Flint East, encountered initial hostility from male organized trade unionists in her attempt to build a parliamentary career. White had cut her teeth in parliamentary journalism, and went on to become the first Welsh woman elected to the National Executive of the Labour Party, in 1958. In November 1944, she eventually overcame the challenge of a favoured miners' representative and gained the nomination. Edward Jones and the miners overlooked White and supported the selection of Joseph Jones of the Yorkshire NUM. The selection meeting was a close contest, with White taking thirty-six delegate votes to Jones's twenty-nine.[42] White took advantage of the fact that her mother's family had been from the area, and by pressing her local connections she was successful in gaining allies in the constituency. Her biggest asset, however, was the support of Arthur Deakin and the Transport and General Workers' Union (T&GWU) in Shotton.[43]

---

[38] Read and Edwards, interviews with author, 1997.
[39] Lloyd, interview with Griffiths.
[40] Eddie Lloyd, interview with author, 1997.
[41] For women in the Labour party in Wales, see Neil Evans and Dot Jones, ' "To help forward the great work of humanity": women in the Labour Party in Wales', in Duncan Tanner, Chris Williams and Deian Hopkin (eds.), *The Labour Party in Wales, 1900–2000* (Cardiff, 2000), pp.241–63.
[42] Thomas Jones, *A Diary with Letters, 1931–1950* (London, 1969), p.527
[43] Baroness White obituary, *The Independent*, 5 January 2000.

For much of the century, the Flintshire seat had fluctuated between Tory and Liberal and, even in the Labour victory of 1945, Nigel Birch held the seat for the Conservatives with a majority of 1,039 over White. The constituency included a number of localities that did not constitute natural Labour territory. In 1950 the constituency was split in two: Birch held the seat of Flint West, though White took Flint East for Labour with a majority of 6,697.[44]

The miners of Point of Ayr represented an industrial proletariat trapped in a rural Conservative enclave that survived until the election of David Hanson for the seat of Delyn in 1992. The Labour Party was always denied success in the seat of Flint West owing to the durability of Liberal support; up to 1979 the Liberal Party still attracted around 10,000 votes, blocking Labour from supplanting the Conservatives. The case of Flint West reveals the depth of Labourism amongst the north Wales miners. Against all the odds, the union was able to challenge the Conservatives, making its presence felt on local councils and within the rural constituency. With the radicalism generated by the Second World War and the enhanced role of the NUM both nationally and locally, the miners became more active in the development of the Labour Party throughout north Wales. The party at constituency level emphasized the urgency of party recruitment during the war, although they operated in the climate of an electoral truce. A popular circular distributed to miners proclaimed that 'Our task in peace and war is to convert a majority of the electorate to Socialism, so as to ensure that when hostilities cease and the war is won the peace is not lost.'[45]

Within the coalfield, the miners contributed greatly to the campaign funds of the party; this was most pronounced in Wrexham, where the union was influential in local branches primarily based around former or existing mining areas. With the termination of the political truce in 1945, the area council of the union urged members to stand in all local elections. The leadership required that the Area Executive Committee (AEC)

---

[44] Arnold J. James and E. Thomas, *Wales at Westminster: A History of the Parliamentary Representation of Wales, 1800–1979* (Llandysul, 1981), p.156.
[45] Circular of Flintshire Divisional Labour Party, 24 February 1941: Patrick Heesom collection.

endorse each candidate in order to receive union funds.[46] With the increased majority for Robert Richards in 1945, the dominance of Labourism in Wrexham was confirmed bureaucratically, culturally and ideologically.

The consolidation of Labourism in the coalfield was not due to the work of the miners alone; other unions such as the National Union of Railwaymen (NUR), and the T&GWU, played significant roles, notably in the industrialized constituency of Flint East. The party here was able to operate in increasingly favourable circumstances. The bulk of the Conservative and Liberal vote became detached from the constituency in 1950. The industrial workers of the massive John Summers steel plant and the two large Courtaulds factories in Flint were able to exercise their influence electorally, playing an important part in the victory of Eirene White.

The T&GWU was dominated by the charismatic Huw T. Edwards, who had replaced Arthur Deakin at the Shotton office. Edwards, a long-serving member of the Labour Party, eventually joined Plaid Cymru because of the tensions between the 'Bevanites' and the 'Gaitskellites'.[47] He had been a member of Flintshire County Council and leader of the Labour group. His politics were formed in the south Wales coalfield, where, as a miner, he experienced the Cambrian Combine strike of 1910–11. However, his years in south Wales had not altered his aversion to British communism. The one positive thing he did have to say about Arthur Deakin was that he saved the British trade unions from domination by the Communists.[48] Edwards remained a critic of Deakin and felt that Bevan should have been Labour leader. Tom Jones, a veteran of the Spanish Civil War, and an ex-miner who had experienced the General Strike in the Wrexham coalfield, replaced Edwards as T&GWU leader in north Wales in 1953.[49]

NUM activists, along with their contemporaries in other unions, were influential in the development of trades councils and Labour electoral strength in certain localities. However, the

[46] North Wales NUM Minutes of special council meeting, 7 December 1945: CRO Flintshire D/NM/39.
[47] Huw T. Edwards, *It was my Privilege* (Denbigh, 1957).
[48] Ibid., p.86.
[49] *Transport and General Workers Record*, August 1990.

Conservative presence proved resilient in both Denbighshire and Flintshire and the party drew support from a number of trade unionists. Hugh Pritchard, the local branch secretary of the Railway Clerks Association, was elected president of the East Flintshire Conservative and Unionist Association in 1949. This was the first time that a trade unionist had been appointed to the highest position in the association. Pritchard argued that this was a measure of the democratic nature of the party.[50]

In Denbigh in 1945, the Labour Party was pushed into third place when Sir Morris Jones took the seat for the National Liberals with a majority of 4,922. A number of Liberal and Conservative candidates were able to hold their seats owing to their industrial backgrounds and their ability to keep working-class votes, not only through deference, but through appeals to a shared experience. Gwilym Rowlands held the seat of Flintshire as a Conservative up to 1945. In 1935 he had won the seat from the Liberals who, except for a short period (1924–9), had held it for eighty years. Rowlands was a native of the Rhondda and the son of a colliery manager; he had himself worked in the pits and had been a member of the SWMF (South Wales Miners' Federation) before becoming a Conservative activist and MP.[51]

The narrow defeat of Eirene White, who cut the Conservative majority to 1,039 in 1945, transformed the Labour Party in north Wales, and she became both the driving force behind the consolidation of Labourism locally and an important figure nationally. Local activists were now convinced that one more push would deliver a Labour victory. White's work in promoting the cause of women in the party throughout the country also enhanced her profile. The debate over steel nationalization became crucial as many of her constituents relied on the industry for employment. White's national profile was important in generating further support in the area. Bevan visited north Wales during the 1945 election and, in 1949, Gaitskell spoke at the Rhos miners' institute, claiming that nationalization had been a success.[52]

With the approach of the 1950 election, both Conservatives and Liberals were fully aware of Labour's strength in the

[50] *Flintshire County Herald*, 18 September 1959.
[51] *Flintshire County Herald*, 21 January 1949.
[52] *Wrexham Leader*, 25 May 1949.

constituencies of Flint West and Flint East. The president of the Holywell Conservative branch, J. R. Hughes, suggested that the Liberals should not put up a candidate in Flint East, but join the Tories to defeat White. The enemy was the same to Liberals and Conservatives – socialism. However, the Liberals were not yet ready to give up their historic roots in north Wales and declined the offer of partnership, standing Stuart Waterhouse in the constituency. White captured the seat with a substantial majority, marking the end of a significant Liberal challenge. In the 1951 election the Liberals declined to fight, Waterhouse claiming that this was because of his own personal business reasons. This had the effect of cutting the Labour majority by half. In Flint West, Birch called on Liberals to vote Conservative as they had more in common with Tory ideals than they did with socialism.[53]

Socialism was not only a word of abuse levelled at the Labour Party by the Conservatives and the Liberals, but it was equated, by many supporters as well as opponents, with the existing policies and practices of the Attlee government. This has been lost in some of the accounts of the Labour Party in this period which view the party as bereft of ideas and solely concerned with administering the capitalist economy. At a meeting in Wrexham in 1951, the socialist solicitor Cyril O. Jones, who had been associated with the left of the MFGB, endorsed the candidature of Robert Richards as he stood 'for all the great principles of socialism'.[54] Similarly, a year later, Tony Crosland told a meeting in Flint that 'in Marxist terms, they [the Labour government] had destroyed pre-war capitalism, but they had not yet established the socialist state'. He called for further extensions of common ownership and a shift towards some form of workers' democracy in the nationalized industries.[55] Miners attended these meetings and became involved in the discussion of policy concerning the future strategy of the Labour government.[56]

With the defeat of the Labour Party nationally in the election of 1951, the post-mortem affected branches in Wrexham and the

[53] *Flintshire County Herald*, 28 September 1951.
[54] *Wrexham Leader*, 12 October 1951.
[55] *Flintshire County Herald*, 1 February 1952.
[56] The Point of Ayr NUM lodge minutes show that there was enthusiasm for the visit to Rhyl of Hugh Gaitskell in 1952 and it was decided that the full lodge should attend the meeting: CRO Flintshire D/NM/774.

two constituencies in Flintshire. The victory of the Conservatives did not lead to the dismantling of the policies of the Attlee government, and the situation in the coal industry remained largely unchanged. This caused a degree of concern for Labour activists, as the rhetoric predicting Tory ruination did not come to fruition. Younger miners in the area, although still firmly committed to the ideals of Labour, were not as active in the union or the party. They had not experienced the pre-war struggles which had led to the adoption of these ideals. Nonetheless, despite the counter-culture of rock 'n' roll, youth movements, the emergence of the Campaign for Nuclear Disarmament (CND) and renewed activity by the CP, the culture of Labourism remained secure. The development of tensions between factions within the Labour Party did not represent themselves in the coalfield, nor were the politics associated with the Cold War affecting the area in any substantial way. Edward Jones retained his belief in the centrist strand of Labourism and carried this with him on to the NEC of the union and the position of vice-president.

In 1953, Eirene White announced that she would not be seeking re-election to the NEC of the party. White took this decision because she wanted to rally moderate socialist opinion and prevent a clash between the extremes of left and right. She argued that factionalism was destroying the party, and Deakin of the T&GWU had only voted against her in the previous year because of her centrist position and for inviting Aneurin Bevan to speak in Flint in 1952.[57] Will Lawther of the NUM remained critical of her protest and could not understand why she initially submitted her name and then later withdrew it. She replied with her view that internal relations within the party were deteriorating.[58] The T&GWU locally was also split over White's position. Huw T. Edwards attacked Deakin's treatment of White, but criticized the local MP for failing to commit herself more fully to the Bevanite cause.[59]

At the 1955 general election, White's majority fell to just over 2,000. Nigel Birch in Flint West consolidated his vote, partly due to the acceptance of the post-war consensus by the Conservatives and his growing popularity in the party. In 1951, Churchill had

---

[57] Baroness White obituary, *The Independent*, 5 January 2000.
[58] *Flintshire County Herald*, 11 September 1953.
[59] Edwards, *It Was my Privilege*, p.83.

claimed that no beneficial legislation would be introduced to favour business over the trade unions. The unions would be consulted on a non-party basis with an emphasis on industrial consensus. This did Birch no harm in his electoral campaign, and in 1955 he gained greater recognition by becoming a Conservative minister. Resigning three years later as Economic Secretary to the Treasury along with Peter Thorneycroft and Enoch Powell over government policy, he retained his electoral base in Flintshire.

The acceptance of the post-war consensus was having a dramatic effect on those who were critical of the limitations of Labourism. Some Labour Party members became sympathetic to the need to dispense with the strike weapon in industrial relations. Arthur Roberts of Flint County Council, when visiting Point of Ayr, noted that the conditions had greatly improved in the mines, though he added that miners were now a significant power and that this power should not be abused.[60] A. S. Nicholas, president of the Industrial Association of Wales and Monmouthshire, condemned as evil those who argued that unions and management were now on different sides of the fence. Reflecting the growth of this consensus across the parties, a new Conservative Divisional Council of Trade Unionists was formed in the Conwy constituency. R. Gough spoke at its first meeting as the Conservative industrial organizer, providing a calming voice to workers who were both Conservatives and trade unionists: 'there are no plans to undermine the legitimate functions of the TUC or other unions and their branches . . . all Tory trade unionists [should] stand for positions [in their respective unions] to free them from the domination of Socialist and Communist parties.'[61]

At the 1959 general election, the Conservative Party was again successful nationally and White narrowly retained her seat with a minuscule majority of just seventy-five votes. The importance of the future of the steel industry again featured prominently in local pre-election debates. In the former Liberal stronghold of Denbigh, W. G. O. Morgan, standing under the banner of National Liberal and Conservative, beat the Liberal candidate

---

[60] *Flintshire Observer*, 14 September 1956.
[61] *Flintshire Observer*, 19 June 1959.

with a majority of 4,625. The Conservatives themselves suffered, as a split in the party soon emerged. The West Flint Conservatives Constituency Association divided when, in 1963, Birch became more vocal in his criticism of the party leadership. He abstained from the vote in the Profumo debate and suggested that the prime minister, Macmillan, should stand down. The dispute locally got worse and the candidate for Flint East, Fred Hardman, criticized Birch and called for loyalty to the leadership in order to sustain electoral dominance over Labour. Eirene White was quick to use this for political advantage and, at a Labour Party dinner in Prestatyn, she compared the state of the Conservative Party to the Labour Party in 1951: 'stale, tired and lacking in purpose'.[62]

The period from the Labour victory in 1945 to the end of the Conservative administration in 1964 was marked by the consolidation of Labourism in the collieries of north Wales. This was not true of other sections of the working class in constituencies outside Wrexham but, in terms of the mining industry, the number of local councillors increased and the nationalization process seemed to offer a stable environment. However, the coalfield was not totally bereft of such political alternatives to Labour as had materialized in areas such as south Wales and Yorkshire. The CP had developed a small membership at a number of pits, and the North Wales District of the party paid special attention to the fortunes of the coal industry and the politics of the area union. But Communists and other perceived outsiders found it difficult to carve out their own place within the culture of the villages.

OUTSIDERS: COMMUNISTS, IMMIGRANTS, CONTRACTORS, AND 'BEVIN BOYS'

The coalfield did not experience a growth of Communist activity in the 1920s and 1930s, although, at some collieries, the system of industrial relations was far from paternalist. This contrasted with south Wales, where the party was able to shape the counterculture of the SWMF, becoming part of its acknowledged political tradition. Communism was weak in the north in part because of the early industrial development of the coalfield; thus,

---

[62]   *Chester Chronicle*, 6 July 1963.

the culture of the NWMA was already well established before the emergence of a coherent Communist doctrine. Up to 1920, the identity of the SWMF remained contested owing to the late development of the industry and the belated centralization of union organization in the coalfield. In 1911 there were 10,500 miners in Denbighshire and 4,000 in Flintshire; the number of miners employed in south Wales had leapt from 128,313 in 1898 to 271,516 in 1920.[63] The industrial economy of the south was booming, while in some sectors, especially coal, the north was in industrial decline. Thus, syndicalism and communism were to form part of the emergent political culture of south Wales, though the dominant strand within the tradition remained Labourist. In the north, the leadership of Edward Hughes, Hugh Hughes and Edward Jones relied on their membership's admiration and deference. This consolidated Labour politics in the coalfield, making it a hegemonic force.

In the late 1930s communism did not exist at all along the north Wales coast, but, amidst the radicalism of the Second World War, a number of branches emerged which drew single-figure memberships from certain collieries. The union leadership and the district Labour Party worked to undermine any notion of a progressive alliance and were firmly against CP affiliation to the Labour Party. A leaflet published in 1943 argued that

> unlike the MFGB, which is free to decide to support or reject or approve conditionally CP affiliation, the latter body is not free to decide and pledge itself to accept and abide by the Labour Party's constitution. If the CP gave such a pledge it would only be because the Communist International ordered or permitted it to do so. The pledge would therefore be worthless . . . The Labour Party, because it is a Socialist Party, stands for democracy – Government of the people for the people. The CI and all its sections stands for 'dictatorship of the proletariat' – dictatorship over the people by the CP in a one party state . . . Communist affiliation would imperil the unity and power of the Democratic Labour Movement.[64]

However, this demonization of the CP did not have a dramatic effect in the pits. The Communist Stan Hughes, of

[63] Chris Williams, *Capitalism, Community and Conflict: The South Wales Coalfield, 1898–1947* (Cardiff, 1998), pp.88–9.
[64] 'North Wales Communist Party and the NUM'. Leaflet published in 1943: CRO Flintshire D/NM/1036.

Hafod colliery, retained the respect of other members of the lodge committee, as did Goronwy Morris of Llay Main. This could well have been due to their espousal of the 'popular front' line. Communist miners concentrated on the fight against fascism and posted anti-Nazi notices in the various colliery canteens. They were also successful in recruitment locally largely beyond the mining industry, and by 1943, there were branches of the party in Wrexham, Chester, Connah's Quay, Shotton, Flint, Llangollen, Aberystwyth, Pwllheli, Conwy, Garth and Ffestiniog.[65] It is clear that Communist strategists viewed the local coal industry as being an infertile environment for recruitment. The T&GWU had already dealt with Communist infiltration at the military supply factory at Marchwiel in Wrexham. According to Huw T. Edwards, Communists from south Wales, London and Ireland were disrupting construction. He took immediate action by sacking the union committee and 'the Communists moved to pastures new'.[66]

The area leadership of the miners' union made it difficult for the Communists to operate on its patch. Requests for the use of union offices for meetings by the party were frequently turned down.[67] The regional organizer of the Labour Party, Cliff Prothero, encouraged this, and argued that the push for affiliation be stopped, as once Communists were elected, their actions were not determined by the organization to which they were elected but by the CP itself.[68] The party responded by inviting Harry Pollitt to speak at meetings with the aim of forming branches in Mostyn, Rhyl, Mold and Denbigh.

The CP in north Wales had worked hard in its attempt to limit the antagonism of the Labour Party. In the 1945 general election, it assisted Richards's campaign in Wrexham. The miners continued to debate the issue of affiliation throughout 1946. The union nationally had been committed to support the party's application following a decision taken by the MFGB conference in 1936. The North Wales Area decided that Edward Jones

[65] North Wales District Communist Party, minutes of district congress 1943: CRO Flintshire D/NM/1036.

[66] Edwards, *It was my Privilege*, pp.61–4.

[67] NWMA minutes of special council meeting, 8 January 1945: CRO Flintshire D/NM/39.

[68] Letter from Cliff Prothero, Welsh organizer of the Labour Party, to NWMA, 14 May 1946: CRO Flintshire D/NM/861.

should press for a referendum on the matter, and should this not be obtained, that he should vote against Communist affiliation.[69] The party found few allies in the wider society of the coalfield. Huw T. Edwards was a critic of the party and had worked to limit its influence in his own union, especially at the large steel plant at Shotton: 'I have never regarded the CP in Britain as being Communist, rather I have regarded them as the willing tool of a Soviet communism.'[70] Edwards was being rather select- ive here if one remembers the role that Horner played in criticizing the 'class against class' phase of the party and attacking unofficial disputes in the South Wales Coalfield. Even the Christians of north Wales warned against the perils of the CP. The bishop of St Asaph, Dr W. T. Harvard, felt that 'com- munism when it is true to its own philosophy, is just as savage, brutal, callous and soul-less as Nazism at its worst'.[71]

With the defeat of the Labour Party in the 1951 general election and the subsequent post-mortem within the movement, the aversion towards Communists hardened. The intensification of the Cold War and developing factionalism added to the general anti-Communist climate. The secretary of the Flintshire Association of Parish Councils, J. Roose Williams, declined re- election due to the furore caused when his CP membership was made public. He stressed that he never brought his politics into council work, but felt that he could not now continue his duties.[72] Roose Williams was a complex character who enjoyed support across the north Wales labour movement. Although a CP activist, Williams remained a committed Christian. In the 1920s, he would travel to various villages by bicycle proclaiming the gospel of Marx and Christ.

Edward Jones also expressed the view of the local miners' union in attacking Horner and communism at successive annual con- ferences when foreign policy was debated. Nonetheless, divisions within the NUM have been exaggerated, and Jones was close to Horner on a range of other issues. Foreign policy could accom- modate factional disputes more easily since it did not threaten miners' solidarity regarding pay claims and working conditions.

[69] North Wales NUM minutes of AEC, 3 April 1946: CRO Flintshire D/NM/39.
[70] Edwards, *It was my Privilege*, p.86.
[71] *Flintshire County Herald*, 4 June 1948.
[72] *Flintshire County Herald*, 19 October 1951.

In 1952, there was a serious disturbance in Flint that led to violence, as the Communist Party sought to recruit members in the centre of town. Party activists distributed leaflets, made speeches in Trelawney Square and came under criticism from a number of lorry drivers from Coventry. The crowd was quite large and an old woman attacked the speakers for having the audacity to stand in front of the war memorial. Several fights broke out and party literature was strewn across the street. The Communists were chased towards the railway station. The police were called and had to block the entrance to the station to stop the crowd getting to the Communists, who leapt on a train for Chester.[73] The following week, J. Gibson, secretary of the Chester branch of the party, told a small crowd in Flint that no more meetings would be held, as the police had stopped them because of the violence. The party did not give up, however, and in October of the same year it organised a rally at Flint town hall addressed by Rajani Palme Dutt. He argued that the aims of the rank and file of the Labour Party were no different from those of the CP.

In terms of its influence on the mining industry, the agitation of the party had little impact. Most miners wanted to see the return of another Labour government and were largely untouched by Communist activity. Edward Jones railed against the influence of the party in industrial matters. In the ballot over the pay claim in 1958, he criticized a pamphlet distributed to rank-and-file miners seeking to persuade them to vote against the offer, which the NUM nationally had urged them to accept.[74] Jones expressed a clear aversion to Communists, but this was not reflected in the wider membership. Although Communists were weak in the local union, they were well respected and seen as being part of the Labourist tradition. Eddie Lloyd from Point of Ayr and Jack Read of Hafod held the view that individuals like Arthur Horner and Will Paynter were solid trade unionists who always fought for the miners first and the party second.

Due to the success of the 1945 Labour government, the ideology of Labourism became dominant. This explains the weakness of the CP in north Wales. Even in south Wales, a

---

[73] *Flintshire County Herald*, 3 May 1952.
[74] *Wrexham Leader*, 21 October 1958.

traditional storm centre of CP activity, a comparison between electoral success in 1945 and its weakness in 1950 testifies to the strength of Labour dominance. In 1945, in the constituency of Rhondda East, W. H. Mainwaring took the seat for Labour with a majority of 972 over the Communist candidate, Harry Pollitt. In February 1950, he retained the seat, again competing against Pollitt, with a majority of 22,182. In essence, the Labour Party in both south and north Wales was able to dilute the effectiveness of the CP by pointing to the successes of parliamentary socialism. This was given added impetus by the developing culture of anti-communism during the Cold War.

Along with the new system of industrial relations, the nature of local identity within the coalfield faced a further challenge with the introduction of foreign labour. An identity of 'Welshness' was characteristic of the labour movement of north Wales but could not be characterized by party affiliation or a commitment to the language. Huw T. Edwards finally split with Labour in 1959 and joined Plaid Cymru, though he stopped short of advocating total independence; his support for the nationalists represented a protest against Labour moderates rather than a pure expression of nationalism.[75] Point of Ayr remained the only pit in the coalfield where the Welsh language was dominant. Gwilym Hughes recalls that when he started in 1930 there was only one Englishman employed at the pit. This situation only started to alter with management changes. At Hafod, the prominence of the language was not as distinct, but the culture of 'Welshness' was articulated through the male voice choir and the miners' institute. At Gresford and the two collieries in Llay there were fewer Welsh-speaking miners, though the majority of the men were Welsh-born. Both Ifton and Black Park collieries remained Welsh workplaces where a sense of national identity was weak.

In contrast to the South Wales Coalfield, the incidence of anti-Englishness was more pronounced in the north and patterned the development of trade union identity in the area. Disputes in the south often had a particular ideological dimension, tinged with syndicalist activity, and, later the influence of the CP. Socialist agitation and revolutionary rhetoric was an absent feature of mining politics in north Wales. Strikes in Denbighshire

---

[75] Interview with Kieth Jones, TGWU, 2000.

and Flintshire in the nineteenth century were specifically aimed at the presence of English managers in the coalfield. One such event led to an outbreak of violence that occurred at the pits around Mold in 1869.[76] Among the general workforce, animosity towards the English was not as pronounced except at the level of camaraderie, although clear distinctions were made and enforced in competing discourses. English miners used different terms for tools underground and remained averse to Welsh cultural pursuits. Petty disputes often led to vocal stereotyping in the local pubs, but an aversion to the English never manifested itself in any violent clashes.

The first major influx of foreign labour to British pits occurred in the immediate post-war period and was a major topic of discussion at general meetings throughout the coalfield. At a meeting of the AEC in Wrexham in 1947, the delegate from Llay Main asked for clarification on the position of the union concerning the employment of Polish labour. The secretary replied that it was a matter for each lodge to decide whether Poles should be admitted to the pits. However, the union did have a particular policy: 'when foreign labour was employed each man must become a member of the union and understand that in case of redundancy, the foreign worker would be the first to go.'[77] Although the foreign worker became a member of the union, he still carried little weight in terms of the system of seniority within the organization. There was an acceptance by the union leaders of the lesser status of these workers, and this was reflected in the policies adopted. In 1948, the NCB labour officer informed the union that they intended to introduce 100 European workers to Black Park and Ifton collieries. The union responded, stressing that management had little input into this area of industrial relations, and reiterated that each lodge would decide whether to accept or reject the said employees.[78] In 1951, the Bersham lodge insisted on the autonomy of the union on this question, warning that the union must guard against the influx of trained men from outside by ensuring the training of younger miners as quickly as possible.[79]

---

[76] See Alan Burge, ' The Mold riots of 1869', *Llafur: Journal of Welsh Labour History*, 3, 3 (1982), 42–58.

[77] North Wales NUM minutes of AEC, 8 August 1947: CRO Flintshire D/NM/39.

[78] North Wales NUM minutes of AEC, 5 April 1948: CRO Flintshire D/NM/39.

[79] North Wales NUM Bersham lodge minutes, 20 November 1951: CRO Flintshire D/NM/1205–12.

The miners who came into the area from Italy, Poland and Hungary were highly skilled. The Hungarian Ymre Csomore had been an overman in charge of eighty men and had worked in pits for eighteen years. Another, Miklos Szabo, had been a fitter in a number of mines and was well qualified in repairing machinery. He had left the pit and worked for the Hungarian state police until the problems associated with the uprising of 1956 forced him to leave for Britain.[80] The foreign workers were quickly absorbed and, after initial problems of acceptance, once underground there was no animosity shown. From the evidence available, one can detect a difference of attitude between particular lodges and the wider membership. At Ifton colliery, the men criticized the union for not taking a more adverse attitude to foreign labour. Peter Morris of the lodge committee informed the labour officer 'that although the branch had voted 10–2 in favour of the employment of Italians, an amendment was moved at a subsequent general meeting that reversed the policy'.[81] At Bersham, the lodge finally agreed to the introduction of up to thirty Hungarians, though they would not fill the skilled positions.[82]

The aversion to the influx of outside labour focused on the defence of jobs for the existing members of the union and the needs of the local labour force. The branch at Ifton took this further and only agreed to the employment of outsiders when all other recruitment strategies had failed. The resolution carried at a general meeting is illustrative: 'we agree to the employment of Hungarian workers on haulage at Ifton Colliery, provided the Lodge receives an assurance from the colliery manager and Employment Exchanges in the area that no British labour is available.'[83] Labour historiography has lost sight of the issue of race and ethnicity with regard to the trade union movement, either viewing it as a peripheral issue or merging it into a general Marxian paradigm of the nature of class politics. The reaction of the wider membership to the question of foreign labour in a

[80] Letter from Ministry of Labour to Edward Jones, 14 December 1956: CRO Flintshire D/NM/861.

[81] Letter from Peter Morris, Ifton lodge, to NCB area labour officer T. Rogers, 7 February 1952: CRO Flintshire D/NM/718.

[82] North Wales NUM Bersham lodge minutes, 10 August 1959: CRO Flintshire D/NM/1206.

[83] North Wales NUM AEC minutes, 6 May 1957: CRO Flintshire D/NM/1482.

period of labour shortage shows that the union attempted to operate a policy of initial exclusion when it came to Polish, Hungarian and Italian workers.

The emphasis on the protection of local workers also stretched to the planned employment of workers from rural Wales. In 1961, a recruitment campaign conducted by the NCB in Caernarfon and Anglesey met with little success. The employer decided to make migration more attractive by initiating a housing scheme in Holywell in order to draw men to Point of Ayr, though this caused friction between the lodge and the management. Jack Griffiths argued that the lodge would not support the recruitment of men into the area on the promise of houses, as this system did not apply to those already employed.[84] The problem of in-migration was a major source of division within the north Wales labour movement. Local lodges and branches were averse to increased levels of industrialization. Tom Jones of the T&GWU caused a storm of controversy between Plaid Cymru and Labour throughout the period by advocating the sinking of new pits in the east and the siting of power stations in the west. Jones felt that English in-migration was a way of promoting the economic prospects of the Principality.[85]

There might have been a symbolic embrace of Labourism and internationalism due to the radicalism of the Second World War and the victory of the Labour Party in 1945 but, in many respects, the traditions of localism remained. Each lodge worked to ensure that the identity of the union and its control over the local labour force was not diluted by NCB attempts to introduce foreign labour into the pits. Nonetheless, a number of Poles, Italians, Hungarians and others were soon accepted, becoming equal members of the union. At Point of Ayr, a number of Poles gained employment along with a German prisoner of war, Eric Muller, who became a popular character in the local village. Two black miners also joined the workforce, one from the Caribbean and the other from the United States. Although experiencing little racial animosity, foreign labourers were somehow seen as representing a dilution of a particular local identity.

---

[84] NCB/NUM minutes of meeting at Point of Ayr Colliery, 17 May 1961: CRO Flintshire D/NM/811.

[85] *Birmingham Mail*, 12 August 1957.

The influx of English miners in the late 1960s was seen as an even greater threat than the relatively small number of European immigrants.

A further example of an outsider group having initial difficulty in being absorbed into the culture of the colliery can be found in the experience of private contractors. Specialist firms entered most collieries soon after nationalization in order to work on difficult procedures such as tunnel drivages. At Point of Ayr, this caused friction for a number of years, especially as the union had initial difficulty in recruiting non-NCB miners. This almost led to a strike in 1954 when the representatives of the lodge spoke at the AEC. They applied for permission to take a strike ballot in order to insist upon full trade union rights for contractors working for Waddingtons at the newly developed number three shaft.[86] After initially hostile responses from the divisional labour director, a strike seemed imminent, though this was averted as membership and recognition were soon granted. The problem of the use of contractors continued to simmer as the local lodge maintained control over the labour force by always insisting on an end-date for work done by private firms.

In 1958, the lodge withdrew from all joint committees at the pit over the issue, but this policy was later reversed at a general meeting after taking advice from union officials.[87] At the other pits in the area, the question of private contractors did not spark as much animosity. The collieries based in Wrexham had their share of contractors but many of these were local miners who had lost their jobs at older pits or been tempted away by the offer of larger salaries. Differing rates of pay between the two sets of workers caused much friction, but this never led to a serious dispute within the collieries as the contractors became members of the union. Many of the contractors at Point of Ayr were Irish, who numbered about four on each shift. The men were latter-day navvies with a 'work hard, play hard' mentality. Younger miners were thrilled by their tales of international travel and sexual excess. They gained a reputation as drinkers and gamblers, with their earnings exceeding those of the indigenous workforce. They worked and socialized together in separate spheres, playing little

[86]   North Wales NUM minutes of AEC, 9 August 1954: CRO Flintshire D/NM/4.
[87]   NUM Point of Ayr lodge minutes, 12 September 1959: CRO Flintshire D/NM/776.

role in the development of the union. Though they were rewarded financially, they were forced from pit to pit, spending many weeks away from their families, and working long hours under dangerous conditions. As members of the NUM, they did not enjoy the same attention from the union as did other employees in terms of grievances. There was a clear pecking order for the lodge when dealing with the problems of the workforce: faceworkers, craftsmen, general underground labourers, surface workers, then contractors. Contractors were also excluded from positions on official committees, although this was never a formal policy.

The mining community could be both liberating and constraining as local perceptions of Communists, foreigners and contractors affected social relations. The animosity at Point of Ayr subsided as miners from Wrexham and other coalfields began to migrate to the villages of Ffynnongroyw, Penyffordd, Mostyn and the resorts of Prestatyn and Rhyl. The problem that remained was that of recruitment of outside contractors into the union. As late as 1963, the Hafod lodge committee informed the AEC that a number of underground workers remained outside the union and that the management was not co-operating fully on the matter.[88] This again shows that the solidarity of the NUM even at the level of recruitment was built on fragile foundations. The union at times worked to exclude outsiders from the existing localized culture but accepted their contributions as trade union members.

The aversion or nervousness of union members towards outside influences had also been true of the Bevin boys and their introduction into the industry during the Second World War. These workers came from a variety of social and occupational backgrounds. The legendary comedian Eric Morecambe was drafted into the industry when he had already begun his career on stage, along with a host of other, diverse individuals. Many of them once recruited settled in the pits but initially found adjustment difficult. In 1945, the representatives from Black Park complained to the AEC about the incidence of non-unionism amongst the Bevin boys, who were reluctant to contribute to, and to become active members of, the organization.[89] In one

---

[88] NUM North Wales AEC minutes, 7 January 1963: CRO Flintshire D/NM/1133.
[89] NUM North Wales AEC minutes, 9 April 1945: CRO Flintshire D/NM/39.

sense, the indigenous workforce viewed outsiders as a separate
body and as not really part of the 'community of the pit'. This
was reflected in the sociology of lodge positions. Throughout the
twentieth century, local mining unions were dominated by senior
faceworkers who often had links within the wider community of
coal society.

The experience of 'outsider' groups and their introduction to
particular mining localities shows that the union and the
community could work against any threat to the cohesion of the
colliery workforce and established practices. Communists, immigrants, contractors and Bevin boys all testify to the brittleness of
the internationalist perspective and perceived solidarity of the
NUM. This process of integration is romanticized by writers
such as Francis and Smith, who view the introduction of foreign
and contract labour as unproblematic. The Point of Ayr case
shows that the union at the local level could be internationalist
and progressive in terms of rhetoric, but concerning policy
commitment, internationalism remained more of a problem.
The fragmentary nature of the mining workforce has often been
ignored in the dominant historiography, with selective groups
hidden from view in order to benefit the particular political
aspirations of authors.[90]

INDUSTRIAL RELATIONS

Contrary to popular belief, the notion of the 'people's war' did
not signify the end of strike activity in the coalfields of Britain. In
particular, south Wales remained a storm centre of industrial
action, with rank-and-file members taking the initiative and
withdrawing their labour. This often occurred without sanction
from union officials and, at times, without the support of
miners active in the CP. The north Wales coalfield was similar: a
number of short stoppages disrupted the production drive
and brought union officials into conflict with the national
government. The radicalism of the war period also affected the
stability of established leadership patterns within the union.
Disputes were increasingly motivated by younger elements of the

---

[90] This issue has been recently explored in Williams, *Capitalism, Community and Conflict*, pp.69-73.

workforce and by those with little previous experience of lodge activity.

Unofficial militancy remained a threat as the local leadership worked to maintain production targets to boost the war effort. In 1942, the Bersham lodge made an appeal for permission to take a ballot for strike action over grievances relating to the delivery of 'house coal', but the application was refused by the area council.[91] Two years later, Edward Jones dealt with the increase in unofficial stoppages by calling a special meeting to discuss the problem. Jones argued that the stoppages were diluting the war effort and that all grievances should be channelled through the normal procedures. The most significant change in the balance of forces within the area was the radicalization of the Point of Ayr activists. Due to the struggle over recognition, control of the lodge fell to veterans of the fight against the POAIU such as Jack Griffiths and David Beatty Edwards. The relationship between management and union at the pit remained strained throughout the period.

The involvement of union officials on the pit production committees at other collieries drew them away from the direct action initiatives of the wider membership and they increasingly criticized disruption at particular collieries. In 1946, the officials met a number of managers to secure 'co-operation and maximum production'.[92] With the advent of public ownership, the changing nature of industrial relations was not immediately apparent. Speaking at Ifton colliery, Edward Jones stressed that the men would have to forget the 'old practices' and commit themselves to the reformed industry.[93] Within six months, a number of small disputes broke out at Llay Main. On one shift, the surface workers withdrew their labour due to poor working conditions. Within a day, the men had held a meeting to discuss the matter and they included in the debate the level of wages earned for a seven and a half-hour shift. The area leadership was called in to arbitrate and worked to break the unity of the men. After a stormy meeting, it was decided that the surface issue should be decided separately from the wages issue. Jones met the

---

[91] NWMA ordinary council meeting minutes, 9 November 1942: CRO Flintshire D/NM/4.
[92] NUM North Wales AEC minutes, 2 November 1946: CRO Flintshire D/NM/59.
[93] *Wrexham Leader*, 10 January 1947.

management and agreed that the men should return to work; under protest, this was carried by forty-three votes to forty-two against an amendment to continue the strike.[94]

In January 1949, the entire workforce at Llay Main again stopped work against the advice of the union officials. The dispute concerned the level of pay for the fixing of newly introduced steel supports. This was followed a week later by a stoppage of 1,700 men at Gresford over the behaviour of a particular deputy; but this was quickly settled.[95] However, production increased at all the collieries in the area and labour leaders emphasized the consensual nature of industrial relations within the region. Jones praised the increased tonnage rates while attacking those opposed to public ownership: '[it] appears to confound the critic who so frequently proclaims that miners are not conscious of their great responsibility in the present economic circumstances.'[96]

The incidence of stoppages during this period shows that the union leadership in north Wales was fully committed to the project of nationalization and wanted to retain the negotiating position that they had enjoyed during the war. The perceptions of the membership did not signify an aversion to the Labourist project, but some miners found adjustment difficult due to the high level of expectation envisaged before Vesting Day. The miners viewed the NCB as a wing of the government, the government was Labour, so they could not understand management intransigence over particular issues. This cautious scepticism never gave way to outright hostility to the pattern of nationalization, or a critique of the Labour government. This was slow to emerge, manifesting itself in the political shifts within the national union only during the 1960s.

An example of the seriousness of NCB attitudes to unofficial disputes emerged in 1951, again at Llay Main. The board announced that it was going to sue forty-one miners for breach of contract after a series of strikes disrupted production. The lodge did not pursue the disputes through the conciliation machinery agreed by the management and the union, and thus threatened the validity of agreed industrial relations practices. The men on strike lost their case and the support of the union, ultimately

[94] *Wrexham Leader*, 20 June 1947.
[95] *Wrexham Leader*, 21 January 1949.
[96] *Flintshire County Herald*, 24 February 1950.

having to pay damages. Another four-day stoppage at the colliery broke out in 1954 over a petty issue of descending the pit too late on a particular shift. The miners met in Wrexham but again officials advised them to return to work while the union negotiated on their behalf. A year later a strike of electricians at Hafod for one week also brought the men into conflict with the union in protest at the introduction of new machinery.[97]

The lodge committee at each colliery played diverse roles in times of unofficial stoppages between 1945 and 1963. At Point of Ayr, the officials supported such initiatives, often promoting industrial action as representatives of the most progressive strand of the workforce. Throughout the post-war period, the lodge at Point of Ayr remained much more militant than the miners it represented. In contrast, the delegate at Bersham deplored the use of the strike weapon in the current economic climate. In 1956, after a series of disruptions, the men finally accepted the wishes of the committee in accepting a compromise over a particular issue for a trial period only.[98] In 1960, the authority of the lodge was again challenged when the 'rippers' decided to strike over the issue of pay. The officials stated that this was unofficial and reported the men to the area office. The behaviour of union officials suggested that nationalization was clearly a project that was received favourably, initiating joint efforts between managers and workers in diluting conceptions of conflicting interests.

Between 1947 and 1955 the number of disputes in the coalfield had increased, mostly without the direction of the particular lodge or the area leadership to co-ordinate them. There had been two at Bersham, nine at Gresford, one at Hafod, six at Ifton and forty-two at Llay Main.[99] All the disputes seemed to lose their momentum once the agent became involved. This clearly shows two strands of activity linking the miners to the politics of Labourism. Firstly, Edward Jones and the majority of lodge officials were content with the nature of the nationalization process and were opposed to strikes. Secondly, the wider membership were initially quick to withdraw their labour but

[97] *Wrexham Leader*, 25 June 1954.
[98] NUM North Wales Bersham lodge minutes, 31 October 1956: CRO Flintshire D/NM/1206.
[99] NCB/NUM pit inquiry into disputes, 1947–55: CRO Flintshire D/NM/338.

soon submitted once the executive involved itself in steering negotiations towards a settlement.

The sociology of disputes throughout the period up to 1964 can be attributed to three main areas of disruption. First, and most important, was that of pay for newly developed tasks. These included the issues that sparked off the strike of electricians at Hafod and rates of pay for 'rippers' at Bersham. Secondly, there was animosity caused through management practices which had not been radically transformed by the policy of nationalization. Workers at Gresford, Ifton and Point of Ayr all complained about the attitude of lower management in addressing the men and allocating tasks. Thirdly, mechanization itself challenged the established patterns of production that had existed for some time. A number of strikes at Llay Main were directly related to the introduction of new techniques associated with the modernization which the NCB wished to pursue. In essence, animosity was not aimed at the Labour government or the nationalization project, but at small-scale localized problems, which the wider membership felt that the consultative machinery was too cumbersome to deal with. This was a classic example of the gap between the formal rhetoric of public ownership and actual local experiences at colliery level.

At Point of Ayr, industrial relations were more volatile as the management proved unresponsive in dealing with the union. In the 1950s, the lodge official, Jack Griffiths, was dismissed as a result of a two-day strike over staffing levels for the introduction of a long-wall face. The area production manager insisted on his reinstatement as this could have led to a dispute throughout the coalfield. This episode highlights the degree of divergence within the structure of NCB management and the pressure that the union could put on NCB officials to discipline a number of maverick colliery managers. The lodge committee at Point of Ayr became increasingly critical of management culture at the pit. In a letter to the AEC in 1961, they intimated that they were seeking to withdraw from all joint committees at the colliery. The executive opposed this course of action, stressing that the consultative agreements made nationally must be adhered to, as they were in all other areas of the NUM.[100] The NCB became

[100] North Wales NUM, AEC minutes, 26 June 1961: CRO Flintshire D/NM/1133.

concerned about the state of industrial relations at the colliery, and the difficulties on a number of occasions reached the district conciliation board. The problem seemed to lie in the appointment of a particular manager, who planned according to contemporaries to rule the pit with a rod of iron. This caused friction between the men and the management, and industrial relations at the pit were only stabilized when he left. It is illuminating how far a particular appointment could transform the industrial relations of a particular area in fostering militancy or moderation.

Between 1945 and 1963 the north Wales miners had to operate in a climate of economic crisis. Miners were cross-pressured by the need for increased coal production and by the threat to some of the smaller pits represented by the introduction of more mechanized techniques of coal extraction. At the same time, the recruitment of labour into the industry was erratic, only picking up significantly in the 1950s. The benefits of public ownership were soon apparent with the acceptance of the Miners' Charter and a more concrete role for the union in terms of industrial relations, codified at the national level. Nonetheless, disputes still arose at each colliery owing to the limitations of the nationalization process. As Allen cogently argues, 'It left each industry it nationalised safely and securely within the control of capitalist market structures, to be shaped, moulded, destined to serve these as certainly as if there had been private ownership.'[101]

The dependence of the industry on the dynamics of the market was soon apparent in the north Wales coalfield when two pits closed during this period: Llay Hall and Black Park. The union did not have a strategy for or against the closure of these pits, as they accepted the logic of the market and the competence of 'experts'. This further cemented the relationship between the miners, the NCB and the Labour government. Pit closures and the odd dispute did not signify a problem with stability. Within the coalfield there was still a feeling that there would always be coal in Wrexham. Further, there was a belief that the Labour Party, if returned to power, would naturally develop a long-term strategy for the industry. Even during the period of Conservative rule, although the miners remained firmly committed to Labour,

---

[101] Vic Allen, *The Militancy of British Miners* (Shipley, 1981), p.32.

there was a view that there would be a secure future. It often took an area or national official to whip up sentiment against the Conservatives, reminding them of the 1926 lockout and the 'hungry thirties'. Arthur Horner, speaking in Wrexham in 1958, highlighted the fact that conditions in the mines were now much better and that the miners had the 'power to make their own futures'. To the NUM leadership at least, the Conservative government was seen as a potential threat to this situation of union/government unity.[102] Thus, the miners were still committed to the ideals of Labourism and the nature and scope of the nationalization process. The political interpretation of industrial disputes during this period has been wrongly used to claim the opposite. Francis and Smith, along with a host of others, have often concentrated on the most active members of the union in order to gauge the perceptions of the wider membership, drawing a distinction between the perceptions of what nationalization was to be and how this hope was quickly dashed. Zweiniger-Bargielowska goes some way to dispelling this simplistic reading, but goes too far in suggesting that nationalization meant little.[103] To the miners of north Wales the process involved a marked improvement at all levels, from rates of pay to an enhanced role for their union representatives. Public ownership represented a period of optimism, which only came under increased scrutiny in the late 1960s.

NORTH WALES MINERS AND THE POLITICS OF PRAGMATISM

Within six months of nationalization, the NCB announced that Llay Hall would probably have to close in the near future. In January 1947, Harry Davies, NUM delegate, had raised the flag of public ownership, proclaiming that 'it was a great day for the younger generation and it was up to them to see that the flag was never hauled down, every man was now of equal status'.[104] The youth of Llay had little time to enjoy the benefits of equal status as the pit closed within a year. The NCB acknowledged that the

---

[102] *Wrexham Leader*, 16 December 1958.
[103] Ina-Maria Zweiniger-Bargielowska, 'South Wales miners' attitudes towards nationalisation: an essay in oral history', *Llafur: Journal of Welsh Labour History*, 6, 3 (1994), 70–84.
[104] *Wrexham Leader*, 10 January 1947.

pit produced coal of a very high quality, but the seams were low, making mechanization difficult. From 1939 onwards the installation of modernized coal-cutting and conveying machinery created problems for the pit, and the future looked bleak. Davies argued that the closure would mean a severe blow to the district and that the union would fight hard to keep the pit open. Throughout 1947, the pit continued to lose money. As soon as the production was covered elsewhere, the NCB announced that the unit would close, with the men having the option to transfer to other pits in the area. Four hundred and thirty-five men worked at Llay Hall including Albert Davies and Ernest Edwards. The closure did not come as a shock to these miners because of the nature of the seams. Further, it was thought that the other pits would absorb the redundant men, so the fatalism of the workforce was kept to a minimum.

The economic climate of the industry did not suggest a cataclysmic run-down in terms of each colliery unit. There was still a shortage of labour in the coalfield, where production had declined rapidly in the pre-war period. The local press still frequently advertised for labour for the mines, and the NCB visited a number of schools to encourage recruitment. Nonetheless, the Coal Board did not include north Wales in its plans for reconstruction, and there were no plans for new collieries. Officials estimated that the mining work force would eventually fall from 8,500 to 6,700 between 1951 and 1965.[105] The closure of Llay Hall did not cause any serious disruption to the system of industrial relations in the area, nor did it lead to a challenge to the orthodoxy of the NCB in terms of its policies for the future of the industry. The closure of Black Park in 1950 was a different matter, and opposition to the closure emerged as a management initiative as much as a union one. This highlights ambiguities within the management structure of the corporation, indicating that different branches of the bureaucracy were often in conflict.

Black Park was one of the oldest pits in the coalfield. At the outbreak of the Second World War, it employed 503 men, mostly residing in Chirk and Oswestry. Along with Ifton, the pit was situated about twelve miles south of Wrexham and relied on a local workforce. Its southerly location proved a handicap; the

[105] *Wrexham Leader*, 17 November 1950.

pit struggled to recruit miners from Wrexham, who did not want to move. In 1950, the divisional director of the NCB intimated that it had to consider the closure of Black Park due to shortage of labour. The local lodge vowed to fight the closure, especially considering the crisis of production in terms of the industry nationally.[106] The AEC debated the issue but no alternatives emerged to challenge NCB orthodoxy. Without further thought on the matter, the union issued a statement:

> It was resolved that we inform our Black Park Lodge having examined all the arguments put forward by the Board in justification of their decision to close Black Park Colliery, we are unable to discover any facts or other evidence which could possibly justify interference with the Coal Board's policy to give effect to the proposals.[107]

The pit finally closed in 1951 with most of the men being transferred to Hafod and Ifton. Many men were happy to move to Ifton as this was in close proximity. What the Black Park incident reveals is the nature of the union's acceptance of NCB policy. This orthodoxy was viewed by miners and their representatives as on the whole pragmatic and legitimate. A number of documents that were subsequently released suggest that there was an alternative to the closure, and even within the corporation the issue engendered a serious debate.

Gordon Nicholls of the Western Area NCB corresponded with F. G. Glossop, another official, intimating a number of reasons for keeping the colliery open. The management themselves at Black Park had not been completely happy with the closure as it would affect the morale of workers in other units in the area. 'The psychological effect on the North Wales mining community would be bad – Llay Hall last year, Black Park this year, which colliery next year?' Those defending the pit argued that it had always been profitable, though officials in the NCB stressed that this argument was not now applicable as the coal used to have a much higher selling price. Further, the coal contained a significant amount of dirt, which would again raise the cost of extraction,

---

[106] North Wales NUM AEC minutes, 4 December 1950: CRO Flintshire D/NM/40.
[107] North Wales NUM minutes of special council meeting, 27 July 1950, re closure of Black Park colliery: CRO Flintshire D/NM/4.

as the coal would have to be washed elsewhere. Robertson, the pit manager, argued for an attempt to improve output by way of the introduction of machines used in mines in the United States. Again, economic reasons went against this; the capital cost would be enormous for small returns. NCB officials argued that the faces at Ifton were mechanized, and transferring the men directly to this pit from Black Park in order to increase production could offset output. The NCB, along with the AEC, wanted to adopt the closure proposals, but Robertson and Nicholls remained doubtful and were optimistic for the future of mining in Chirk.[108]

The NCB stuck to the 'labour shortage' problem to justify the closure and faced no serious challenge from the union. Black Park was in close proximity to Ifton, drawing labour from the same area and thus competing in the employment market. Both pits could not be economically manned, so the corporation was faced with the closure of one of them. In terms of output, Black Park had suffered most with falling tonnage, and modernization had proved more successful at Ifton. A number of Polish workers had complemented the labour force for a time but quickly left because they could not settle. This was no doubt due to the aversion that the union had exhibited when the idea of Polish labour was floated. Thus the colliery was to close and future projects were to be concentrated at Ifton.[109]

The closure of Black Park shows that the union found itself powerless at the local level in developing counter-strategies that would be accepted by the area union and the NCB. The failure to adopt a strategy by the NUM that would counter this 'market orthodoxy' remained a major lacuna in the policy of the union from 1947 through to the dispute of 1984–5. As early as 1950, the corporation was closing pits for other than geological reasons, as the Black Park case clearly shows. At the end of the 1950s, six collieries remained in north Wales: Point of Ayr, Gresford, Bersham, Hafod, Ifton and Llay Main. The 1960s were to bring another round of closures and send shock waves through the coalfield and its mining localities.

---

[108] NCB North Western Area memorandum from G. Nicholls to F. G. Glossop Esq. concerning Black Park and Ifton Collieries, 9 February 1950 (private and confidential): CRO Flintshire D/NM/4.
[109] NCB report on Ifton and Black Park collieries, 28 December 1949: CRO Flintshire D/NM/40.

From the onset of nationalization through to the victory of the Labour Party in 1964, the defining characteristic of the NUM in north Wales was continuity. Edward Jones, as the full-time official, ensured that the union remained committed to the goals of the national union, and no rank-and-file challenges to the leadership of the area emerged. The organization remained compliant in its conciliatory role in the industrial relations of the industry. The years after 1945 saw the consolidation of consensus, as all the miners of north Wales became fully unionized. Involvement in the production drives and administrative functions of the NCB raised the status and profile of the union. In terms of the number of pits in the area, the economics of coal were in decline. Though each remaining pit suffered at particular times from a shortage of labour, this worked to stabilize the union to a greater extent as leadership positions at the branch and area levels were held by individuals for a number of years.

The membership at each pit still largely remained aloof from the politics of the union in terms of active participation, and the rise of fascism and the outbreak of the Second World War did not alter this. The wider membership still distanced itself from the everyday activities of the union and, overall, saw membership as an insurance policy to be utilized in times of crisis. The organization remained politically cautious and took this position into the policy-making processes of the NUM. In 1952, Edward Jones announced that the area would not be following the path of south Wales in discontinuing work on Saturdays due to cuts in the health service announced by the government. The pits in the area continued to produce coal at a healthy rate and, in comparison with other areas, maintained a stable record of industrial relations. As the manager of Bersham colliery illustrated, 'the relationship between the workers and officials is as good as you can find anywhere, and any little argument we have can always be straightened out around the table'.[110]

The implementation of the nationalization programme and the codification of safety legislation led to a significant improvement in the welfare of the miners, but the union still had to deal with fatalities as a fact of life in the coal industry. On 4 July 1952, an accident occurred at the Point of Ayr in which six men were

[110] *Wrexham Leader*, 22 February 1952.

killed, with others sustaining injuries.[111] The accident occurred in a newly developed shaft involving contractors. As usual, a benevolent fund was set up and the perils of mining were again brought home to the wider population. A year later at Ifton, fires broke out underground and temporarily closed the pit. Edward Jones and other union members rushed to the scene: fortunately no one was hurt, but the workforce of 1,200 remained idle for a number of days.[112] A week later a roof collapse at Llay Main killed a miner, which further highlighted the need for sophisticated support systems and safer working practices. Disasters, accidents and compensation claims were the main concerns of union officials. The literature on mining unionism has tended to concentrate on politics and disputes. This perhaps tells us more about the ideological position of historians than it does of NUM officials. In north Wales, union activists can be characterized more appropriately as social workers than as overtly political animals planning and executing strikes.

The local concerns of the union at each pit took precedence over wider claims of comradeship and solidarity. Llay Main began to face particular difficulties in 1959, and the NCB announced that the workforce would be reduced, but with transfer offered to other pits in the area. This again posed a threat to the unity of the union, as the question of seniority became a problem for the recipient lodges. In response to the difficulty of Llay men and their settlement at Hafod, the lodge representative appealed for a more comradely attitude in the treatment of transferees.[113] This was in contrast to the rhetorical internationalism espoused by particular branches in formulating motions for the area conference. The Point of Ayr lodge called for the boycott of South African goods in protest at the apartheid regime, while remaining critical of the use of outside contractors. Within the workplace, there was clearly a pecking order of occupations which the lodge prioritized in times of crisis. Foreign workers, contractors and youth were under-represented in the structures of decision-making and found officials unresponsive to their claims.

[111] NCB report on accident at Point of Ayr Colliery in the no. 3 shaft sinking, 4 July 1952: CRO Flintshire D/NM/40.
[112] *Wrexham Leader*, 23 January 1953.
[113] North Wales NUM, AEC minutes, 14 September 1959: CRO Flintshire D/NM/1482.

The degree of consensus between NCB officials and the NUM in north Wales expressed itself in leadership aversion to stoppages that were unconstitutional, but also in relation to the issue of absenteeism. In the late 1950s, this became a recurrent problem for all areas, and absentee committees appeared in the coalfields. Jones was quick to point out to NCB officials that such institutions had been in operation for a number of years in north Wales, and the union and the management had always worked together on such issues. At Bersham colliery in 1963, the lodge agreed to the sacking of three men owing to their atrocious attendance record.[114] The nationalization process intensified this level of deference towards management, and a number of respondents concluded that, after initial problems, the idea of 'them and us' began to subside. Gwilym Hughes, a lodge official at Point of Ayr, described how a large gathering attended the funeral of Mayfield, the colliery manager, who had coped with the problems of nationalization and the disaster of 1952.[115] However, this did not suggest a thorough attachment to moderation, as the subsequent appointment of Spedding as manager ignited the first wave of serious militancy at the pit since 1926.

In terms of the national union, north Wales retained its autonomous voice and role after reorganization and benefited from the federated structure of the institution. Edward Jones became vice-president of the NUM in 1954, and secretary of the Miners' International, an amazing achievement for an individual from one of the smallest areas of the union. In 1960, Jones addressed his last conference as agent in Llandudno, where he concluded emotionally that 'without nationalization the industry would have become decadent'.[116] The union under the auspices of Jones had little time for factionalism, and though disputes emerged in the 1950s, they did not represent a challenge to his orthodoxy. The election in 1961 to replace Jones was marked by its relatively faction-free nature, and each candidate argued for continuity with the previous leadership. The eventual victor, voted in by the single transferable vote system, was Josiah Ellis of

---

[114] NCB/NUM minutes of meeting held at Bersham colliery, 16 February 1963: CRO Flintshire D/NM/625.

[115] Gwilym Hughes, 'My life at Point of Ayr colliery' (unpublished manuscript, 1974), p.90 (in possession of author).

[116] *Wrexham Leader*, 5 July 1960.

Hafod. Ellis was one of eleven children from a mining family and had worked in various pits in the Wrexham area for many years. His manifesto was completely bereft of politics and he merely stated that he wished to pursue the interests of the union through the promotion of its rules and constitution.[117] All the candidates shared a similar background of initial politicization from the point of production, lodge activity and Labour Party membership. Ellis sealed victory on 56 per cent of votes cast.

In his first year, Jos Ellis faced an impending crisis in the coalfield. The fall in demand for coal nationally affected small coalfields such as north Wales. Further, the problems of mechanization were having a serious impact on morale in terms of industrial relations. At Bersham, the men were critical of any further implementation of new technology as they felt that this would lead to large-scale redundancies.[118] The men at Gresford came out on a three-day strike in protest at the level of pay and the deteriorating relationship between the workforce and the officials. Some men were claiming that they were being victimized because of their refusal to perform particular tasks. At Llay Main, 120 loaders withdrew their labour in a dispute over pay.[119] At Point of Ayr, the lodge remained critical of the management and the inadequacy of communication on particular issues relating to the pit. Ellis, in the tradition of Edward Jones, operated within the structures of the negotiating procedures agreed by the NCB and the NUM. He continued to accept unquestioningly the management orthodoxy in terms of new technology and the reduction of the labour force at particular pits. In 1962 at the annual area conference, he made this clear by stressing that 'we must not be satisfied to wait for mechanization, we must press for it, and in fact we must demand our share of it'.[120] The Wilson government, in the shape of a massive pit closure programme, would implement the logic of this strategy.

Within the next decade, the coalfield was to lose half its workforce, leaving one colliery in Wrexham and one in Flintshire.

[117] Election pamphlet of Josiah Ellis for the position of North Wales Area agent, 1961: CRO Flintshire D/NM/1145.
[118] NCB/NUM minutes of meeting held at Bersham colliery, 13 December 1961: CRO Flintshire D/NM/625.
[119] *Wrexham Leader*, 3 July 1962.
[120] North Wales NUM annual report, 1962: NUM, Wrexham.

The Wilson years were a period of crisis for both the industry and the hegemony of Labourism in the coalfields. The early sixties was a time when the NUM failed nationally to adopt a coherent strategy in terms of new technology and pit closures. NCB orthodoxy in relation to these areas went without challenge, and the union continued to 'fiddle while Rome burned'. Nonetheless, the period from 1947 through to 1963 represented the 'golden age of Labourism' in two significant ways. First, the miners achieved one of their main policy goals with the nationalization of the industry. Secondly, in mining localities in particular, the appeal of Labourism became almost total and its policies were promoted by all sections of the party, the union and the local population of particular villages. The level of factionalism within the area union and the constituency parties was almost non-existent as the emphasis remained on returning a Labour government after thirteen years of Conservative rule. Unlike other areas of the NUM, north Wales was to maintain this commitment to Labour leadership orthodoxy.

This chapter has highlighted a number of issues that justify the focus on the north Wales coalfield in terms of broadening our understanding of working-class labour organizations. It is clear that the effects of nationalization resulted in further enmeshing the NUM within the politics of Labourism and thus limited the chance of the acceptance of alternative strategies. Owing to the longevity of the rule of leaders such as Edward Hughes, Hugh Hughes and Edward Jones, lodge/area relationships were patterned by a system of deference that undermined the emergence of militancy. Due to the decline in the number of miners and the distance between collieries, activists had to operate within a culture of intense electoral competition in which they were a minority, unlike their peers in Yorkshire and south Wales, who enjoyed domination by Labour in particular constituencies.

The dominance of Labourism in the north Wales coalfield in the period from 1947 to 1963 was a two-sided coin in terms of its impact on the union and the mining communities in the area. Its positive aspect secured public ownership, improvements in health and safety, increased pay at particular collieries and an enhanced role for the union at the local and national level. In negative terms, Labourism immediately closed off any radical alternatives to the left of the Labour Party in the planning of a strategy for the coal industry: the CP offered little that was distinctive. In particular, Labourism failed to provide the union with a coherent plan to deal with the rapid decline of the industry during the 1960s.

The pros and cons of the nationalization process and the policies of the Labour government of 1945 have been debated at length elsewhere. Commentators have often lost sight of the fact that the ideology of Labourism cannot be separated from the initiatives and priorities of individuals in particular coalfields. To the miners of north Wales the politics of the Labour Party represented an attempt to control the excesses of the capitalist economy through the institutions of the state. The miners themselves participated in this project as the only viable alternative to the capitalism of the Conservative Party, which was identified with the 1926 lockout and the decline of the industry. Compared with what was to come in the late 1960s and 1970s, the miners looked back on this period as the 'golden age' of the industry. They perceived it as the dawning of a new era. The power of the coal owner had been eradicated and the consumer boom of the 1950s and 1960s enhanced the self-esteem of each miner, his family, trade union and local community.

Bersham miners breaking production records in the Queen Seam, 1968. © British Coal Corporation. Reproduced by permission of the Public Record Office.

Face workers withdrawing roof supports at Hafod Colliery in 1952. © British Coal Corporation.

Above Miners' cottages, Old Row, Chirk Green, 1960. Chirk provided labour to both Black Park and Ifton collieries. © British Coal Corporation.

Opposite above The breakthrough connecting Hafod and Bersham collieries, 1963. Tom Ellis, Bersham manager and future Labour MP for Wrexham, in the centre shaking hands with Jim Hislop, manager of Hafod. © British Coal Corporation.

Opposite below Christmas carols underground at Bersham Colliery. © British Coal Corporation. Reproduced by permission of the Public Record Office.

Top left 'The Negotiator'. Joe Gormley, NUM President, shows his hand to a miner at the Llay miners' welfare. © Mel Grundy.

Top right Ted McKay, North Wales NUM Area Secretary, at the Gresford disaster memorial 1982. © British Coal Corporation. Reproduced by permission of Flintshire Record Office.

Below The pit by the sea; Point of Ayr Colliery. © British Coal Corporation. Reproduced by permission of the Public Record Office.

Tensions clearly visible on the Point of Ayr picket line in spring 1984. Most of the pickets in shot were from south Wales. © Jeff Pitt.

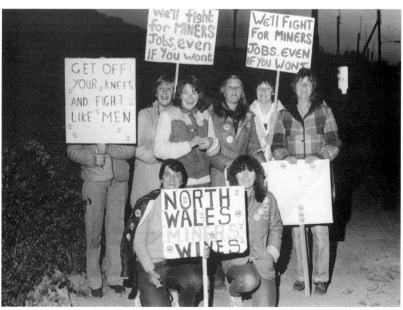

Point of Ayr striking miners' wives mobilize their forces in spring 1984. © Jeff Pitt.

During the year long National Miners Strike of 1984-85 men at Bersham Colliery near Wrexham broke the strike in November 1984 leaving only 15 men who stayed true to the union, until the bitter end, four months later on March 11th 1985 — the last men to return in Wales.
Standing L→R Joe Smout, Keith Hett, Idwal Poole, Emlyn Williams.
Kneeling L→R Dave Prince, Bobby Williams, Raymond Jones, Chris Hughes, Michael Hett, J. R. Murphy, Mike Delaney, Martin Green, Dave Felton and Dave Evans. Not present, Mark Britner.

Above 'Hats off' for the last tub of coal from Bersham Colliery, 18 December 1986. © Vic Cleveley. Reproduced by permission of Flintshire Record Office.

Opposite above The fifteen men at Bersham Colliery who stayed true to the union, until the bitter end, during the year-long National Miners' Strike of 1984–5. © Vic Cleveley. Reproduced by permission of Flintshire Record Office.

Opposite below Reflections and laughter on the last shift at Bersham Colliery, December 1986. © British Coal Corporation. Reproduced by permission of Flintshire Record Office.

Memorial erected by the North Wales NUM in May 2001 to celebrate the history of coal mining in the village of Ffynnongroyw. © Kevin Jones.

II

MINERS, LABOUR AND PIT CLOSURES, 1964–1971

> Dai Pearce and Big Joe,
> They finish today,
> Friday the thirteenth,
> Unlucky they say.
>
> It is for the Board,
> They're losing a team,
> In evaluation it's
> Like losing a seam.
>
> They work bloody hard,
> These men from Chirk,
> And they're always willing to do any work.[1]

In terms of labour history and, more specifically, the history of the British miners, the 1960s provide an image of hopes dashed regarding Labour socialism. The tensions within the 'contentious alliance'[2] of the party and the trade unions manifested themselves, leading to growing militancy within particular trade unions and a rejection of the pragmatism associated with the Wilson government. This chapter will reassess the decade of the 1960s and its impact on the NUM through the lens of the north Wales coalfield. The election of Harold Wilson in 1964 was to be a double-edged sword for the industry. The number of pits rapidly declined, along with a push for mechanization in those that remained. Yet the attitudes of miners remained buoyant as many began to enjoy the benefits of the 'affluent society'.

A new wages agreement culminating in the National Power Loading Agreement (NPLA) in 1966 brought a powerful unifying force to the politics of the NUM, or so it seemed at the

---

[1] Extract from 'Redundant miners' by Keith Hett, from *Bersham Pit Bottom and Other Poems* (private publication, 1986).
[2] For a detailed account of the relationship between the trade union movement and the Labour Party, see Lewis Minkin, *The Contentious Alliance: Trade Unions and the Labour Party* (Edinburgh, 1991).

time. The introduction of the NPLA complemented the migration of miners from declining coalfields to more prosperous ones,
thus affecting the balance of power in the union, in some respects
both nationally and locally. By 1970, the industry had been
significantly streamlined and the relationship between the
Labour Party and the NUM reached a crisis point in particular
areas, notably Yorkshire, Scotland and south Wales.[3] The experience of the late 1960s created the foundation for such
radicalism, leading to the successful strikes of 1972 and 1974. In
terms of leadership, continuity remained apparent, with the
moderates retaining control of the National Executive Committee (NEC). Nonetheless, pockets of radicalism were emerging
and becoming increasingly critical of the structure and politics of
the union. The North Wales Area of the NUM suffered a series
of shocks in this period, most notably in the closure of four pits,
leaving only Bersham and Point of Ayr. However, the area
remained autonomous, retaining its identity and representation
on the NEC. There were a number of tensions in this period
between the union bureaucracy and the wider membership,
though they were not sufficient to challenge the nature of
Labourist politics.

To the miners of north Wales and other sections of the
working class, the nationalization of coal was certainly not
unproblematic, but it strengthened their commitment to the
Labour Party. By the late 1950s, miners were aware of the
precarious situation in terms of the economics of the energy
industry because of the increased use of gas and oil. However,
this awareness was not something new: from the nineteenth
century onwards, the coal trade had always been affected by the
market; nationalization did not alter this but it provided a
cushion. Even through the dark days of the late 1960s, when
criticism of Wilson was at its most vocal, the commitment to the
ideals of Labourism within the mining industry remained strong.

---

[3] After 1966, the rate of pit closures increased and the NCB embarked on a
programme of rationalization that saw its management structure streamlined and the
closure of a number of administrative units. Each pit was also given greater autonomy,
and the language of competition became the norm for officials. See Norman Siddall,
'Winning horses: a paper based on a talk given to NCB production staff conferences,
autumn 1967': CRO Flintshire D/NM/1460.

With the benefit of hindsight, many Welsh miners saw the Wilson years as a positive experience when compared with the free-market excesses of the Thatcher years and the events leading up to the strike of 1984–5.

The Wilson period is illuminating, not in signifying the 'strange death of British Labourism', but in terms of 'business as usual' in its attempts to foster a socialist programme in an un-favourable economic climate. Both historians and political scientists have treated particular periods as closed boxes or dramas with a beginning and an end. The Wilson years were neither the beginning nor the end of anything. Although tensions were created, the period was marked by continuity in terms of the trade union link with the Labour Party, with electoral support in the coalfields remaining strong.[4] In terms of the NUM leadership, the emerging tensions were settled within the same structures and patterns of authority. Personal animosities usually outweighed the politics of left and right, and certain areas retained their deferential attitude to the 'labour establishment' within both the union and the party. The politics of pragmatism far outweighed the ideological convictions of the Wilson critics, who remained outside the party, and within the coalfield the dominant political creed remained firmly committed to the 'parliamentary road to socialism'. Socialism had been largely translated into the specific advances associated with public ownership and welfare reforms.

In examining the Wilson record, it is necessary to establish the difference between myth and reality. In terms of myth, it is a fantasy to suggest that before 1964 the proletariat was eagerly awaiting the dawn of a new era and the delivery of a socialist society. Furthermore, the Labour Party did not promise a New Jerusalem that was then diluted by the bureaucratic careerists in the Parliamentary Labour Party (PLP). In reality, the miners viewed a Labour victory as a positive move away from the politics of the Conservative Party and a reaffirmation of the goals of nationalization through union involvement in the planning of

[4] Labour won the 1964 election with 41.1 per cent of the vote. In 1966 the share of the vote increased to 48.1 per cent. For a detailed analysis of the sustained manual, working-class support for Labour, see Alan Campbell, Nina Fishman, John McIlroy, 'The post-war compromise: mapping industrial politics, 1945–64', in Campbell, Fishman, McIlroy (eds.), *British Trade Unions and Industrial Politics: The Post-War Compromise, 1945–64* (Aldershot, 1999), pp.69–113.

the industry. Wilson himself did not achieve this goal; his attempts at economic planning were well intentioned but ill thought out and not applied with conviction. The zest with which modernization was applied did not take account of emerging problems of unemployment and the dilution of cohesive communities, in particular in areas traditionally associated with heavy industry. Nor did it take account of the tension between the modernization agenda and the values and priorities of significant sections of the labour movement. The key resource that the party mobilized to bridge the gap was a conception of 'loyalty', which inevitably favoured the interests of the Labour government.

Both the myth and the reality of the Wilson era had the effect of creating tensions in the labour movement generally and in the NUM in particular. Although this did not lead to an outright attack on the politics of Labourism, it opened channels of dissent, articulated by leadership challenges in specific coalfields. In 1963, many British miners were not aware of the contradiction between modernization and support for traditional industries. Party loyalists were dismayed at the scale of the havoc that the government's agenda wreaked on the coal industry. For some, the prospect of alternative employment came as a blessing, but for others it was welcomed with sadness. Amongst activists, claims of betrayal were levelled at the Wilson administration, leading to attacks on local party functionaries.

Most people alive at the time remember with sorrow where they were when the death of the US President John F. Kennedy was announced. Harold Wilson was speaking at the Civic Hall in Connah's Quay to the Labour Party faithful, with a number of north Wales miners in the audience. Kennedy's assassination was to be a potent image of the 1960s, heralding social and political shifts across the United States. Likewise, in Britain the decade was to usher in a period of de-industrialization and cultural transformation that threatened patterns of continuity in colliery villages.[5] The miners in attendance were soon to be shocked themselves by the pace of the run-down of their coalfield, presided over by their political leader who seemed to show little

---

[5] The impact of the 1960s is charted in great detail in Arthur Marwick, *The Sixties: Cultural Revolution in Britain, France, Italy and the United States, c. 1958–c. 1974* (Oxford, 1998).

sympathy that the coalfield would be reduced from over thirty pits at the turn of the century to only two by 1974.

Wilson was seen as the man who would stand by coal and promote the welfare of the miners as a central plank of the government's agenda for Britain, having pledged this at the 1960 party conference. This pleased miners, as he had been one of the architects of coal nationalization. The union itself was still secure and its political stance remained centrist. The politics of the Cold War had helped to undermine the effectiveness of the Communists, and those who did hold prominent positions, such as Will Paynter and Lawrence Daly, were often critics of the policies of the Soviet Union. Daly had previously broken with the Communists in 1956, creating a seedbed of left realignment. The union president from 1961, Sidney Ford, a pragmatic leader, provided a balance to the left-wing general secretary Will Paynter. The 1947 consensus that was the foundation of the nationalization process was slowly becoming strained both externally, due to the workings of the capitalist economy, and internally, due to political shifts within specific areas of the union.

The rate of pit closures in the late 1950s seemed to suggest that a number of collieries were being closed for more than just geological reasons. In many areas, this provoked little reaction, as the number of pits still exceeded the number of miners who wanted to work in them. Further, the appointment of Alf Robens in 1961 as chairman of the NCB intimated that the future of the industry would be secure, with the NUM playing an essential role. Robens had been a leading light in the Labour Party, and could perhaps have become its leader if circumstances had been different. Robens had been an official with USDAW, the trade union representing shop workers and others in the retail sector. He had been a rising star in the Labour shadow cabinet before his appointment to the NCB by the Conservatives. Although he was to have a dramatic impact on the industry, it is ironic that both the unions and others in the industry had been opposed to his appointment. His association with the right of the Labour Party had not endeared him to the left in the NUM. Nonetheless, he went on to be remembered as one of the best chairmen of the corporation and maintained a good relationship with union leaders in a number of areas. This seems difficult to understand, as the industry was dramatically run down during the 1960s. But

Robens was able to maintain a fair relationship with the miners, their leaders and their communities.

Robens played the role beautifully, speaking at NUM conferences, attending funerals of union leaders and putting himself about in all areas of the British coalfields. However, the relationship went beyond the ability of Robens to elicit consent and demonstrated the depth of Labourist commitment within the industry. He often spoke at NUM weekend schools, lambasting the policies of the Conservatives and promising a different approach by a future Labour government which would place coal at the centre of energy provision for the nation. Once Labour was in government and pit closures followed, he was not afraid to attack Wilson and others, pressing for the development of a coherent fuel strategy. Echoing the views of miners' leaders, he stressed that, 'when we closed a pit employing say 2,000 men, these jobs were lost for ever in the area, and the cost of introducing new industry was so expensive, in fact, that realistic figures have never been published'.[6]

In his autobiography, Robens claims that he resented the fact that the NCB was taking the blame for closing pits.[7] He argued that it was purely a decision of the Labour government and that they were outdoing the Tories in undermining the future of the industry by introducing a fuel policy which was designed to lower the amount of coal needed for energy supplies.[8] It is clear that the government manipulated the NCB, but it still played its role in advocating rationalization; a number of hasty decisions, particularly in Cumberland and north Wales, led to some questionable closures. This prompted the development of a more radical approach to closures within the union, especially amongst activists. Robens himself noticed this but argued that it was merely down to a new brand of extremist. He continued to lavish

[6]   Lord Robens, *Ten Year Stint* (London, 1972), p.155.
[7]   Speaking at a weekend school in north Wales, Robens argued against the expansion of nuclear power, as this would endanger the survival of the coalfield's remaining pits. *Liverpool Daily Post*, 13 October 1969.
[8]   In 1969, Robens himself was aware of the developing tensions between the union and the Labour Party. He called for a minimum programme of closure to prevent the crumbling of the miners' morale. Robens also called for a more developed system of planning in partnership with the TUC. Address by Lord Robens, NCB chairman, to the Institute of Metals, 11 March 1969: CRO Flintshire D/NM/1459.

praise on people like Horner, Paynter and Watson in Durham.[9] By 1963, these stalwarts of the labour movement had all retired. Robens concentrated on building a new pantheon of favourable NUM officials epitomized by Joe Gormley of the Lancashire Area.

In other coalfields, particularly Yorkshire, the left continued to crystallize around Communist dissidents and disgruntled members of the Labour left who were averse to Wilson's pragmatism. Vic Allen has charted the development of the left in Yorkshire, where a number of educational initiatives had radicalized several miners' leaders, culminating in the election of Arthur Scargill to the area presidency in 1973. This process had begun in the late 1950s, when attacks on the consensual nature of the conciliation scheme emerged through unofficial channels.[10] The Doncaster Panel emerged as a crucial forum for rank-and-file dissent. The north Wales coalfield remained immune from the political shifts in the national union and continued to exhibit its familiar characteristics of autonomy and moderation.

The rate of pit closures alarmed many and, by 1968, only 317 collieries remained open; there had been a thousand at the time of nationalization. This culminated in the attack on the platform at the 1968 Labour Party conference as the modernizing zeal of Wilson continued to destroy coalfields.[11] The period was marked by the inaction of the right of the NUM, though the left also found itself a prisoner of a Labourist project which it had played a part in constructing. The whole notion of a nationalized industry operating within a capitalist economy raised problems for the left, which it failed adequately to address.[12] Even

---

[9] Robens, *Ten Year Stint*, p.40. Robens was able to play a dual role as guardian of the miners' interests and a self-conscious modernizer adept at seeking rationalization of the industry while minimizing potential sources of conflict by remaining close to moderates in the national union.

[10] Resolution to the 1958 annual conference seeking the amendment of clause ix of the Conciliation Agreement. See Andrew Taylor, *The Politics of the Yorkshire Miners* (London, 1984), p.29.

[11] David Howell, 'Wilson and history: 1966 and all that', *Twentieth Century British History*, 4, 2 (1993), 174–87.

[12] The Communist general secretary Will Paynter had a particularly close relationship with Sir William Webber, the industrial relations officer of the NCB. Both argued that it was the restraints affecting government policy that were creating a crisis in the industry and not the nature of nationalization. See Roy Church, 'Employers, trade unions and the state, 1889–1987: the origins and decline of tripartism in the British coal industry', in Gerald D. Feldman and Klaus Tenfelde (eds.), *Workers, Owners and Politics in Coal Mining: An International Comparison of Industrial Relations* (Oxford, 1990), p.53.

Communist officials such as Horner and Paynter did not coherently see beyond the 'socialism' of the Attlee governments of 1945–51.

The relationship between miners, their union and the Labour Party is one that has often been overlooked by many authors on the left. This is ironic, as here lies the secret of the pattern of British trade union development and working-class politics. Though tensions were apparent in the 1960s between miners and Labour, the right in both union and party was always able to maintain ascendancy. The role of sponsored MPs and dominance in constituency Labour Parties (CLPs) ensured that key areas would remain on board. This was not a one-way process. The view that Labour was the representative of the interests of the industry goes some way to explaining the popularity of Robens on the right and a figure like Scargill on the left. Robens recalls that at a particular meeting he was being harassed by a woman over the closure programme. Her friends attempted to silence her, stressing that it was Lord Robens she was speaking to. The woman was not deterred: 'I know it is, he's one of us though. He's Labour like us, isn't he? We put him where he is.'[13] Critics within the industry who twenty years later disagreed with the tactics of Scargill still held a place in their heart for him because he had come from a similar occupational and class background. The concept of 'one of us' and the strength of a shared identity goes some way to explaining the resilience of Labourism in the British coalfields and beyond, even in the climate of industrial decline in the coal industry in the 1960s.

The South Wales Area, which often provided coherent critiques of Labour Party policy, was also affected in the 1960s by the scale of pit closures, but the consensus between the NCB and the union remained relatively stable. Soon after the 1964 election victory, Will Paynter opposed the use of industrial action over wages and was in agreement with Robens in criticizing the level of absenteeism in the Welsh pits.[14] The executive committee, supported by a delegate conference, also decided against industrial action on the issue of closures.[15] The Aberfan disaster

---

[13] Robens, *Ten Year Stint*, p.293.
[14] Ibid., p.283.
[15] Hywel Francis and David Smith, *The Fed: A History of the South Wales Miners in the Twentieth Century* (London, 1980), p.430.

of 1966 did little to consolidate the relationship between the union and the NCB,[16] although, overall, party loyalty proved durable even in these days of uncertainty and the electoral dominance of Labour in south Wales seemed secure. The Carmarthen by-election in the same year, which delivered a victory for Plaid Cymru (followed by a dramatic fall of the Labour vote in Rhondda West and Caerphilly), sent a warning shot across the bows, but miners remained relatively compliant in response to calls for Labour loyalty.

The North Wales Area was relatively immune to the tensions developing between class, party and nation. Although the coalfield was in crisis, established relationships and 'class percep-tions' remained relatively untouched by the disappointment of the left in and outside the NUM. Criticisms of government policy were often contained within the 'logic of Labourism'. Traditions of deference and party loyalty outweighed the push for radical solutions. If anything, it was the essence of Labourism that was strengthened during this period. At the annual conference of the north Wales miners in 1965, the level of optimism regarding the Wilson government was apparent. Jos Ellis gave a colourful speech and noted that the miners now had a government that would be sympathetic to the plight of the coal industry. In terms of industrial relations, he stressed that the use of strike action only damaged the future of the coalfield. Ellis also lavished praise on Alf Robens for his agitation for a national fuel policy.[17]

In terms of the structure of the union, only six lodges remained by 1965: Llay Main, Gresford, Bersham, Hafod, Ifton and Point of Ayr. For all the collieries, the next few years were crucial in determining their futures. Llay Main had recently experienced trouble due to increased mechanization, Gresford was suffering from geological problems and Bersham was struggling to keep up production from the Ruabon Yard seam. The most promising pit was still Point of Ayr, which had adapted well to the use of power loading.[18] In 1965, Percy Jones became

---

[16] Iain McLean, 'On moles and the habits of birds: the unpolitics of Aberfan', *Twentieth Century British History*, 8, 3 (1997), 285–309.

[17] NUM North Wales Area annual report, 1965: CRO Flintshire D/NM/119.

[18] NUM North Wales Area annual report, 1965. Membership of each Lodge was as follows: Llay Main 995, Hafod 861, Bersham 790, Point of Ayr 541, Gresford 1,848, Ifton 1,111, and a small group of 14 members at the privately owned Smelt Colliery: CRO Flintshire D/NM/119.

head of department for the union, remaining a committed servant of the north Wales miners through to the 1990s.[19] Jones had been an office worker at Llay Main and, along with other officials, was active in the Labour Party, being a councillor for Hawarden. There were still no recognizable political divisions within the union and the sole Communist, a councillor in the Rhos and a lodge official, was a pragmatist.[20] A branch of the CP remained in Rhos but was very small, never amounting even to a faction within the area's politics.

Although NCB projections from 1964 were quite promising, Jos Ellis and the Wrexham leadership were increasingly aware of the gradual switch to oil heating throughout the coalfield. This led to the development of tensions between the local Labour Party branches and the union. Ellis, on a number of occasions, attacked the policy of Wrexham Borough Council in its promotion of a smokeless fuel policy, going so far as to say that its implementation would bring unemployment and poverty to the area. The union found an unusual supporter in the local Liberal Party. Wilfrid McBriar, the prospective parliamentary candidate for Wrexham, called for a new deal for the miners and a halt to all pit closures.[21] The call for a meeting was refused by the AEC because they were not keen on a 'political gathering' on the issue of closures. The NCB was not a cohesive unit and there were criticisms of the rate of closures within the management structure. Tom Ellis,[22] the manager of Bersham colliery, warned that 'if the Board decided to close all uneconomic pits the social consequences would be disastrous; about 212,000 men would become unemployed'.[23] Yet loyalty to the Labour Party remained, it being viewed as more favourable to coal than the

[19] The head of department was an unelected position within the organization. However, Jones went on to wield significant power as an adviser to the agent and AEC members while being shielded from the pressures of the wider membership.
[20] Article by Stan Hughes, 'Why I turned to communism', *Wrexham Leader*, 28 April 1964.
[21] Letter to Jos Ellis from Wilfrid McBriar, 14 December 1965: CRO Flintshire D/NM/599.
[22] Ellis remained a maverick figure in the NCB. He fully embraced the ethos of nationalization but remained critical of the pace of change from privatized management techniques to the new spirit of co-operation. At Bersham, Ellis frequently deviated from area policy in terms of developments to ensure the future of the pit. See Tom Ellis, *Miners and Men: Mining Engineering* (London, 1971), pp.88–9.
[23] NCB Bersham colliery minutes of colliery consultative committee meeting, 14 January 1965: CRO Flintshire D/NM/1297.

Conservatives. Before the 1966 general election the NUM manifesto bluntly stated that:

> Experience since 1945 has shown that we are far more likely to obtain a fair and reasonable solution of the problems facing the coal-mining industry, and certainly, more humane consideration, with a Labour Government in office than under a Tory administration . . . the Labour Government has not done all that we would have wished, but let us, nonetheless, recognise that despite all the difficulties, the Government has given very substantial assistance to the coal-mining industry.[24]

In north Wales, this situation was ironic, as the area was to lose three pits in the two years following the re-election of Wilson. Coal imports into the area continued to rise. The North Wales TUC Advisory Committee had warned of this as early as 1962. The production per week in the coalfield was around 44,000 tonnes, though the existing demand was around 80,000 tonnes; the shortfall was filled by coal from the Midlands, which created tensions within the NCB and the NUM. The Wrexham Trades Council also used this argument and consistently campaigned for the NCB to consider sinking a new pit in the Wrexham area.[25]

The campaign for further development was neutralized by the problem of absenteeism and the inability to recruit miners locally. There seemed to be a calm before the storm in 1964, and at Llay Robens told the delegates that the shadow that had been hanging over north Wales on his last visit had now been lifted. The progress made with mechanization had been a success, and co-operation between management and men complemented it. The NCB also joined with the union in pushing for the use of coal locally. The area manager, Gordon Nicholls, pleaded with the governors of the Denbighshire Technical College to 'use coal or take responsibility for the bringing of the industry to its knees'.[26] This unity within the industry was used by Jos Ellis and the leadership to criticize the politics of local government. In a statement made to the *Wrexham Leader*, Ellis stated that 'it appears

[24] Manifesto of the NUM for the general election of 1966: NUM, Wrexham.
[25] North Wales TUC regional advisory committee: notes of a meeting between Lord Brecon, minister of state for Welsh Affairs, and the trade unions at Rhyl, 26 April 1963: CRO Flintshire D/NM/1076.
[26] *Wrexham Leader*, 24 July 1964.

our enemies are not the coal owners but rather the people we appoint to undertake duties as councillors in local government'.[27] Robens also illustrates this in his autobiography:

> The attitude of some councils I found infuriating. On the one hand they went cheerfully ahead putting in oil to replace coal under the boilers of swimming baths, schools, town halls and so on. And then in the next breath, authorities in the mining areas, who collected large sums of money in rates from the coal industry, were moaning because we closed pits.[28]

On the industrial relations front, the number of strikes in the coalfield began to diminish. Discontent in the area was normally confined to the bureaucratic structures of the conciliation agreement. At Point of Ayr in March 1964, twelve miners at the pit were sacked for failing to carry out a task at the instruction of the manager. The men were subsequently reinstated but the umpire at the meeting held to discuss the issue ruled that the action of the manager had been lawful. Owing to the position of the industry and the difficulty in motivating recruitment, the union found that it had a strong bargaining position and could often challenge NCB decisions which lodges would normally have little chance of reversing. Activists took this view at the time. Vic Roberts, the future president of the area, recalls that the position was quite comfortable: 'the Board couldn't sack one of us and they couldn't sack all of us.'[29]

A dispute of some importance occurred at Bersham in 1964 over a price list for the Ruabon Yard seam. Although the union accepted the amendments of the management to the agreement, they forced them to delete references intimating the possible closure of the pit. Closure was now being taken seriously as the reports from the NCB were often schizophrenic in terms of future security or an immediate closure.[30] The corporation had a simple classification system for its collieries in the North Western Division. Pits were placed in the categories A, B or C. On A list were continuing collieries with a long-term future such as

[27] *Wrexham Leader*, 29 January 1965.
[28] Robens, *Ten Year Stint*, p.10.
[29] Vic Roberts interview, 1997.
[30] North Wales District Conciliation Board minutes of district disputes committee, 22 October 1964: CRO Flintshire D/NM/347.

Gresford, Ifton and Point of Ayr. The B category was for collieries with a doubtful future and Hafod was in this class. Both Bersham and Llay Main were in category C in 1965, classed as short-life uneconomic collieries.[31]

A major problem for the union was the inconsistency of classification, with pits moving from one band to another in a period of months, making it difficult for the union to argue its case concerning particular collieries. This troubled Joe Gormley of Lancashire, the future NUM president. E. J. Kimmins, the NCB area director, informed Jos Ellis that, after consultation with Gormley, he agreed that 'joint efforts had to be developed and maintained in developing a more favourable climate of increased production and efficiency'.[32] Industrial action was seen as a negative force in undermining this process, and the symbolism of Robens and his relationship with leaders such as Gormley and Sam Watson was important in diluting the effectiveness of arguments emerging from the left. This was evident in a dispute at Gresford when thirty-four workers walked out over a pay dispute. The lodge immediately stressed that they would not support the men involved. This strengthened the position of the NCB in the stage-two meeting of the conciliation scheme, and the men subsequently lost one week's wages.[33]

The numerous disputes were still highly localized in nature and lacked a clear political dimension. The leadership of Robens for the NCB and Sidney Ford for the NUM helped to minimize this, as did the fact that the Labour Party was in power. Disputes in north Wales diminished further with the settlement of the wages question and the signing of the NPLA. This provided a uniform system of payment throughout the British coalfields and strengthened the bargaining position of the union nationally, though weakening it locally. Vic Allen and others have argued that this was the catalyst for the development of militancy.[34] The experience of the NPLA in north Wales seems to suggest that the changes adumbrated by Allen were not as clear-cut as is claimed.

[31] NCB North Western colliery classification, November 1965: CRO Flintshire D/NM/1160.

[32] Letter from E. J. Kimmins, area director, North Western Area NCB, to Jos Ellis, North Wales NUM, 8 June 1967: CRO Flintshire D/NM/255.

[33] Conciliation meeting held with representatives of NCB/NUM concerning a dispute that arose on 26 April 1965: CRO Flintshire D/NM/346.

[34] Vic Allen, *The Militancy of British Miners* (Shipley, 1981), p.18.

The post-1966 political culture of the NUM, both locally and nationally, was more a force for continuity than a trend towards militancy.

The issue of a uniform system of wages for the coal industry had been a concern of the MFGB from the 1890s onwards. With the onset of nationalization, the task of unifying areas around a national agreement seemed possible, though the union itself was still divided on the extent of uniformity and the place of incentives in localized bargaining procedures. The Lancashire Area provides a striking example, under the leadership of Gormley, whereby wage rates were often decided at pit, or even seam, level, thereby enhancing the role of local officials.[35] Support for, or opposition to, a 'day wage' system was largely dependent on the level of earnings in particular coalfields. Lancashire enjoyed relatively high pay rates, and this coloured its view of incentives in future debates at national conferences. Even within the NCB, there was a positive view towards a NPLA as it would help to co-ordinate development within and between coalfields. Robens himself praised the union for its pursuit of this claim and the impact it had on the development of the industry after 1966.

In north Wales, the situation had been similar to Lancashire, and the existence of the POAIU had been a constant bulwark against a district initiative. With nationalization and mechanization of the remaining pits, the national union felt more confident in pressing its case. Jos Ellis, speaking at the district conciliation meeting in Chester in 1962, called for an area power loading agreement that would cover the 'basic principles'. The union felt that it was necessary to establish 'norms' at the area level in order to avoid the secretary having to negotiate from pit to pit.[36] It is interesting to note that the issue was not backed by the suggestion of militant action. Ellis wanted the conciliation board to set up a subcommittee to consider the whole matter so that an agreement would be forthcoming and be acceptable to both sides. In 1964, the NCB took the initiative and each area worked to secure agreements but negotiations were fraught with difficulties owing to the number of tasks underground that had to be graded and classified. The level of bureaucracy involved was

---

[35] See Joe Gormley, *Battered Cherub* (London, 1982), pp.65–7.
[36] Minutes of North Wales District Conciliation Board, Chester, 19 February 1962: CRO Flintshire D/NM/347.

proving to be a debilitating factor in forging agreements and leaders like Gormley and Ellis were happier in the role of settling disputes over pay quickly in the traditional manner. The North Wales AEC, in the same year, called off negotiations with the corporation because they did not agree with the points put forward by the area as a basis for discussion.[37]

The left within the national union continued to campaign for national uniformity, with Will Paynter making it his priority as general secretary in 1966. The approach of the left was greatly helped by the extent of mechanization and the potency of the symbolism of nationalization, which had a limited but effective impact in raising the consciousness of miners to transcend local animosities. Nonetheless, there was a ceiling to the level of this consciousness, and the disputes surrounding the NPLA were to return to haunt the NEC in subsequent years. North Wales voted in favour of the agreement. However, Colin Newell of Ifton clashed with the president, Jack Griffiths, at a miners' weekend school in Rhyl, remaining critical of Paynter in his pursuit of the NPLA. The miners at Ifton were initially worse off, and Newell stressed to Paynter that north Wales was not being treated as fairly as some of the larger areas.[38]

The acceptance of the NPLA by both the NCB and the NUM is celebrated in most quarters as the catalyst for wage militancy. On the surface, this seems correct as the unity in the strikes of 1972 and 1974 can be explained in terms of the increased power of the NEC to speak with one voice. But it was the right of the union that gained most, along with the Labour Party, in determining the future policies of the union. The NPLA took away the power of local negotiators to determine pay rates. In this sense, radicalism was somewhat diluted, as a national dimension could now be more easily included on the agenda for wage claims. But, importantly, the stratification of the labour force at pit level remained static in terms of bargaining capability and the capacity to influence the direction of lodge politics. Faceworkers were still in a majority in terms of the union hierarchy and the 'out-bye' workers remained under-represented as traditional patterns of authority continued. Vic Allen is wrong to suggest

[37] Letter from North Wales NUM to L. Plover, NCB industrial relations director, 8 January 1964: CRO Flintshire D/NM/346.
[38] Colin Newell interview, 1997.

that mechanization and the NPLA damaged morale and undermined the power of the faceworker.[39] The damage to morale did not come from the timidity of the agreement in fostering unity, but from fact that it undermined the ability of particular workers to influence rates of pay at the colliery level. Moreover, the faceworker continued to occupy the position of the earlier checkweighman in terms of union influence and the protection of differentials.[40]

Until the introduction of incentives in the 1970s, the NPLA remained a cause of disagreement amongst workers in all of Britain's coalfields. In north Wales, a number of faceworkers preferred the option of working for private contractors as their pay with the NCB had been codified in the agreement. Tony Bellis of Point of Ayr still claims that the NPLA made 'good men idle and idle men happy'.[41] A number of men from the Lancashire coalfield also agree with this notion, as they had to endure a drop in wages and a dilution of their earning capability.[42] The most beneficial aspect of the agreement was the favourable terms it created for craftsmen. They had often resented the fact that they were paid less than faceworkers when they had already endured low pay in order to complete the four-year apprenticeship schemes.[43] On the left of the national union, all were united in the belief that the NPLA allowed the NUM to negotiate with the NCB on an equal footing, bringing traditionally moderate areas more firmly into national bargaining procedures.

The benefits of the NPLA were clear for both the NUM and the NCB, but since it altered relationships at pit level minutely and still favoured certain jobs, it failed to unify the workforce as a whole. A number of oral testimonies from the north Wales coalfield suggest that the principle was a credible one but the

---

[39]   Allen, *Militancy of British Miners*, p.92.
[40]   After the introduction of the NPLA, conflict underground often manifested itself between NPLA-graded workers and those who were general labourers. This became more acute when the waiting lists for face training started to expand. Traditionally the progression from haulage work to coal face would take less than a year. By the 1970s, the average wait was six years and the gap between the pay of out-bye workers and face workers remained significant.
[41]   Tony Bellis interview, 1997.
[42]   Interview with Alf and Brian Gildart, both former miners at Bickershaw and Parsonage Collieries in the Lancashire coalfield, 1997.
[43]   John Alan Jones (electrician from Point of Ayr) interview, 1997.

practice delivered little.[44] Subsequent pay claims still upheld wage differentials, with those on the highest grades gaining most from a particular settlement. The surface strikes of 1969 illustrate the inadequacy of the equalizing strategy of the NPLA. The events of 1966 owed more to compromise than to a commitment to an 'ideal type' of wage parity within the coal industry. The NEC was evenly split on the issue and the level of sectionalism within particular collieries exposed the fragility of union solidarity. As Gormley recalls in his autobiography,

> [It] was ironic that the policy went through with the vote of COSA, the white-collar section of the union associated with the Right; even though they couldn't benefit from it in any way, it was their vote which got the agreement signed, and it makes me sad that they should have been so maligned, in the years which followed, by the very people who did benefit.[45]

The period of the NPLA negotiations highlights the complexity of the relationship between diverse sections of labour institutions. The rhetoric of unity and equality was important as a mobilizing force in terms of agitation and in keeping the membership in line with a particular policy. But the existence of the union was based on a set of principles, which were often contradictory. The leadership of Gormley in Lancashire and Ellis in north Wales was an example of this process. Both men wanted a strong united union but neither could lose sight of the need to protect certain sections of the membership over levels of earnings. Paynter and Daly, on the left of the national union, saw the NPLA as the final step towards fulfilling the aim of a truly 'national union'. The politics of pragmatism and the politics of principle continued to exist uneasily within the NUM. Furthermore, the NPLA did little to undermine the level of localism and its influence on the character of respective area unions.

---

[44] Interviews with opponents and advocates of the NPLA suggest that the principle was right but it altered little. Noel Campbell, an electrician at the Point of Ayr colliery, recalls that as an apprentice his senior craftsman was happy because his wages almost doubled, though a number of other workers such as Eddie Lloyd and Colin Newell were pessimistic about its effects; some gained and some lost but seniority in terms of the division of labour remained static.

[45] Gormley, *Battered Cherub*, p.66.

Labour politics in north Wales in the 1960s

At the 1964 general election, support for Labour amongst the north Wales miners remained secure. In Wrexham, James Idwal Jones commanded a healthy majority of 13,238, easily beating the opposition of a National Liberal and Conservative candidate, and J. Thomas of Plaid Cymru who mustered 4,673 votes. In Flint East, Eirene White retained the seat but still only marginally with a majority of 3,956. Nigel Birch in Flint West was again helped by a significant Liberal vote which limited Labour prospects. The emerging support for Plaid Cymru and 'cultural nationalism' did not manifest itself in an attack on the politics of Labourism within the coalfield. Jones reminded the miners that without the nationalization of the coal industry by the Attlee government in 1947 there would have been no pits remaining in north Wales.[46] The 'labour aristocracy' in the coalfield was for the moment secure, but the imminent closure of a number of pits revealed fractures in the relationship between party and union.

A year later James Griffiths, Secretary of State for Wales, met the AEC in Wrexham. Griffiths wanted to reassure the union that he would do all in his power to keep the local coal industry alive. Jos Ellis warned that the increased use of oil was seriously undermining the local market for coal and causing the miners concern about their future. The union started to challenge the orthodoxy of the NCB and the Labour Party in questioning the viability of particular pits. The executive had still not adopted a clear policy on closures, and Llay Hall and Black Park had closed with little opposition from the union. Ellis told Griffiths that the union was calling in their own engineer from the NUM headquarters to monitor the situation at Llay Main since the management continued to stress losses of profitability.[47]

The union maintained its financial support for Labour branches in Flintshire and Denbighshire, but animosity remained, particularly in Llay, where the pit was experiencing problems. Criticism was levelled at Jones by miners and local party members. The first signs of tension emerged between the

---

[46] *Wrexham Leader*, 9 October 1964.
[47] NUM North Wales report on meeting between North Wales Area NUM and James Griffiths, secretary of state for Wales, 21 October 1965: CRO Flintshire D/NM/602.

union and Wrexham Borough Council. Throughout 1965, the union attacked the council's aim to heat the town's planned development of a swimming baths with oil. They had already carried out the replacement of coal that provided heating for Wrexham Technical College. Ellis argued that it was ridiculous to choose oil when Wrexham was at the heart of the dying coalfield. Denbighshire County Council was more sympathetic and pledged that it would use coal to heat buildings wherever possible. The chairman, R. E. Rowlands, claimed that all council members had the interests of miners at heart.[48]

The relationship between the elected councils in mining communities and the dominant trade union exposed the problems facing Labour councillors committed to coal but having to operate within the confines of what appeared to be the most economical fuel policy.[49] Structural constraint is evident, although this is not to say that more could not have been done to counteract the decline of the industry. This was certainly the view of the people of Llay and the attitude they took against the party in Wrexham. The Llay Labour Party protested to the headquarters in London over the alleged lack of interest shown in the plight of the pit by the local MP. Members felt that he should have co-ordinated a number of meetings in order to discuss the issues. Jones had not even visited the village when the threat of closure was announced. J. H. Owen, the local councillor, was particularly vociferous in attacking the MP, arguing that the Tories were doing more at the local level in questioning the decisions of the NCB. This may have been true on the surface, but the Tories were more concerned with gaining political capital from the issue as a general election loomed. The Labour Party in Llay also went some way to exposing the fragility of coalfield unity. Owen argued that a completely different response would have been forthcoming if a closure had been announced in the Rhos.[50]

[48] *Wrexham Leader*, 7 December 1965.
[49] Once elected, miners found that they could not merely speak for the union and the coal industry. Once in the council chamber, they were faced by the demands of competing interest groups and a normally hostile group of council officials and policy advisers. This was the experience of John Alan Jones, a miner and council representative who became frustrated with the pessimism of council administrators in attempting to challenge government policy. John Alan Jones interview, 1997.
[50] *Wrexham Leader*, 28 January 1966.

Jones was quick to reply to his critics and wrote to the North Wales AEC to combat the claims of the Llay branch. He referred to his speech on the second reading of the Coal Industry Bill, proposing that plans for the closure of uneconomic pits be accelerated. Jones claimed that he resisted the bill due to the position of the Wrexham pits and felt that he could maximize the case against closures in Westminster rather than in the coal-field.[51] This did not pacify the miners of Llay, but they pinned their hopes on a favourable election result that would give the party a firmer mandate to deal with economic problems, particularly those of coal.

In the Rhos, disquiet emerged at the proposed run-down of the industry. There was no outright criticism of the Labour Party, but the work of the Communist Stan Hughes on the Public Amenities Committee of the local authority suggested rising dissatisfaction. Miners felt that Hughes would press the claims of coal against the expanding use of gas throughout the region. The optimism of the labour movement in both Denbigh-shire and Flintshire expressed itself in the general election of March 1966 when Harold Wilson returned to power with a healthy majority. In Wrexham, Jones increased his majority to 17,443 despite local criticisms of his activity in the coalfield, and Eirene White in Flint East pushed her majority to 8,482. Tom Ellis, the manager of Bersham, came within 3,000 votes of taking Flint West from Nigel Birch.

It is apparent that, although there had been disquiet within particular branches of the Labour Party locally and at certain pits, the miners themselves were only seeking solutions through the traditional channels of union, party and parliamentary pro-cess. The debate concerning the future of the industry remained confined to Labourist orthodoxy, stressing the need for negoti-ation, compromise and an unquestioning loyalty to the party. In terms of alternative political strategies, the coalfield was bereft of the oppositional policies that were emerging elsewhere. Welsh nationalism was the dog that failed to bark in terms of its impact on the miners. There was to be no Carmarthen in the north and, in 1966, the vote for Plaid Cymru in Wrexham dropped

---

[51] Letter from James Idwal Jones MP to Maldwyn Lloyd, North Wales NUM, 29 January 1966: NUM, Wrexham.

dramatically to just over 2,000 votes. The party received a boost in 1968 when the veteran local socialist Cyril O. Jones joined because of the timidity of Labour. However, this development did not lead to an exodus from Labour to Plaid. Four years earlier, Huw T. Edwards of the T&GWU had rejoined Labour from the nationalists, though he found initial difficulty in finding a branch that would accept him.[52] The Mold branch refused his application because he had earlier stated that the best way to obtain the objectives of Plaid Cymru was to infiltrate other parties.[53] Again, this highlights the strength of Labourism and the local animosities that existed when individuals broke with commitments in terms of political affiliation: the treachery of MacDonald in 1931 had had a profound effect on Labour's collective memory.

The attraction of nationalist politics was further diluted in 1969–70 by the radical wing of the nationalist movement initiating a violent campaign. A bomb scare at Gresford colliery emerged after a telephone call was received stating that a number of explosive devices had been placed in the underground workings. This episode preceded the Welsh explosives case in which John Jenkins and Frederick Alders were charged with causing a number of explosions. Both defendants were accused of being members of the Mudiad Amddiffyn Cymru (Movement to Defend Wales). Jenkins was an army sergeant accused of the theft of explosives from Hafod colliery in 1968. The trial was held in Mold and both men were jailed as a result.[54] Although Plaid Cymru distanced itself from the tactics of other nationalist groups, this did not help them in their attempt to woo traditional Labour voters. The party subsequently failed to dent Labour's domination in the Welsh coalfields at successive general elections.

The pit closures of the Wilson period did not seriously alter the north Wales miners' commitment to the Labour Party. In

---

[52] Huw T. Edwards, *Hewn from the Rock* (Cardiff, 1967), pp.236–7.
[53] *Rhyl Journal*, 1 April 1965.
[54] *Wrexham Leader*, 10 April 1970. Two nationalist extremists were killed when their own bomb exploded as they were trying to plant it on the Chester to Holyhead railway at Abergele in order to kill Prince Charles en route to his investiture as Prince of Wales at Caernarfon. Today a commemorative march in the town still attracts a small number of nationalist republicans from Scotland, much to the embarrassment of Plaid Cymru and Labour devolutionists. The march is complete with a 'colour party' exhibiting paramilitary trappings, including the burning of the 'Union Jack'.

1965, the leadership in Wrexham still unquestioningly accepted the economic case for rationalization. In responding to rumours of imminent closures, Ellis continued to promote a pragmatic approach: 'if these collieries are to be closed I expect the closures to take place over a phased five-year period to avoid any unemployment.' The union and local Labour parties concentrated on attracting inward investment rather than constructing a case against the contraction of the industry on a point of principle. The NUM was doing this in other areas, notably Yorkshire, through the initiatives of a well-organized left. In 1967, James Idwal Jones claimed that he was happy with the economic policies of the Wilson government. He pointed to the inward investment well under way with the siting of the Firestone Tyre Company and a BICC works in the Wrexham area.

Nonetheless, the cohesion of the area leadership was not immune to challenges on the question of closures. Joe Williams, a lodge official, warned that Jones could well lose his seat in Wrexham if the government did not change its policies on the coal industry. He argued that all socialists were in favour of progress but not if this meant throwing people out of work. Williams backed this statement with an apparent threat to the future of Hafod. Tom Ellis, the vice-chairman of the Wrexham Labour Party, replied to Williams in the *Wrexham Leader* and argued that 'the miners of this area would be ill advised to sever their connections with the Labour Party'.[55] The miners of north Wales had no choice but to maintain their commitment to the party locally and nationally: they felt that an alternative Conservative administration would be worse. Thus, the link between the miners and Labour remained, based on principle and pragmatism. No coherent left had emerged in the coalfield to counteract the orthodoxy of the leadership, and disgruntled activists had to concentrate on traditional strategies.

The AEC continued to campaign throughout the coalfield against the use of alternative fuels. Jos Ellis criticized Rhyl Town Council for choosing oil central heating in the town hall, claiming that 'this will destroy the industry of which the miners have always supported Rhyl through tourism'. There had been a tradition of an exodus from the Wrexham coalfield to the resort

---

[55]   *Wrexham Leader*, 14, 17 and 23 November 1967.

during the 'miners' fortnight' in July/August each year. Even representatives of the NCB showed disappointment with the move. Rhyl had an affinity with a coal-mining area, especially with Point of Ayr in close proximity. Members of all lodges in the area attending executive meetings in Wrexham were increasingly worried about the amount of coal imported from the Midlands. They were also pessimistic about the operation of the national-ized industry, as it seemed to be following an uncoordinated pattern in terms of coal distribution.[56]

Between 1964 and 1970 the hopes and aspirations of the Wilson years were dashed, for, by 1968, three of the major pits in the area had been closed. This created a strain within the union and the Labour Party but, again, the period was marked by political continuity. Unlike other coalfields, no serious challenges emerged to question the commitment, of the AEC. Jos Ellis did not see beyond a deferential attitude to the government and saw the campaign against the increased use of oil as the only effective policy against pit closures. The position of the leadership was helped by the perception of the wider membership. Throughout this period, there was still a shortage of labour, with men seeking to leave the industry to take jobs in local factories. The cam-paigns launched to question the closure of Llay Main, Hafod and Ifton were significant in that they lacked a 'grass roots' dimen-sion. The radicalism of sections of the workforce was absent from north Wales colliery politics.

THE POLITICS OF PIT CLOSURES

After one year of the Labour government, it was clear that the mining industry would not be immune to the modernizing zeal of Wilson, and the pace of pit closures was accelerated. Gordon Nicholls of the NCB stressed that there had been slight improve-ments at one or two collieries in north Wales but this was nothing to what was required to maintain a viable future. An improvement was noticeable at Bersham, which now had two mechanized faces in production but had recently experienced trouble with faulting. At Gresford four faces were in production

---

[56] NCB Hafod colliery consultative committee meeting, 6 February 1968: CRO Flintshire D/NM/709.

and experienced continuing geological problems. Hafod had initial difficulty with the scale of mechanization and the prospects for the future were dependent on the pit coming to grips with new technology. Owing to a much tighter market for coal, an emphasis was placed on quality. Ifton suffered as a result because of the high dirt content of its product. Llay Main was in serious difficulty as all three faces were experiencing 'floor lift' which curtailed production. The most prosperous pit was Point of Ayr, where the introduction of new machinery had largely worked well.[57]

Llay Main was under immediate threat as it had been experiencing problems since the late 1950s. Miners hoped that the election of a Labour government would save the pit, and a number of local people criticized the inaction of the party in arguing the case for Llay. In 1962, the divisional chairman of the NCB warned that the colliery could not survive on its present output.[58] The workforce was cut to allow for further mechanization, but geological problems persisted. In October 1965, the *Wrexham Leader* reported that the pit was under threat of closure and that the NCB was watching developments closely. The union delegate, Tom Jones, stressed that mechanization was now almost complete but costs had become a concern.[59] Within a month, the NCB announced the closure, which affected almost 1,000 men. Firstly, management used the profitability argument, aware that the union could not or would not seriously challenge economic orthodoxy. Secondly, they quickly announced that men would be needed at other local collieries. This was an attempt to lessen the blow to those wishing to remain in the industry.[60] The workforce at Llay had already been cut to 917 and there was a general feeling of pessimism about the pit. This factor led to an absence of resistance within the union to the closure, except from the Point of Ayr lodge, which, was, ironically the safest pit in the area.

---

[57] North Wales Area consultative committee meeting, 25 October 1965: CRO Flintshire D/NM/346.
[58] Minutes of Llay Main lodge meeting with area NCB officials, 2 January 1962: CRO Flintshire D/NM/757.
[59] *Wrexham Leader*, 22 October 1965.
[60] NCB notes of a discussion with North Wales NUM (Llay Main), 26 November 1965: CRO Flintshire D/NM/762.

Jack Griffiths of the AEC initially opposed the closure plan and called on the national officials of the union to assist the area in assessing the situation and challenging the views of the NCB. Within a month, however, the union had accepted the argument of the corporation that other pits in the area would close unless men from Llay Main transferred to Bersham and Gresford. It was resolved that the union had a weak case for keeping the pit open, and a special executive meeting decided not to oppose its closure. The AEC commissioned a report from the national union that upheld the economic rationale of the NCB. Keith Saunders, the engineer of the NUM, warned that, 'having regard to the conditions obtained at present in Llay Main it was not very hopeful that the colliery could be properly maintained without incurring an expenditure considerably in excess of proceeds'.[61]

It was this lack of a coherent critique of the NCB by the area and the national union, which proved to be the most damaging aspect of the post-nationalization consensus. The bureaucracy that cemented the union to the ideals of management did not contain channels whereby the economic orthodoxy of NCB officials could be challenged. The centralization of NCB activities outside colliery units complemented the efficiency plans introduced by the Robens regime. The corporation was to be completely reorganized, with new areas; for example, the North Western Division became the North Western Area and large-scale amalgamations were initiated. The five former areas of East Lancashire, Burnley, Cumberland, North Wales and West Lancashire amalgamated and were controlled from Manchester.[62] The North Wales Area was keen to protect its autonomy within the NCB, as it had done by securing its independence within the NUM. The closure of Llay workshops was seen as a threat to this autonomy, and the union immediately involved the national union to campaign against the initiatives of NCB officials, who had already announced the colliery closure.

In January 1966 Will Paynter spoke on behalf of the union at a meeting with NCB officials and argued for keeping the

---

[61] North Wales NUM special AEC minutes, 16 November 1965: CRO Flintshire D/NM/1133.
[62] NCB circular: 'News from the coal industry', 3 February 1967: NUM, Wrexham.

workshops open. With the attendance of the general secretary, Jos Ellis felt that he should also press criticism on the corporation over closure of the pit, although the area had done little to save it. Ellis complained that the speed of closure could not be justified, since the union had invited the national union engineer to make a report. In response, the management decided to stop production immediately by pulling out of the 36s District. Ellis maintained that production was halted in order to dilute the effectiveness of a union investigation that could have provided counter-claims to those of the NCB. He also hinted that black-mail had been the policy of the day, with the management consistently pressing home the view that, unless there was speedy closure of Llay Main, other pits in the area would be in jeopardy. The union was also concerned that, as soon as the closure was announced, recruiting officers from the West Midlands entered the village, which seemed to contradict the view of NCB officials on the need for local manpower.

Robens reacted to both Paynter and Ellis by refusing to con-sider the colliery, since this was not in the remit of the meeting. He merely argued that the centralization plans of the NCB were the most efficient for the future of the industry and that the workshops would have to be closed.[63] After the meeting, the union failed to develop a strategy for challenging the decision. This highlights union commitment to the existing structures of decision-making which evidently favoured the NCB and the government. With the closure of the colliery in March 1966, Gordon Nicholls of the NCB was pleased at the smooth opera-tion and praised the degree of consensus between the corporation and the NUM:

> Management and union feel the closure to be a good thing indeed for the people employed in mining in North Wales; it will secure the future of other collieries which are short of men. Further, many men are already living near the pit where they will be working so there is no disruption.[64]

In fact, the closure of Llay Main did not secure the future of the Wrexham pits: within eighteen months two more were to

[63] Verbatim notes of a meeting between the NCB and the NUM, 19 January 1966: CRO Flintshire D/NM/762.
[64] *Wrexham Leader*, 3 December 1965.

close, with the remaining two placed in serious jeopardy. Far from causing little or no disruption, the closure was catastrophic for the village of Llay. The population of the village was around three thousand, over half of whom were dependent on the pit for their livelihood. The men were not all absorbed locally, which caused concern for the union, as a number were enticed to the Midlands by an offer of more money and a better standard of housing.

In 1967 the annual conference of the North Wales NUM looked back with regret at the closure of Llay Main because the pit contained the best coking coal in the country. The union in effect had become a prisoner of a consensus that it had played a role in constructing. The hegemony of Labourism was proving to be both friend and foe. Jack Griffiths, in his presidential address, stressed that the union had to think beyond the politics of economic orthodoxy and 'not to forget that the union was built on ideals and principles and we must at all times endeavour to keep this in mind when serving the interests of our membership. A movement without ideals must eventually fall.' Jos Ellis himself acknowledged that there would probably be more pit closures as the Labour government seemed to be adopting a similar policy to the Conservatives in pursuit of profitability. Public ownership was clearly no longer a barrier to this process: 'It appears therefore, that we can no longer depend on the old nationalization philosophy of the good and productive pits carrying the poor and uneconomic pits.'[65]

The uncertainty of the period in terms of the future viability of the coal industry was not shared by the bulk of miners themselves. Those who had experienced a number of pit closures in the coalfield felt that developments in terms of coal would be forthcoming. The NCB promoted this view and all through the 1960s it called for the recruitment of young men to local collieries, promising them a secure future. There was some disquiet at the shortage of land available in Rhyl to build council housing for the use of miners. This affected the plans of the NCB to encourage recruitment to Point of Ayr. The aim was to provide ninety houses for miners from other areas, particularly Lancashire, as the pit could provide a secure future for those

---

[65] NUM North Wales Area annual report, 1966: CRO Flintshire D/NM/120.

coming from a dying coalfield. Prestatyn and Holywell Councils had also been approached for the provision of more housing, though this sparked a minor debate highlighting the intensity of local feeling against in-migration. In many ways, the symbolism of coal did not carry the same weight in Flintshire as it did in Denbighshire. Local identities had been constructed through rural images, and many remained averse to calls for greater industrialization.

As far as miners at Point of Ayr were concerned, the crisis in the industry was not treated with the nervousness present in other coalfields. Employment opportunities beyond coal were widely available, and the pit was perceived as largely immune to the increasing pace of closures. The pit was consolidating its successful transition to mechanization, breaking production records on a regular basis. Jack Griffiths expressed optimism in an interview with the local press: 'the picture is certainly much better, we are very encouraged by the results and are anxious to see another successful face established as quickly as possible.'[66]

The Wrexham coalfield was still shell-shocked by the closure of Llay Main when the area experienced further turmoil at Hafod. The pit had recently absorbed some of the men from Llay Main and there had been rumours circulating from late 1965 that closure was imminent. At a number of colliery consultative meetings the following year, the management denied reports in the local press that operations would cease in 1967.[67] In August of that year, the closure of the colliery was announced to the consultative committee without the knowledge of the AEC. This was a break with tradition, as the AEC was usually the first to be consulted on such matters. The situation was not helped by the fact that Jos Ellis was out of the country on a study visit to the Soviet Union as part of an NUM delegation.

The NCB statement released on the closure read: 'the colliery had been losing quite heavily, the marketing position was extremely difficult and although the output was 14,000 tonnes below budget at the end of July they had been unable to sell the coal which had been produced.' The NCB claimed that the statement made by the minister of fuel and power concerning the

---

[66] *Rhyl and Prestatyn Gazette*, 27 October 1967.
[67] Hafod colliery minutes of colliery consultative committee meeting, 5 October 1966: CRO Flintshire D/NM/709.

reduction of the size of the industry had obviously aggravated the situation and the colliery would close in November. The AEC was shocked by the decision, especially as the agreed procedure on closing pits had not been adhered to.[68] The lodge committee had appealed some months earlier for the option of working seams that had last produced coal in the 1920s, but this was rejected by the management.[69] Jos Ellis, for the union, was quick to oppose the closure but did not level blame at the NCB or the Labour government. Instead, he criticized the local authorities and the public for the increased use of alternative fuel supplies such as oil and gas. In contrast, the men at the pit were arguing the case against closure and challenging the views of the management. In answer to a question regarding reserves at the colliery, the NCB claimed that coal reserves were estimated at sixty years at current production rates. However, the area director stressed that the development of the 'four foot' seam, which was favoured by the unions, would only make matters worse, as the pit had been sustaining heavy losses since Vesting Day.[70]

The AEC quickly arranged a meeting with the NCB to oppose the plans for closure, but there was no talk of any direct action to save the pit. The men were already despondent and several of them had already left, with others lining up for redundancy. The union mobilized a force of its most able representatives led by Ellis, along with P. T. Devaney, the Bersham delegate, Jack Griffiths and Jack Read. The delegation argued for the development of the 'four foot' seam as being the solution to the problems facing the colliery. Griffiths pointed out that 'the ordinary workmen were losing confidence in the Board and decisions such as these created a bad image for the Board and nationalization'.[71] Even the NACODS representative could see that the 'four foot' seam was a viable option but was aware of the

---

[68] North Wales NUM minutes of special meeting of AEC, 17 August 1967: CRO Flintshire D/NM/41.

[69] Relations between management and men had been very good as Tom Ellis had recently moved from Bersham to manage the pit, which was close to his heart, as his father had previously worked there. However, the consensus soon fractured as the union decided to fight to keep the pit open, much to the disappointment of Ellis who wanted a speedy closure. See Ellis, *Mining and Men*, pp.104–5.

[70] Statement by E. J. Kimmins, NCB area director, to the Hafod colliery consultative committee, 15 August 1967: CRO Flintshire D/NM/709.

[71] Minutes of NCB/NUM meeting held at Llay about the closure of Hafod colliery, 12 July 1967: CRO Flintshire D/NM/762.

weakness of the marketing situation of the colliery. The meeting did not resolve the problem and the NCB stuck to their 'market viability' argument. Meanwhile, the union made every effort to press its campaign to save Hafod. James Idwal Jones, who had earlier been criticized for his inaction over the closure of Llay Main, appealed to the prime minister for a postponement of the decision so that reports could be taken from both sides. The Rhos Parish Council also protested strongly but added that if the closure was inevitable it should be phased so as not to increase unemployment dramatically in one swoop.[72] Robens reacted swiftly and rejected the council's argument for a reprieve; he announced 135 vacancies at neighbouring pits and the chance of further jobs in Yorkshire and the Midlands. Along with Hafod, the NCB had announced 173 other closures, thus causing turmoil in the NUM locally and nationally.

The union concentrated on challenging the closure through the traditional channels of conciliation, but events were fast overtaking them. The orders that Hafod had supplied to Connah's Quay power station and the Courtaulds factories in Flint and Greenfield had already been transferred to other pits in the area. The lodge officials argued that this was deplorable and a deliberate ploy by the NCB marketing department to undermine the morale of the workers and dilute the effectiveness of arguments for saving the colliery.[73] Meanwhile, the AEC informed the national union of the situation and the NEC agreed that the North Wales NUM had a strong case in fighting the closure. Keith Saunders was to visit the pit on 10 October. Jos Ellis had already protested to the secretary of state for Wales, Cledwyn Hughes, and stressed that the union would fight, because the pit had masses of coal reserves. The executive had already persuaded the NCB that the procedure adopted by the management was not in accordance with agreed principles. The corporation was forced to withdraw the announced date of closure.[74]

In the middle of September, the union's case strengthened when the Labour government announced that a number of pits

[72] *Wrexham Leader*, 22 August 1967.
[73] Minutes of Hafod colliery consultative and safety committees, 21 September 1967: CRO Flintshire D/NM/709.
[74] NUM North Wales AEC minutes, 27 September 1967: CRO Flintshire D/NM/41.

would be given a temporary reprieve. The government was also facing criticism from other unions over proposed incomes policies. After a meeting with the NUM in Scarborough, the government agreed to postpone the planned closures affecting sixteen pits including Hafod. However, it was bluntly stated that these measures were only adopted to deal with the problems of the winter; thereafter closures would continue.[75] The union thus had a stay of execution which would only last until March 1968, but it gave them six months to prove viability.[76] The union busied itself with the construction of a powerful report to keep the pit in production by the time it met the NCB in November. The case for closure was largely economic: the pit had lost money and the reduction in the local market for coal had made the environment difficult for sale of the product. Ellis, for the union, argued that the losses since Vesting Day should not contribute to the decision because recently the colliery had gone through a period of improvement in terms of profit. To the men at the pit, the 'four foot' seam was an extremely viable option, and the social consequences of the closure would be a massive blow to industry in north Wales. Saunders also spoke in favour of keeping the pit open and produced a comprehensive report which argued for a long-term future.[77]

The increased activity of the union over Hafod, compared with the relatively low level of activity over Llay Main, can be explained by the circumstances of the pit. It was just four miles from the centre of Wrexham but provided work for over one thousand men from the close-knit villages of Rhos, Johnstown and Penycae. The NUM branch secretary at the time of the closure had worked at the pit since 1924. When the pit had previously closed for a period of seven months during the slump of the 1930s, shops were closed and never reopened, with many families driven apart by the experience.[78] On 12 December 1967, the NCB replied to the AEC on the proposed utilization of the 'four foot' seam. It was admitted that this project would

---

[75] Government press statement, 29 September 1967: NUM, Wrexham.
[76] Letter from Sidney Ford to Jos Ellis, 10 October 1967: CRO Flintshire D/NM/710.
[77] NUM document re meeting to be held on 10 November 1967 to appeal against the closure of Hafod colliery: CRO Flintshire D/NM/710.
[78] NUM North Wales Area report on the proposed closure of Hafod Colliery, 1967: CRO Flintshire D/NM/121.

prolong the life of the colliery, but the coal would not be suitable for the domestic market and it would have to be crushed for industrial purposes. This process would inevitably reduce the profitability of the product and weaken the position of the colliery nationally; thus, the colliery would close in the new year. The union again rejected this view and wanted further negotiations with the secretary of state for Wales. They also pressed their claims about the profitability of the pit with the Welsh Economic Council.[79] Ellis made it clear to James Idwal Jones that the union would continue to fight the closure and was disheartened by the apparent reluctance of the Labour government to listen to arguments about the viability of particular pits.[80] More importantly, Ellis emphasized that the importation of coal into the area was totally unacceptable at a time when pits continued to close in north Wales. The market for coal in the area far exceeded the amount produced in the local pits, and so more local colliery developments would be beneficial, economically and socially. Furthermore, unemployment in the Wrexham area was on the increase, with 3.8 per cent of the population out of work and only 150 vacancies available at other collieries.[81]

It is interesting to note that, as with the earlier closure of Black Park, there were divisions within the NCB over the closure of Hafod. Tom Ellis, the manager, highlights this in his narrative of events.[82] The north Wales branch of BACM (British Association of Colliery Management) agreed with Ellis over the problem of coal imports from other coalfields, stressing that managers in the area should work jointly with the NUM in saving the industry in Wrexham.[83] The north Wales TUC advisory committee proved

[79] NUM North Wales Area special area executive committee minutes of meeting, 12 December 1967. The problem for the miners was that the Welsh Economic Council never had the full backing of the Labour Party and the trade unions, ensuring its weakness in influencing policy at Westminster. For details of the construction of the Welsh Office and its constituent bodies, consult John Osmond, *Creative Conflict: The Politics of Welsh Devolution* (Llandysul, 1977), pp.99–106.

[80] Letter from Jos Ellis to James Idwal Jones, MP for Wrexham, 22 December 1967: CRO Flintshire D/NM/711.

[81] North Wales NUM report of submission to Welsh Economic Council, December 1967: CRO Flintshire D/NM/711.

[82] Tom Ellis, 'Death of a colliery', *Transactions of the Denbighshire Historical Society*, 21(1972), 94–108.

[83] Letter from R. Thomas, hon. sec. north Wales branch of the BACM, to North Wales NUM, 12 June 1968: CRO Flintshire D/NM/722.

to be of little support, as the NUM delegation found when it addressed the body in January 1968. The secretary of the committee merely expressed the view that, although the unions did not want to see a rise in unemployment, they had to admit that the pit had been uneconomic for some time. All doors were now closed, and even the Welsh Economic Council failed to get a decision from the Welsh Office, and passed the matter to the Ministry of Power. The union criticized all these institutions for their inaction and felt that no other strategy could be adopted to save Hafod. Richard Marsh, the minister of fuel and power, finally contacted the union to state that the pit would close in March 1968.[84] The union accepted the closure and the heart was ripped out of the north Wales coalfield.

The Rhos Labour Party, as a last resort, appealed to Harold Wilson personally to intervene to stop the closure. John Alfred Clarke, the chairman, sent a telegram to the prime minister two weeks before the pit was due to halt production. In a written reply from Downing Street, it was stressed that consideration had been given to the plight of Hafod, but a number of new industries were in the development stage in Wrexham to offset the potential hardship that would follow. Wrexham Rural District Council was positive about the development of light industries on the Vauxhall Industrial Estate and called for a further six months of production at the pit so that there would be a smooth transition. In the following May, it was evident that the Hafod issue had caused friction between the community and the Labour Party and in the local elections there was a very poor turnout, with the Conservatives taking two seats from Labour. The promise of jobs for all miners had not materialized, and two months after closure the Wrexham and District Employment Exchange reported that 400 Hafod miners were still out of work.[85]

With the battle to save the pit over, the AEC of the union was scathing about the inadequacy of the procedures involved in the decision. Jos Ellis wrote to Cledwyn Hughes alarmed at the closure and, in particular, the role played by the Welsh Economic Council. Hughes stated that the criticism levelled at the

[84] NUM North Wales special AEC minutes, 17 February 1968: CRO Flintshire D/NM/41.
[85] *Wrexham Leader*, 14 May 1968.

council was quite unjustified and stuck to the line of argument
that viewed efficiency as central:

> It is of course a matter of regret that some collieries have to close if the coal
> mining industry is to become fully competitive with other forms of energy
> by 1971. But this process of contraction within the industry is inevitable if
> the industry is to survive and prosper.[86]

At the annual conference of the North Wales NUM in 1968,
the mood was sombre owing to the closure and the difficulties
experienced by the other pits in the area. Jack Griffiths, in his
presidential address, claimed that the union could not oppose the
changes in the industry, but had to utilize them to raise the living
standards of the members who remained in the existing pits.[87]
However, criticism of the Labour government was apparent in a
number of speeches, and Griffiths talked of the ineffectiveness of
the campaign against closures both locally and nationally:

> All this has produced very little reaction from a government which we
> miners helped substantially to gain power . . . I am afraid that the closure
> of the colliery [Hafod] is now looked upon as an exercise in economics and
> the effect on people incidental.[88]

For the people of the Rhos, the area would never be the same
again. Coal had played a central role in the identity of the
village. The impressive miners' institute supported social amenities, political gatherings and popular entertainment. With the
closure of the pit, the last archetypal mining village in north
Wales was consigned to memory.

The dust had hardly settled on Hafod when, in August 1968,
the union was hit by another bombshell. Despite the fact that
Ifton had just developed a new face, it was reported in the local
press that a closure date might soon be announced as the pit had
been unprofitable since April.[89] The area director announced

---

[86] Letter from Cledwyn Hughes, secretary of state for Wales, to Jos Ellis, 3 April 1968:
CRO Flintshire D/NM/711.
[87] Increasingly this became the view of the NUM right. Joe Gormley, the future
president, had long argued that the union should concentrate on raising wages for those
who remained in the industry, viewing closures as an economic fact of life.
[88] NUM North Wales Area annual report, 1968: CRO Flintshire D/NM/122.
[89] *Wrexham Leader*, 16 August 1968.

that the pit would close on 23 November. The Ifton branch
secretary, Colin Newell, argued that there were considerable
reserves at the pit and the case they had against the decision was
a strong one. The union again called in Keith Saunders to assess
the situation. He reported that the colliery had a viable future
and that closure should be contested by the union. The NCB
took little notice of the case against their decision and started to
reduce operations at the pit.[90] The executive again opted to
protest through the avenues of conciliation that had made little
difference to the future of Hafod. They busied themselves with
the production of reports of the social consequences and contested the corporation's view of the profitability of the pit. The
union had a strong case in terms of the unemployment question,
as Ifton was situated at the junction of five employment exchanges. Labour at the colliery was dependent on a number of
villages: Chirk, Chirk Green, Black Park and St Martins with
some miners also residing in Oswestry. Only six months before
the announcement of the closure a number of men had moved
from Hafod to Ifton with the promise of a secure future at a long-
life colliery.[91] The case was again taken to the Welsh Economic
Council, but the outcome seemed obvious as previous protests
had aroused little reaction.

The NCB also produced a comprehensive report and their
case for closure seemed to be stronger than that produced to
justify the closure of Hafod. The pit had lost money and had a
number of geological problems, with serious faulting on Q16s
and Q24s faces. A major fault was physically possible to
surmount but economically non-viable. Further, the product
from Ifton was harder to sell because of its inferior quality. T. H.
Jones, the Ifton delegate, was still not convinced. Jones recalled
that, in 1928, the life of Black Park was said to be over 100 years,
with Ifton and Black Park seams providing the gateway to the
Wynnstay reserves which could supply the best coal in north
Wales.[92] Saunders accepted the points raised in the NCB's
submission concerning the faulting and the loss of money over

[90] NUM North Wales special AEC minutes, 19 September 1968: CRO Flintshire
D/NM/41.
[91] NUM report on the social consequences of the closure of Ifton colliery, 1968: CRO
Flintshire D/NM/722.
[92] Notes of meeting, 16 August 1968, between NCB/NUM North Wales executive on
the future of Ifton colliery: CRO Flintshire D/NM/721.

previous months, but argued that there could be a successful future: 'with thick, good quality seams beyond the fault, it would appear that justice is hardly done when a halt is brought to all operations at this stage.'[93]

The union put the blame squarely on the NCB for facilitating the importation of coal to the area and undermining the development of further reserves. In terms of electricity generation, 460,000 tonnes were imported, of which 300,000 came from north Wales collieries. Domestic coal was also brought in from the Midlands. The union protested against this but the corporation stated that both south Wales and the Midlands had always had a share of the north Wales market.[94] In a meeting with all the unions and the NCB prior to the closure of Ifton, Jos Ellis made a passionate speech and argued that the basic principles of nationalization had been cast aside:

> Instead of big areas like Yorkshire and Derbyshire carrying the smaller areas it seems that every area is going its own way. If it is not profitable, it will go out . . . In a small area [like north Wales] this was a greater blow than the closure of three small pits in say Yorkshire or Derbyshire.[95]

Ellis went on to argue against importing coal from the larger areas and urged that all the coal produced locally should be used in north Wales. The union could see that the fight to save Ifton was a lost cause, and one final attempt to persuade the Secretary of State for Wales to intervene and pressurize the government came to nothing. Ellis met George Thomas, who was now Wilson's man in Wales, to express concern over the lack of representation of the mining unions on various public bodies such as the Welsh Economic Council and the Welsh Hospital Board.[96] The pragmatism in the approach of area leaders is apparent: the policy was to gain further representation and influence in existing institutions instead of developing critiques of

[93] NUM report by Keith Saunders on Ifton colliery, 10 October 1968: CRO Flintshire D/NM/722.
[94] NCB North Western Sales Region: north Wales marketing appraisal (statement by regional marketing director), 15 August 1969: CRO Flintshire D/NM/722.
[95] Notes of a Meeting between NCB/NUM/National Association of Colliery Overmen, Deputies and Shotfirers (NACODS)/Colliery Officials and Staffs Association (COSA)/BACM, 15 August 1968: CRO Flintshire D/NM/722.
[96] Jos Ellis, notes of a meeting with George Thomas MP, secretary of state for Wales, 11 September 1968: CRO Flintshire D/NM/722.

their powers, procedures and policies. Ellis and the rest of the north Wales leadership could not or would not see alternatives beyond a Labourist consensus. George Thomas contacted Ellis in November, the month of closure, and reiterated that, even allowing for transport costs, the price of coal from English coalfields was consistently lower than that produced in north Wales.[97] Gwyneth Dunwoody, the parliamentary secretary to the Board of Trade, contacted the AEC and stressed that there were no grounds for continuing production at Ifton. Moreover, 2,400 manufacturing vacancies were to be created in the area of both Hafod and Ifton to make good the loss of jobs.[98] The union now felt that no more could be done and reluctantly accepted the decision. Ifton colliery closed on 23 November 1968 and the job losses of over 1,000 miners ended a history of coal in the Chirk area spanning four centuries.

As the 1960s drew to a close, only three pits remained in the coalfield: Point of Ayr, Gresford, and Bersham. Point of Ayr was the most successful, though the lodge committee remained critical of the performance of the management. In 1966, the area president Jack Griffiths admitted that the output was the worst for thirty years and 'if the pit would have been privately owned, the management would have been sacked years ago'.[99] The union felt that the corporation was deliberately undermining the morale of the men and trying to close the pit. The scale of mechanization and the introduction of long-wall faces, along with the high quality of its coal, had helped to secure its future. The NCB had decided to concentrate its operations at Point of Ayr, but it still had problems with the recruitment of labour. Families from Wrexham were initially reluctant to transfer to the coastal villages surrounding the pit. Miners from Wrexham saw themselves as different from those on the Flintshire coast, save for an occupational similarity and a general commitment to Labour politics. Although concentrated in small villages, Wrexham miners retained an identity that was linked to a large town in close proximity to the city of Chester.

[97] Letter from George Thomas to Jos Ellis, 5 November 1968: CRO Flintshire D/NM/722.
[98] Letter from Gwyneth Dunwoody, parliamentary secretary to the Board of Trade to Jos Ellis, 19 November 1968: CRO Flintshire D/NM/722.
[99] NCB Point of Ayr colliery consultative committee minutes, 7 December 1966: CRO Flintshire D/NM/816.

The climate of uncertainty was no better at Bersham. In 1966, Ken Moses became the manager before going on to become a leading light in the NCB. Moses immediately set out his stall and argued that the men had to be increasingly flexible in the interests of production. The saviour of Bersham was the development of the Queen Seam, and throughout 1968 it went on to achieve the highest rate of face advance in the North Western Area.[100] Gresford faced an uncertain future and was to close within the next three years. The hopes pinned on the election of Wilson in 1966 had been quickly dashed as tensions emerged in the party–union relationship as a result of local pit closures. Nonetheless, commitment to the party and the politics of pragmatism remained secure. As this survey of the politics of pit closures has shown, the period remained marked by continuity, not conflict. The behaviour of the NCB and its pursuit of profitability was condoned by a Labour government which was unable or unwilling to envisage a planned policy on energy provision that went beyond the constraints of the capitalist economy.

THE COMING OF THE ENGLISH

The shortage of manpower, especially at Point of Ayr, led to a period of in-migration of English miners, mostly from the Lancashire coalfield. Families from the closed Bradford and Mosley Common pits settled around the villages in the vicinity of the colliery and the resort towns of Rhyl and Prestatyn. This led to significant developments in terms of the changing identities of the villages and had a partial impact on the politics of the union. In-migration has been a significant feature of the coal industry since the nineteenth century, in some cases with a dramatic effect on the politics of local unions. In south Wales, for example, a number of the many English workers who entered the coalfield, such as A. J. Cook and others, worked to undermine the established politics of the district associated with the leadership of Mabon and other moderate Labour figures. Francis and Smith also illustrate, although they exaggerate, the way in which Communists and syndicalists from Spain and Italy were able to

---

[100] Letter from Ken Moses to Bersham lodge secretary, 18 March 1968: CRO Flintshire D/NM/1385.

settle quickly in the Valleys around 1910 and ensure that a left identity would remain a potent political force in the SWMF.[101]

In contrast, the Nottinghamshire coalfield experienced a large influx of miners from other areas, which did not transform the moderate approach to trade union politics, as the local branches retained a particular identity and autonomy. The Kent coalfield provides another case of transformation, as many victimized miners left for the coalfield after 1926 and were able to establish a progressive approach to union politics via the Communist Party throughout the twentieth century.[102] The north Wales coalfield remained distinctive in that the workforce was almost totally indigenous. From the earliest colliery developments, labour had been primarily drawn from the localities surrounding the pits. Along with other areas, the north Wales collieries became open to a number of overseas workers after the Second World War, but not in significant numbers. Overall, the pits had been exporters of labour. After the 1926 lockout a number of unemployed miners moved to Pennsylvania in the United States; the founder of the union, Edward Hughes, had initially moved to the Durham coalfield before returning to the area. Even in the 1960s, miners were still moving from Wrexham to pits in the Midlands and south Wales.

In 1968, after the closure of Hafod and with the imminent closure of Ifton, the NCB announced that more miners would be needed for Point of Ayr. A number of men transferred but remained in their own localities and chose to travel by transport provided by the NCB. Some of the Wrexham miners found that they had to rise at four in the morning in order to make it in time for the morning shift. The men from Chirk could catch a quick sleep as the Hanmers bus sped through the Welsh countryside. The Wrexham men became known as 'jackos' and they returned the compliment by labelling the indigenous workforce 'seagulls'. There was no overt tension between the two groups but there was a high level of group solidarity. Teams were often made up of men from one or the other, which at times led to disputes over the allocation of overtime, though the union activists were mixed and contained both 'jackos' and 'seagulls'. The main body of

---

[101] Francis and Smith, *The Fed*, p.13.
[102] For a profile of the Kent NUM, see Malcolm Pitt, *The World on Our Backs: The Kent Miners and the 1972 Miners Strike* (London, 1979).

in-migrant labour, however, came from the rapidly declining Lancashire coalfield. Lancashire miners made a limited but nonetheless significant impact on the politics of the union.

The link between Lancashire and north Wales had always been a tenuous one. From the 1870s onwards activists from Lancashire had attempted to recruit around the pits of Flintshire and Denbighshire with varying degrees of success until the north Wales miners organized themselves under the guidance of Edward Hughes in the 1890s. In the post-nationalization climate, Edward Jones and later Jos Ellis worked closely with Lancashire in forming an alliance of some of the smaller areas of the union to defend challenges from the left in their plans for centralization. This was epitomized by the work of Joe Gormley, who retained his belief in supporting the claims of areas over the interests of the national body. Nevertheless, north Wales retained its centrist approach to national union policy and resisted becoming a fully-fledged member of the right faction. As vice-president, Jones promoted himself as a reconciler who was impatient of the ideological posturings of competing groups.

During the 1960s, the rapid decline of the Lancashire coalfield led to miners considering moves to other areas. Between 1960 and 1964, twenty Lancashire pits closed. The bleakest year was 1968, with six closures and the loss of 5,800 jobs including Mosley Common.[103] This pit had caused much concern in the Lancashire Area, with Gormley himself stressing that the men, and particularly those he claimed as militants, were responsible for shutting it.[104] The Communist lodge official, Mick Weaver, was a thorn in the side of the leadership. When the pit closed, a small group came to north Wales along with others from Bradford and Bickershaw collieries.

Les Kelly, who went on to become the full-time official for north Wales in the late 1980s, was one miner who came to Point of Ayr in 1968 in a group of around thirty. Kelly himself had been a union activist at Bradford as branch secretary of the small Lancashire and Cheshire Kindred Trades Workers, which amalgamated with the NUM in 1968. Soon after starting at Point of Ayr, Kelly became interested in the politics of the union;

---

[103] David Howell, *The Politics of the NUM: A Lancashire View* (Manchester, 1989), p.15.
[104] Gormley, *Battered Cherub*, pp.52–7.

he was elected to the lodge in 1971, becoming the secretary in 1973. Initially he was struck by the dominance of facemen on the committee. Kelly was an electrician and felt that craftsmen were under-represented in the union locally and nationally. He also noticed that Jack Griffiths, the area president, was actually a member of the NCB staff as superintendent of the colliery baths. This alarmed the men who had come from Lancashire, because there was the potential for a conflict of interest between the management and the union. The miners from Bradford were welcomed and only suffered a touch of animosity, usually mani-fested in the shape of anti-English camaraderie underground and in local pubs.[105] Kelly grew to be a dominant figure in terms of lodge and area politics and he was able to unite the differ-ent experiences of the Lancashire, Wrexham and indigenous workers. A significant group of Lancashire miners settled in the village of Mostyn about three miles from the colliery. A cul-de-sac on the council estate of Maes Pennant became known as 'Manchester Square' due to the number of English miners in-habiting the housing. A number of oral testimonies illustrate that, although there was little animosity shown to the men and their families, the level of 'Welshness' and localism in the village remained. The children of those miners are still regarded as English to this day, such is the strength of the bond between the village and a Welsh identity.

Brian Woods, who had come from Mosley Common, was happy at Point of Ayr because of the low level of strikes. He remembered that during the 1960s it was 'difficult to get a full week in at the Common'.[106] Although many like Woods found little difficulty in settling, others had a more challenging experi-ence, especially those who had come from large towns like Leigh. The north Wales coast seemed to be a barren outpost in terms of local amenities, public transport and cultural pursuits.[107] A number of miners longed to be back in England and, even today,

---

[105] Les Kelly interview, 1997.

[106] Brian Woods (faceworker at Mosley Common and Point of Ayr) interview, 1997.

[107] Lancashire miners were especially critical of the lack of a 'working-class club culture' in the villages surrounding Point of Ayr. Many felt that the pubs were merely forums for local gossip, and English miners came to rely on holidays in Blackpool to get their diet of cabaret and fish and chip shops. One consistent gripe was that you needed to catch a bus to get to the nearest betting shop. Brian Gildart, a former Parsonage miner from Leigh, often organized coach trips back to the town in order for the miners to visit the local Labour club.

families who moved from Leigh still regard Lancashire as home. The experience of English youth was also marked by the lack of amenities in the coalfield. The children of Bradford miners had been used to the metropolitan influence of Manchester and its culture of music venues, sporting events and cinemas.[108]

It was often the women who had most difficulty in adapting to a different environment, as they were tied to the home and responsible for childcare. Women from Greater Manchester found themselves virtually prisoners in the villages. Previously they could have walked to town for the shops, but in Mostyn and Trelogan in the 1960s, bus services remained poor. Medical centres and sources of entertainment were also some distance away in the towns of Prestatyn and Rhyl. Lancashire, Wrexham and local women did not stray from their familiar circle of friends. At weekends, women and their partners would travel to Labour clubs in Leigh as a means of escape and entertainment. Many of the families returned to Lancashire on a regular basis to keep in touch with relatives and friends. Wrexham miners also often ventured back to the Rhos and the familiarity of the miners' institute.

A number of women worked part-time but in low-paid occupations that were unresponsive to union organization. Pontins Holiday Camp in Prestatyn provided buses to transport local labour employed to clean chalets. Politically, female representation in the local Labour Party branches was minimal, with many women mirroring the voting habits of husbands and partners in local and general elections. In the local pubs, the sexual division remained constant, males inhabiting the 'tap room' and females residing in the lounge. But, under the veneer of community cohesion, alcohol abuse, the neglect of children and domestic violence were constant features of working-class life. Nevertheless, although patriarchy in the villages was apparent, a number of 'hen-pecked' husbands were identified in the workplace as unable or unwilling to participate in the cultural pursuits of other miners: gambling, drinking and sport.

Both married and single miners sought solace from the limitations of village life by attending nightclubs in Rhyl. The

---

[108] Youth culture in Lancashire is assessed in Dave Haslam, *Manchester England: The Story of the Pop Cult City* (London, 1999), pp.83–108.

Ritz was a popular spot, along with the Lido in Prestatyn, booking acts such as the Beatles and the Kinks. The bonds of friendship extended from the workplace into the community, with both employment time and leisure time enjoyed in the company of familiar faces. The cultural pursuits of the women were more significantly influenced by the domestic situation. Single, younger women often mirrored their male counterparts by attending pubs and dances. For married women the pursuits were more settled: bingo, dart leagues, Tupperware parties and coffee mornings.

The men quickly settled into working at Point of Ayr. Some were dismayed that the men at the pit had voted to start the period of night shifts on a Sunday; in Lancashire and most other areas production on the night shift started on Monday. The pit itself continued to prosper, with production records broken throughout 1968–9. The *Rhyl and Prestatyn Gazette* reported that there was a strong bond between management and men and a healthy atmosphere; 'in fact Point of Ayr with its 150 Joneses, its contingent of Lancashire lads, its Jamaicans, Spaniards and Germans, among the 600 labour force is known as the happy colliery.'[109] The 'quasi-cosmopolitan' nature of the pit provided younger miners, who had left school with minimal qualifications, with an informal education. Miners under the age of eighteen had to work for two years under the close supervision of men who were close to retirement. In this situation, older miners acted as informal tutors of work skills, geography, history, politics and social relations.

The pit might have been a melting pot of different experiences and accents but this did not have a significant impact on the political complexion of the union. Les Kelly throughout the 1970s continued to raise the profile of the area with limited success. The Lancashire contingent complemented the developing critique of deference shown to the agent, particularly in the 1970s during the McKay leadership. This rank-and-file disquiet gained further impetus with the politicization of the younger miners, particularly the craftsmen whom Kelly had encouraged to play a greater role in the affairs of the lodge.[110] Nonetheless, criticism of the

[109] *Rhyl and Prestatyn Gazette*, 16 February 1968.
[110] In particular, a number of electricians who started work in this period were to go on to form the nucleus of the striking miners in 1984–5.

Wrexham leadership lacked coherent organization and did not seriously threaten the environment of consensus. The absence of a significant left force in Lancashire accounts for the limited impact which the immigrants had on the politics of the North Wales Area and the attempted changes owed more to style than to substance. The coming of the English seemed to have a greater impact on the notion of community, as opposed to altering radically the political culture of the union, and Labourism as a manifestation of lodge politics remained untouched.

The 1960s represented a period of transition for the mining communities of north Wales, though politically the continuities are more evident. Economic orthodoxy and industrial decline in the name of technological modernization quickly extinguished the perceived radicalism of the Wilson victory in 1966. The NUM retained a cautious leadership throughout the period, though pockets of radicalism could be detected in certain coalfields, notably south Yorkshire which helped to tilt the union to the left. The rank-and-file initiatives which swept through Yorkshire were absent from north Wales, and the emphasis on legality still patterned the language of political action. Cyril Gregory of the Gresford lodge made it clear in 1970 that 'there would be no strikes in the coalfield without a national ballot', an insistence that was to prove to be divisive in the 1980s.[111]

Radicalization owed little to disillusionment with Wilson, or to activity geared towards more socialist measures in the nationalized industry, or the wider society. The emphasis was on improvement for the membership, in terms both of levels of pay and on the ability of the union to bargain effectively without the constraint of industrial relations legislation. Jos Ellis and a number of miners from the coalfield joined the various demonstrations opposing the legislation of Edward Heath in 1971 and called on local lodges to vote in favour of strike action over the issue of pay.[112]

The north Wales miners entered the 1970s depleted in numbers but retaining their autonomy and a commitment to Labour politics. At the annual delegate meeting in 1971, the 'old guard' retained their official positions with Jack Griffiths of Point

---

[111] *Wrexham Leader*, 22 September 1970.
[112] *Wrexham Leader*, 23 February 1971.

of Ayr once again taking on the mantle of the presidency. The coalfield would soon be a two-pit area, but still it resisted attempts at amalgamation. The union felt that the miners of Denbighshire and Flintshire could best be represented and remembered by a labour institution based in Wrexham. As Griffiths pointed out at the annual conference in 1969, 'the greatest darkness cannot put out the light of a very small candle'.[113]

[113] NUM North Wales annual report, 1969: CRO Flintshire D/NM/123.

III

THE POLITICS OF COAL, 1972–1982

I look at my wage slip
And wonder why
They say coal's expensive,
It must be a lie.

We are a quarter mile down,
And two miles inside.
We are cold, wet and hungry,
But still full of pride.

We are all NUM,
And we all pull together
Cos once you're a miner,
You're a miner for ever.[1]

The defeat of Harold Wilson in 1970 marked a watershed in the politics of the British labour movement. The general election victory of the Conservatives under Edward Heath led to the most extensive industrial conflict since 1926, with the miners playing a central role. Heath suggested that the Conservatives would break with tradition and cast off their 'one nation' image. In the handling of strikes, Heath signalled that he meant business and withstood the threats of a number of public-sector unions. Trade union opposition to the government crystallized around the Industrial Relations Bill, the central plank of the Conservative manifesto in 1970.

The government's aim was to seek a legal solution to the behaviour of trade unions. The subsequent legislation was to give the state influence over individual labour organizations. This was the most significant aspect of the bill, as each union would have to register and accept particular conditions of 'good practice'. The unions were quick to respond, and on 21 February 1971 the

---

[1] Extract from 'The price of coal' by Keith Hett, from *Bersham Pit Bottom and Other Poems* (private publication, 1986).

TUC organized a 140,000-strong demonstration, agreeing on a general policy of non-collaboration in terms of registration. Five dockers, known later as the Pentonville Five, who had been fined by the Industrial Relations Court, were jailed for refusing to pay, but later freed under the threat of a general strike. Enoch Powell and others in the Conservative Party were calling for a more resilient approach, but Heath gave in and returned to a corporatist policy.[2]

In 1972, the NUM under the presidency of the recently elected Joe Gormley was still reeling from the effects of the massive wave of pit closures. The left had been strengthened by the developments in the Yorkshire coalfield, but the right was still able to mobilize itself as the election of Gormley had shown. Gormley had beaten the Communist Mick McGahey of the Scottish Area by 117,663 votes to 92,883.[3] This led to developments that exacerbated factions within the union, with left activists becoming increasingly restless. Arthur Scargill, for instance, was making his presence felt in the Yorkshire coalfield where the fusion of the Communists and Labour left activists was having a significant impact on union politics.[4]

The Conservative attack on organized labour went beyond anti-trade union legislation as the government increasingly curtailed the activity of strikers under the criminal law. North Wales became the *cause célèbre* when the building trade unions attempted to end the growth of 'lump labour'[5] on a number of building sites. Flintshire and Denbighshire had been weak spots of construction unionism, with only 10 per cent of workers organized. During the Union of Construction, Allied Trades and Technicians (UCATT) strike of 1972, pickets from Flint, Denbigh and Wrexham led the campaign against the 'lump'. Three strikers were later jailed for conspiracy, unlawful assembly and affray. Ricky Tomlinson, a plasterer from Wrexham and later a popular

<hr/>

[2] Powell felt that nationalization was intolerable in a free society and was increasingly critical of Heath's policy on trade union reform. See Robert Shepherd, *Enoch Powell: A Biography* (London, 1996), p.421.
[3] Joe Gormley, *Battered Cherub* (London, 1982), p. 77.
[4] Details of the left in Yorkshire from the perspective of a rank-and-file activist can be found in David John Douglass, *Pit Sense versus the State: A History of Militant Miners in the Doncaster Area* (London, 1994).
[5] 'Lump labour' was a system introduced into the building industry using private contractors to work on sites, thus undermining the strength of unionized workers. See Leslie Wood, *A Union to Build: The Story of UCATT* (London, 1979), pp.21–2.

actor of *Brookside* and *Royle Family* fame, was one of the defendants who received a custodial sentence.[6] The militancy on the
building sites was perhaps a sign that, even in traditionally
moderate areas such as north Wales, workers were becoming
increasingly restless.

STRIKES AND SOLIDARITY

Between 1969 and 1972 the pressure for concerted action
amongst the miners had been growing. With the added
ingredient of a Conservative government, the ground seemed
ripe for an attack on the policy of pay restraint. At its annual
conference in 1971, the NUM agreed a resolution that claimed a
minimum basic weekly wage of £26 for surface workers, £28 for
underground workers and £35 for NPLA workers. The conference also initiated a rule change that allowed strikes to be
called with a 55 per cent majority of favourable votes, as opposed
to two-thirds, which was the previous rule. The subsequent
overtime ban, which was initiated in pursuit of this claim,
brought home to miners the inadequacy of their basic wage.[7] On
a national ballot, 59 per cent of miners voted in favour of a strike
from 9 January 1972. The nature of this dispute was to colour
the perceptions of the left of the NUM and the right of the
Conservative Party for the next decade and have far-reaching
implications for both governments and unions.

Members of the NCB and the Conservative government were
initially shocked at the result of the ballot, as they were sure that
Gormley would provide a barrier to the left.[8] Rather surprisingly, all areas threw their full weight behind the dispute, and
the factions within the union came together to co-ordinate the
course of action. A special delegate meeting of the north Wales
miners urged all lodges to give full support to the ban on
overtime and recommended that members vote in favour of
strike action.[9] The local press was quick to stress that a strike

[6] For details of the strike and the subsequent court case, see Jim Arnison, *The
Shrewsbury Three: Strikes, Pickets and 'Conspiracy'* (London, 1974).
[7] Malcolm Pitt, *The World on Our Backs: The Kent Miners and the 1972 Miners' Strike*
(London, 1979), p.113.
[8] Andrew Taylor, *The Politics of the Yorkshire Miners* (London, 1984), p.179.
[9] NUM North Wales special delegate meeting, 22 October 1971: CRO Flintshire
D/NM/151.

might put the future of the Wrexham pits in jeopardy. The *Wrexham Leader* reported that 'housewives' in the village of Rhostyllen, which fed Bersham colliery, were worried about future employment if the strike went ahead. This was a familiar tactic of the press, emphasizing the declining purchasing power of women during industrial unrest. Nonetheless, all the pits in the coalfield voted for strike action and seemed united in their quest for higher wages.

Wrexham was without coal within a day of the strike. A number of pickets manned the entrances of Bersham and Gresford to ensure that only coal for hospitals, pensioners and concessionary loads to miners would be allowed. Cyril Gregory, the pragmatic Gresford delegate, stressed that the men were unanimous in favour of the dispute, particularly as the action had been sanctioned 'the proper way' by a national ballot. He claimed that many of the men working on the surface in the north Wales pits would be better off on social security. The union was also despondent about the future of the industry and resigned itself to the fact that the pits would close irrespective of the strike.

The area union decided to step up the action after the first week of the strike and organized a demonstration for the end of January in Wrexham. The AEC called for widespread support for the rally, which Labour branches and trades councils throughout the region attended. Lord Maelor, himself a former miner, headed the march through the town and the men sang 'Cwm Rhondda'. Stickers and posters had been produced and donations received from Plaid Cymru and the International Socialists. Around 2,000 people attended, and local Labour MPs Barry Jones and Tom Ellis spoke in favour of the miners' action, pledging to keep up the pressure in the House of Commons. In the local press, Jos Ellis recalled that there had not been scenes like this in Wrexham since the 1930s. Tom Ellis predicted that 'the strike is going to be a historic one. I am sure in my own mind . . . that this strike is going to have an effect on the future development of politics and industry in this century.'[10]

The Point of Ayr pickets staged a twenty-four-hour demonstration outside the Courtaulds Castle works at Flint in an effort

[10] *Wrexham Leader*, 7, 11 January, 1 February 1972.

to stop coal deliveries, for early in the strike trucks had challenged the strength of the picket line. The Labour Party became fully involved with the campaign locally, and the branches in Denbighshire and Flintshire were unanimous in their commitment to the miners' cause. Anthony Meyer, the Conservative MP for Flint West, also made his presence felt. He had taken the seat after the retirement of Nigel Birch in 1970 and went on to challenge Margaret Thatcher's leadership of the Conservative Party in 1989.[11] Speaking in the House of Commons, he explained that he 'represented miners at the Point of Ayr who no doubt never voted for him', but he maintained that 'there is no group of my constituents among which I would rather rely in adverse circumstances'. In a speech to his constituents in Rhyl, Meyer claimed that if he had been a miner he would himself have rejected the government's offer: 'It is impossible not to sympathise with the miners . . . they do a dirty job for a reward that compares badly with what others get. I would not like to do their job for any amount of money.'[12]

The programme of picketing in north Wales continued to be successful, with a challenge primarily coming from the local coal merchants who continued to cross picket lines. Cyril Gregory reported to the press that several coal merchants were also deliberately putting out leaflets encouraging customers to transfer to a system of oil heating. More pressure was applied and pickets were deployed to the British Celanese factory in Wrexham, which was already on short time and had attempted to bring in secret supplies of coal.[13]

The problem with the coal merchants continued and the union was threatened with legal action by Derrick Roberts, a merchant from Llay, who had been continually turned away by the pickets at Gresford. Gregory stated that he would not be allowed on to the yard even when the strike was over if he continued to attempt to pass the pickets.[14] The miners had now been on strike for almost a month, and there seemed to be no cracks in the solidarity of the membership. A week later the

[11] Anthony Meyer, *Stand Up and Be Counted* (London, 1990).
[12] *Liverpool Daily Post*, 17, 18 January 1972.
[13] *Wrexham Leader*, 18, 21 January 1972.
[14] Letter from Gwilym Hughes and Partners, solicitors, to Jos Ellis, North Wales NUM, 16 February 1972: CRO Flintshire D/NM/1192.

government declared a state of emergency. The AEC intensified its picketing and decided that an allowance of £20 per week be made to lodges to cover further food and travelling expenses for pickets.[15] At Gresford miners intensified their actions and succeeded in stopping management from going underground to carry out safety work. This became a serious issue, as the future of the pit was already uncertain.

At the national level, the unity of the men was apparent and, on 1 February, the 'Battle of Saltley Gate' commenced which would provide the lasting image of the strike. A mass picket of miners and a number of other trade unionists from the Birmingham area closed the Saltley coke depot by direct action.[16] Arthur Scargill was clear about the significance of this particular confrontation between capital and labour: 'We took the view that we were in a class war. We were not playing cricket on the village green, like they did in 1926. We were out to defeat Heath ... because we were fighting a Government.'[17]

Meanwhile, the secretary of state for employment, Robert Carr, announced that he would set up a court of inquiry under the chairmanship of Lord Wilberforce. The court heard oral evidence on 15–16 February and recommended increases for the miners, which the union initially declined but accepted later, with supplementary demands included.[18] The NEC, by a majority of sixteen to nine, voted to recommend a return to work, much to the criticism of the left in the union. The NUM agreed to ballot its members on the offer and, on 23 February, with an overwhelming vote for acceptance, the miners decided to end the action. The strike had lasted seven weeks. The Kent Area viewed the settlement as a compromise and was angered when the strike was called off before the result of the ballot. The left eventually accepted the result and joined the rest of the NEC in welcoming the fact that the strike had brought a successful settlement to the campaign for a wage increase.

The North Wales AEC had, from the outset, accepted the decision of the NEC and recommended the lodges and the

[15] North Wales NUM special AEC meeting, 26 January 1972: NUM, Wrexham.
[16] For a full account of the events leading to Saltley Gate, see Pitt, *The World on our Backs*, p.166.
[17] Arthur Scargill, 'The New Unionism', *New Left Review*, 92 (1975), 13.
[18] For an account of the NUM's presentation to the court of inquiry, see John Hughes and Roy Moore (eds.), *A Special Case? Social Justice and the Miners* (Harmondsworth, 1972).

membership to do likewise.[19] The majority voted in favour of the proposal and the north Wales miners ended their first area strike since 1926. The men at all three pits – Gresford, Bersham and Point of Ayr – had been solid in their support for the union, as had the membership in the rest of the British coalfields. Nevertheless, this did not signify a renewed unity amongst the federated areas. Both left and right within the organization misread the situation and so enhanced the level of factionalism in the national body. The militants felt that the action was the first step in a rising climate of militancy, whereas moderates viewed the dispute as a last resort in securing a substantial pay claim. The aftermath entrenched political differences in the union and did not represent a harbinger of a more fixed unity. In retrospect, Gormley retained mixed views about the outcome of the dispute.

> I am not sure whether that strike performed a good service or a bad. It was good in that it united the lads, and showed them the strength that unity could bring. On the other hand, its success led to an attitude of mind, prevalent today [1982], where people, the moment they don't get what they want, think and talk of strike action immediately.[20]

Gormley was aware of the threat that the left posed to his position. It had been a strike of the wider membership, and many initiatives remained beyond the direction of the national leadership and NEC. The left in Kent, south Wales, Scotland and Yorkshire welcomed this development, viewing it as undermining the resilience of the right in the union bureaucracy. With the events of 1972 etched on their consciousness, they pressed for further control of area and national bodies. The events of Saltley Gate remained fresh in the mind of Scargill and showed what direct action could achieve: 'here was living proof that the working class had only to flex its muscles and it would bring down governments, employers, bringing society to a standstill.'[21]

[19] North Wales NUM special AEC meeting, 19 February 1972: CRO Flintshire D/NM/41.
[20] This view is a thinly veiled attack on the politics of Arthur Scargill who had just become NUM president at the time of the publication of Gormley's autobiography. Gormley, *Battered Cherub*, p.118.
[21] Scargill, ' The new unionism', 19.

In Kent and Yorkshire and, to a lesser extent, in other areas, the dispute released powerful forces that led to greater involvement of the membership in determining the strategies of the respective unions. The analyses of both Malcolm Pitt for Kent and Vic Allen for Yorkshire stress that the strike marked a watershed in the politics of the NUM. However, one must not lose sight of the continuity in terms of political pragmatism that still characterized the attitudes of the union and of coalfield communities. In the ballot which led to the action, only 55.8 per cent of the membership voted in favour of a strike in a high turnout of 86 per cent of those eligible to vote. If the earlier two-thirds majority voting system had not been changed, the action would not have been approved. In essence, the mining community was still politically cautious.

The north Wales coalfield is a stark example of the left failing to materialize. The number of miners who could be characterized as 'left' probably amounted to no more than a dozen. Nonetheless, the unity of the NUM, once the decision was taken by a ballot vote, was strong and the actions of each area gained legitimacy even amongst those who had voted against the strike.[22] The normally cautious Tom Ellis, MP for Wrexham, was aware of the growing attacks on the trade unions that were emerging as a backlash from the Conservative Party. In a letter to Jimmy Williams of the Bersham lodge, Ellis claimed that he was 'getting very worried about the Labour Party and our prospects for the future and the next election, we need in my view more people to be speaking out for the brotherhood of man and true socialism'.[23]

Ellis and a number of AEC members in the coalfield felt that they were being pressurized by two opposing political forces that were working to undermine the political traditions of the north Wales miners. On the one side, the Conservative Party wanted to change the role of the law in industrial relations and dilute the

---

[22] The absence of a Labour government to dilute the militancy directed at the state was significant as the 'Labourist consciousness' of the miners could be mobilized against the policies of Heath. Wilson and others in the Labour Party knew that the strike could be used to damage the government and humiliate Heath. In the 1966–70 period, the Labour Party had operated in the opposite way by providing a barrier to developing radicalism.
[23] Letter from Tom Ellis MP to Jimmy Williams, NUM Bersham lodge, re article in *The Times* condemning the actions of the trade unions, 31 January 1973: CRO Flintshire D/NM/1472.

autonomy of working-class organizations; on the other, there was an effective left wing in the union working to transform the NUM. The seeds of resistance were sown in this period as north Wales became involved in the endemic factionalism of the NUM. As yet, the leadership of Jos Ellis was in line with the tradition of pragmatism in the coalfield, which was not overly coloured by factional affiliation in either direction. This was to change dramatically in two years' time with the election of an outspoken official.

As the Heath government continued to grapple with the prob- lem of industrial relations and the state of the British economy, politics within the coalfields were in a state of flux. The wages question was far from settled, and in 1973 there were again calls for action to back claims for higher pay. Pits were still closing and increasingly there were debates in the national union over what course of action should be taken to stop the run-down of the industry. The north Wales leadership had soon to contend with the loss of another pit in its rapidly shrinking coalfield. Early in 1973, the NCB had reported that Gresford was in serious danger and would have to close unless rapid improvements led to increased production. Keith Saunders, the NUM engineer, was called to investigate and stressed that recent trends in the for- tunes of the pit would make it difficult to justify a report that would be contrary to that of the corporation.[24] Nonetheless, the AEC decided to inform the NEC that they would oppose the closure owing to the devastating effect that it would have on the local economy.

The lodge committee at Gresford had hoped that the NCB would allow them to work their way into the seams that had been used by the old Wynnstay colliery, which had closed in 1927. This could have provided a secure future for the pit, according to Jack Read and Jos Ellis. The NCB area director informed them that this was not viable, as the existing seams were not suitable for development and further expansion would prove to be too expensive.[25] The union stuck to its proposals and forced the colliery into the review procedure to argue the case for continued

[24] North Wales NUM minutes of AEC meeting, 27 June 1973: CRO Flintshire D/NM/1133.
[25] Letter from J. R. Hunter, NCB area director, to Jos Ellis, NUM North Wales, 18 March 1974: CRO Flintshire D/NM/1192.

production. On 9 May 1973 the first review meeting took place and the area director set out the case for closure.[26] The NCB announced that the pit would close in September 1973, the men being offered jobs at the remaining two pits in the area or alternatively in other coalfields. The AEC, still smarting from the inability to develop a strategy to save Hafod and Ifton, immediately pledged that a concerted campaign would be mounted to ensure a future for Gresford. There would be a three-pronged approach to the decision: it would be argued that the Quaker Seam should be developed, a reduction in manpower to ease costs and promote efficiency would be agreed with the parties involved, and political pressure would be applied in all quarters.[27] Tom Ellis was sympathetic to the union's case and visited the colliery as part of an NUM delegation. He argued that 'there was an abundance of reserves at the pit and that it had nine unexploited seams containing high quality coal'.[28]

The union's immediate task was to try to engineer a stay of execution while they gathered relevant evidence to secure the future of the pit. The AEC approached ministers, MPs, local authority officials and NCB managers, though the corporation rejected all subsequent appeals. The union also stressed that it would push for greater levels of productivity to ensure the immediate success of the Quaker Seam.[29] Jos Ellis was aware that the case was initially weak, following the report by Saunders and the union's inability to rebuff adequately the claims of the NCB, but he still felt that Gresford was too important for the area to surrender. The AEC worked in conjunction with the local authority and produced a comprehensive report, which stressed the need to maintain current employment levels in the Wrexham district. The report argued that the pit was ideal for the production of domestic coal, but admitted that, for the sake of efficiency, the colliery would have to operate with a workforce less than half the present size.[30]

[26] In the previous twelve months, the pit had lost four faces prematurely, and two others were abandoned owing to the scale of faulting. NCB statement by T. G. Tregelles, area director, on Gresford colliery, 9 May 1973: CRO Flintshire D/NM/663.
[27] NUM Gresford lodge committee minutes, 12 May 1972: CRO Flintshire D/NM/666.
[28] Statement on meeting between NUM and John Morris QC, secretary of state for Wales, 9 May 1974: CRO Flintshire D/NM/670.
[29] NUM North Wales special meeting of lodge officials, 6 June 1973: CRO Flintshire D/NM/41.
[30] T. M. Haydn Rees, 'The case for the redevelopment of the mining industry with particular reference to Gresford' (Clwyd County Council, 1973): NUM, Wrexham.

In August 1973, the NCB informed the union that there was no chance of the pit breaking even and that closure would go ahead as planned. Jos Ellis remained critical of the outcome and pronounced the review procedure to be a farce since NCB personnel, who had already made a decision on the closure, heard appeals against their own decisions. He claimed that all appeals should be made to a panel of independent mining engineers that would then make a joint and binding recommendation to both the NCB and the NUM.[31] On 9 November 1973, Gresford colliery wound its last ton of coal and the pit closed. All seemed lost, but there was one ray of hope. As the energy crisis in the Middle East unfolded, the union called for the redevelopment of the colliery. Officials again approached the NCB and elicited a more promising response. The area director agreed to look again at the reserves at Gresford in the context of the changed energy situation and the rise in demand for coal.[32]

The union sent a five-man delegation to the NCB headquarters in London to try to revive the prospects for the colliery. Along with the support of the local Labour MPs and representatives from the local authority, it argued that, in the changed economic climate, Gresford could produce urgently needed coal. Lawrence Daly for the national union aligned himself with the campaign to save Gresford, but the NCB soon dampened enthusiasm. The corporation argued that even the changing energy needs of the nation did not justify the level of capital expenditure which the pit required.[33] The AEC felt that they could do no more to save the pit and reluctantly accepted closure.

As had been the case with Hafod and Ifton, the North Wales Area sought to fight colliery closures through a process of negotiation, rather than applying the industrial muscle which the union apparently had at its disposal as a result of the 1972 strike. Both Jos Ellis and the president, Jack Griffiths, had recognized the futility of the search for consensus but still maintained this strategy for challenging closures. The failure during this period, both locally and nationally, to demand and develop a

[31] North Wales NUM special AEC meeting, 24 September 1973: CRO Flintshire D/NM/41.
[32] North Wales NUM minutes of AEC Meeting, 1 April 1974: CRO Flintshire D/NM/1133.
[33] North Wales NUM AEC meeting, 29 August 1974: CRO Flintshire D/NM/1133.

comprehensive strategy for fighting closures was to prove disastrous for the union as the events of the 1980s showed. This is not to suggest that the left wing's call for industrial action was the only alternative. The union could have developed a coherent policy that went beyond the scope of the review procedure, providing an avenue of discussion that could have gained legitimacy and the support of the Labour Party in opposition. In one sense, the failure to adapt and harness the rising wage militancy to the issue of closures was a sign of the weakness of such militancy as a unifying strand going beyond basic trade union sectionalism. The north Wales miners, though sympathetic to the course and nature of the 1972 strike, remained cautious in terms of developing their own initiatives locally in establishing channels of conciliation and negotiation.

The last meeting of the Gresford lodge was a sombre affair, as Wrexham continued to lose its identity as a town built on coal. Albert Davies, the secretary, noted that it was a sad day for the pit but miners had to face the future as they had done in the past. Jack Read, the veteran trade unionist from Hafod, remained until the end, when the salvage operation was completed. In his final entry in the lodge minute book, tinged with emotion, he reflected on the closure: 'It is with great sadness that I pen the following now that my Lodge has ended and the workforce has left apart from me and the salvage team. There does not seem any more purpose in what I do.'[34] Read had worked in a number of pits in the Wrexham coalfield and had lost a brother in the Gresford disaster. He moved to Bersham, where he retired in 1979 and continued to involve himself in the affairs of the union, particularly the welfare of retired miners.

The last entry in the Gresford minute book illustrates the link between the pit, the workforce and the community. Brave men who have battled with nature itself and with other workers through constructing a 'work hard, play hard' mentality have been known to weep openly at the closure of particular pits. This attachment to place historically has coloured the political culture of mining communities. However, occupational identity was not always complemented by formal political commitments. The 'far

---

[34] NUM Gresford lodge committee minutes of the last meeting, 20 November 1973: CRO Flintshire D/NM/660.

left' has never fully grasped this dimension of the class-consciousness of British miners. It helps to explain why miners and their trade union representatives repeatedly rejected abstract political theories. This identity was also an inclusive one with gender differences posing no threat to a particular occupational attachment. Women of mining families identified with the pit at an early age, attracted by the inherent masculinity of the occupation, the bonds of fraternity it produced, and the social/cultural networks that it constructed. Even in the 1980s, mining communities would not provide a fertile ground for feminist politics.

The North Wales Area was now down to two pits, Bersham and Point of Ayr. This encouraged the union to adopt a more resilient approach to its autonomy and the need to bolster the defence of the local union against the emergent left and its influence on the NEC. In the middle of the furore over the closure of Gresford, the NUM again threatened to shake the foundations of the government's economic policy. It embarked on its second national strike in two years. At the 1972 NUM annual conference, miners called for wage increases that would give faceworkers £40 a week and surface workers £30. Even the moderates in the union united when it came to the inadequacy of the miners' income in comparison with other blue-collar occupations. Gormley, in characteristic style, had set out his stall in 1971:

> I am not going to be a miners' leader if I cannot claim a bigger minimum wage for the lads who go underground than the lads carting the dustbins around London. I tell you, I am getting off my knees, I have been on them too long. I don't intend to be on them any longer.[35]

The pay claim was lodged early in 1973 but it was blocked by the government's policy of pay restraint. The membership accepted a reduced offer by the NCB, but at the conference in July the claim was again submitted. Global events also worked in favour of the miners as the oil-exporting states cut oil production, leading to an escalation in prices. At a special meeting of the North Wales AEC on 29 October, there was a discussion of the

---

[35] Joe Gormley cited in David Powell, *The Power Game: The Struggle For Coal* (London, 1993), p.187.

wages question. The feeling was that the recent NCB offer was unacceptable and that north Wales should campaign for the proposed overtime ban in line with the policy of the NEC. The ban was to commence from the first coaling shift on Monday, 12 November and it was resolved that the lodges should take immediate steps to ensure compliance with the action.[36] Meanwhile, Gormley was still hoping to broker a settlement to avoid escalation to a strike which the left was demanding.[37] The NEC voted not to put a new offer by the NCB to a national ballot, and an all-out strike seemed likely. The NCB this time wanted to pose a more sustained challenge in the dispute than it had done two years previously. A confidential memorandum, which had been formulated at a meeting of area directors in London on 22 November, set out the policy of the corporation in terms of the conduct of pit management and how they were to handle the dispute. The document stressed that the work being done by BACM members was to be referred to at all times as 'pit keeping' and not strike-breaking. Further, in answer to questions from the press, the future of the industry was to be raised continually, to the effect that the overtime ban was threatening its viability. Each manager was told to keep a log of events, in terms of what meetings were held with the men and the differences within the union. The policy for the NCB North West Area also indicated that NACODS members were to be kept on the side of management at all costs. This included giving deputies full pay if they were turned away at the pit gates by the presence of pickets.[38]

In a national ballot of the membership, the miners voted with an 81 per cent majority in favour of strike action. On 7 February, Heath called a general election under the slogan of 'Who governs?' There was pressure from some in the union to call an end to the strike while the election campaign progressed but the left were in the ascendancy and the decision of the NEC was to continue with the action, much to the annoyance of

[36] North Wales NUM special meeting of AEC, 9 November 1973: CRO Flintshire D/NM/41.

[37] The 1974 strike was a dispute that both the NUM right and the Conservative government were keen to avoid. See John Campbell, *Edward Heath: A Biography* (London, 1993), pp.561–97.

[38] NCB memo to colliery managers re NUM overtime ban (highly confidential), 26 November 1973: NUM, Wrexham.

Gormley. He called a special meeting of the NEC the day after Heath's announcement and candidly recalled the occasion in his memoirs.

> It may have surprised some of the members, but I suggested straight away that we should suspend the strike. For a start, I said, the very fact this election has been called means that we've won the battle. It doesn't matter a damn who wins the election – whichever party it is will be bound to reach a settlement with us.[39]

In north Wales, the leadership was close to Gormley and critical of the political dimension that had been brought into the dispute by the left. Cyril Gregory of Gresford and Jimmy Williams of Bersham criticized the rhetoric of McGahey, the vice-president of the NUM, who claimed that a strike would bring down the government.[40] Williams cautiously expressed the view that the men at Bersham had split views on the strike but would vote in favour because of their frustration at the level of wages. Gregory added that the salvage men at Gresford felt it was their duty to support the men who were fighting to secure a future in the industry. The AEC set about preparing for the strike with support from other unions and expected no serious trouble on the picket lines. Jos Ellis told the *Wrexham Leader* that 'the men were fully behind the ballot vote and would be solidly supporting the strike'. Jim Morris of the Denbighshire section of the T&GWU made it clear that his members would not cross NUM picket lines. The miners focused primarily on the opencast sites at Acrefair and Brymbo and coal-burning industries throughout the district. Gresford played a full role in the action, although only a minority of the workforce remained working on salvage operations.[41]

With the announcement of the general election and with the views of Gormley gaining support in some coalfields, the AEC called a meeting of all lodge officials on 9 February. It was decided that the strike would continue as planned under the auspices of the AEC until the NEC instructed otherwise.

[39] Gormley, *Battered Cherub*, p.141.
[40] A number of Labour MPs also voiced criticism of the views of McGahey and signed an Early Day Motion in the House of Commons as a protest.
[41] *Wrexham Leader*, 1 and 8 February 1974.

Arrangements for picketing were quickly formalized. Point of Ayr would be responsible for Flintshire, with Gresford and Bersham targeting Shotton steelworks.[42] A liaison committee was set up to co-ordinate the efforts of all the unions involved: NUM, T&GWU, COSA and NUR. The stocks of coal at each pit were relatively low and it was suggested that the committee obtain domestic coal from other areas owing to the small amount on the ground in the pit yards. The NUM felt that it needed to sustain public support by maintaining the distribution of essential supplies.

The pickets were well organized and proved effective from the first day of the dispute to the last, with some minor skirmishes at particular venues. The Bersham lodge based regular pickets on the Wrexham Industrial Estate and faced little dissent from their fellow workers. At Point of Ayr, a significant number of young miners were involved and they concentrated their efforts at Connah's Quay power station and the large Courtaulds plants in Greenfield and Flint. All apprentices were fully involved in the action, including those attending courses at the technical college in Wrexham.[43] The pickets at Gresford soon encountered a small problem which was an irritation to the union and those staffing the picket lines. Throughout the first week, the clerical staff had continued to work. They were undecided over the issue because their counterparts in Lancashire were ignoring the policy of the NUM and crossing picket lines. The AEC intensified the number of pickets at Gresford and the clerical staff decided that it was in their best interests to keep away from the colliery while the strike was in progress.[44] After two weeks on strike, the miners were helped by an allowance paid to pickets by the national union. Money had been allocated from the Industrial Action Fund and north Wales received £300, though the miners were warned to use the money as carefully as possible, as no assurance of a further allocation could be given.[45]

As the end of February approached, the action of the north Wales pickets proved to be highly effective, raising criticisms

---

[42] North Wales NUM meeting of lodge officials, 9 February 1974: CRO Flintshire D/NM/41.
[43] Notes of area liaison committee, 11 February 1974: CRO Flintshire D/NM/41.
[44] *Wrexham Leader*, 15 February 1974.
[45] Notes of area liaison committee, 19 February 1974: CRO Flintshire D/NM/41.

from local industry and the Conservative Party. Ken Davies of Brymbo steelworks voiced concern about the future of the unit if the picketing continued. The miners had been successful in halting the delivery of oil to the works, and Jos Ellis claimed that it was a peaceful and necessary exercise with little trouble.[46] Anthony Meyer again expressed some sympathy in the local press for the plight of the miners, though he warned that the dispute was having an appalling effect on the country. Jack Griffiths of Point of Ayr replied to his letter, justifying the actions of the union and claiming that they had widespread public support.[47] The situation at Gresford was still causing concern, and the COSA representative on the liaison committee made it clear that those continuing to cross picket lines would be reprimanded once the dispute ended. A further boost came when the dockworkers at the small port of Mostyn announced that they would not handle any coal.[48]

On 24 February, the report of the pay board, which had been requested to consider the issue of miners' pay, was released four days before the polls closed in the general election. This report showed that the miners were entitled to a rise above their current offer. The incoming Labour government met the NUM and a deal was struck which most areas accepted. The surface rate for the industry was set at £32, the minimum underground rate at £36 and NPLA at £45, along with a number of incidental benefits relating to holidays and shift allowances. The left claimed that more benefits could have been extracted, but Gormley was quick to point out that 'at the end of it all, we had brought the miners back to the position in which, in the national interest, Ted Heath himself should have wanted to see them – at the top of the industrial wages league'.[49] Criticism of the settlement not only came from the left in the union. A letter from the Point of Ayr lodge to the AEC attacked the differentials that still existed between the various categories covered by the award. There had been particular discontent at the pit at the level of the increase granted to members of NACODS and other managerial personnel.[50]

[46] *Wrexham Leader*, 22 February 1974.
[47] *Rhyl Journal*, 7 February 1974.
[48] Notes of North Wales Area liaison committee, 11 February 1974: CRO Flintshire D/NM/41.
[49] Gormley, *Battered Cherub*, p.145.
[50] North Wales NUM minutes of AEC, 1 April 1974: CRO Flintshire D/NM/1133.

The experience of the strikes of 1972 and 1974 in north Wales made little impact on the political culture of the coalfield. No coherent left emerged, and the leadership of the lodges was still largely based on a system of deference and patronage. There was no Communist presence in the area, and the left in the Labour Party found it a hostile region in terms of recruitment. In line with the thinking of Gormley, the north Wales miners viewed the strikes as industrial struggles over the level of wages and not as a political struggle, as some on the far left were at pains to advocate. The aim of the left was to challenge this apathy, and Scargill in particular wanted an escalation of the use of industrial action to secure further improvements.

THE CONSTRUCTION OF A FACTION

With the retirement of Jos Ellis in 1975, many thought that the North Wales Area would cease to exist. The Bersham lodge wanted an amalgamation with Lancashire but others on the North Wales executive felt that local leaders could best look after their own miners. In December 1974, the national union sent a delegation to the coalfield to discuss the future of the area in the context of the retirement of Ellis and the closure of Gresford. Scargill led the delegation and felt that a merger with another area union was the best possible solution. This would also cut the strength of the right on the NEC. The local leaders argued that the interests of the members would best be served by retaining an office in Wrexham where an agent could continue to operate. Scargill stressed that this seemed to be nonsense as the area now only had Point of Ayr and Bersham, which gave them just over a thousand members.[51] The delegation filed its report to the General Purposes Sub-Committee, and the NEC was to make a final decision. A meeting of the AEC was called and the president used his casting vote to support a resolution that would request the NEC to approve the appointment of a new secretary.[52] Scargill made his position clear, namely, that he would not support the claims of the area. The left, in general,

---

[51] North Wales NUM notes of a special meeting of the AEC, 14 December 1974: CRO Flintshire D/NM/41.
[52] North Wales NUM special meeting at the miners' institute, Wrexham, 25 January 1975: CRO Flintshire D/NM/41.

remained convinced that the eradication of small areas would bolster its power on the NEC.

While waiting for the decision of the NEC on the future of the area, the AEC went ahead and made plans for the election of a successor to Ellis. Two nominations would be permitted from both Point of Ayr and Bersham, with one from the recently closed Gresford colliery. The elected candidate would also sit on the NEC for the North Wales Area.[53] The annual delegate meeting of 1975 was the last attended by Jos Ellis. He was pleased that the NEC had finally decided that an agent would be appointed to keep alive the tradition of the coalfield as an autonomous area. Ellis closed his farewell speech by thanking all the members he had served, proud of the fact that they had fought the closure of Gresford.[54] The retirement of Ellis along with Griffiths, the president, left a vacuum that perhaps could have given the left an opportunity. But no such grouping existed in the coalfield, so again the campaign for the official remained faction-free, owing more to personalities and the animosity between Flintshire and Wrexham than it did to the politics of the candidates. The election for secretary took place on 13 May and five candidates submitted nomination papers. The result was to be decided using the single transferable vote system. Ted McKay, the eventual victor, had been a miner for twenty-five years at Point of Ayr, a lodge committee member and a town councillor. In his election pamphlet, he proclaimed that

> I have always believed that union leaders should reflect the thinking of men in the pit. To achieve this they should not only meet with the local lodge; but with every one, from the shearers to the screens. This must mean meeting and seeing men at the pit.[55]

Jack Read, the veteran of Hafod and ex-secretary of the Gresford lodge, also stood, becoming an early favourite because he was well known across the coalfield. Arthur Smith, the delegate from Bersham, had little support at his own pit, which was

---

[53] North Wales NUM special AEC, 11 March 1975: CRO Flintshire D/NM/41.

[54] North Wales NUM report of annual delegate meeting, 7 April 1975: CRO Flintshire D/NM/129.

[55] Edward McKay election manifesto for the post of area agent, 1975: NUM, Wrexham.

fielding two candidates. Jimmy Williams (Yanto),[56] the branch
secretary, had been involved in the politics of the union as a
young man and had proved to be a competent negotiator.
Throughout the campaign, he emphasized the importance of the
politics of Labourism: 'I firmly believe that one cannot separate
the Labour Party from our Great Trade Union Movement
because some of the many social benefits which were enacted in
Parliament, and which we now enjoy came about through the
united strength of the movement.'[57]

The final candidate was another Point of Ayr man, Elwyn
Williams, an electrician who had been on the lodge committee
since the age of twenty-two. Because of the number of candidates, it was felt that certain pits would split the vote and might
let in Jack Read, but this did not happen. Smith finished bottom
of the poll along with Read, and the final battle came down to
Jimmy Williams and McKay. McKay took the post with 452
votes against 363 for Williams. However, a number of objections
were raised and a special AEC was called to analyse the result.
Some delegates alleged that the ballot papers were opened at the
area office before the committee had gathered. The AEC
accepted this had happened but claimed that the boxes had only
been opened for posting in one parcel to the Electoral Reform
Society (ERS). The ballot box from Point of Ayr was taken to the
home of Jack Griffiths for the night; this also raised objections
because he had nothing to do with the management of the
election. Many felt that the contest had caused a degree of
bitterness, and there was an uneasy atmosphere on the Point of
Ayr lodge for some time after. McKay was successful, and he was
declared elected on 2 June 1975. The objections raised by
certain members were passed on to the national president for his
observations but the result would stand.[58]

As soon as McKay took up the post, he faced internal conflict.
The Bersham lodge still contested the validity of the ballot. The
ERS had originally made a mistake on the first count by

[56] Williams had been active in the union from an early age and enjoyed a good
working relationship with Tom Ellis, the Bersham manager, who seemed at ease working
closely with the union. See Tom Ellis, *Mines and Men: Mining Engineering* (London, 1971),
pp.89–98.
[57] Jimmy Williams (Yanto) election manifesto for the post of area agent, 1975: NUM,
Wrexham.
[58] NUM North Wales special AEC, 21 May 1975: CRO Flintshire D/NM/41.

allocating the results in alphabetical order to the names on the ballot sheet, giving the appearance that Jimmy Williams had come bottom of the poll when in fact he had come second, though this was soon rectified. The matter was taken up with Gormley, but he was in no doubt that on all counts McKay had been elected. McKay was quick to call for unity and to let the issue drop. In a letter to the Bersham lodge, he wrote: 'we hope that your Lodge will accept the position as it is now. We cannot do anymore than ask you not to lower the tone of this union by making statements to the press who have never been friends of ours.'[59] This turned out to be an ironic appeal against the press because in later years the newspapers proved to be great friends of McKay, providing a platform for his attacks on the left in the union.

At Point of Ayr there was still unease at the result and the involvement of Jack Griffiths in the whole affair. Miners at the pit felt that Griffiths was clearly pushing for the election of McKay and using his influence in the area to ensure his success. He had been making attacks on Jimmy Williams that soured the atmosphere leading up to the contest. Griffiths was quick to defend himself, and in a letter to the Bersham lodge, claimed that he had nothing against Williams personally but felt that McKay was simply the best man for the job.[60] Elwyn Williams, one of the defeated candidates, remained critical of the way in which the campaign had been conducted. McKay had fought a tightly organized election, sending letters to individual miners and mobilizing support within the wider membership. However, he did not even have the full support of his own lodge, and the disunity that was to follow led to discontent throughout the coalfield. The only unequivocal support that McKay received was from the management at Point of Ayr.[61]

The new regime at Wrexham soon settled in by implementing a series of rule changes. At a special conference on 26 August a number of resolutions were passed, although the Bersham lodge

---

[59] Letter From Edward McKay to Bersham lodge committee, 18 June 1975: CRO Flintshire D/NM/1147.
[60] Letter from Jack Griffiths to Jimmy Williams, Bersham lodge, 9 September 1975: CRO Flintshire D/NM/1147.
[61] *Point of Ayr Magazine*, 1975: NUM, Wrexham.

was absent.[62] This was hardly a popular mandate for change, as half of the membership took no part in the proceedings. It was proposed that the AEC should now consist of two representatives from each lodge with one being the delegate. The president was to be elected from one of the four members at the annual conference. The AEC would consist of four members and the full-time officials.[63] The system that was introduced further ensured that there would be no rank-and-file representation in the area. As for access to the NEC, this was also blocked since it was written into the rules that the agent would always hold this position. The structure helped the McKay leadership to construct a faction which was to be a bulwark against the left nationally and the critics of policy locally.

At the annual delegate meeting in 1976, the domination of Point of Ayr was complete, with Peter Thomas replacing Griffiths as president, and McKay began to stamp his politics on the union.[64] He warned of the power of the left and the threat that it posed to the small areas. This tone had been largely absent in the years of Jones and Ellis, but it now seemed to be the driving force of the new leadership. McKay pushed himself on the national scene with a sense of urgency:

> At the moment we have a threat to the continuation of the North Wales Area. The threat that we have comes from within the union, for make no mistake the campaign by the Big Left Wing Areas to kill off the small Areas has nothing to do with fair representation or democracy, it is a hard political fact that North Wales is one of the Areas that stands in the way of a take over by the Left, and we must consider what would be the result of that, not only on the miners, but on the whole of the working people.[65]

It was the threat of the unity between the Labour left and the CP in the NUM that caused him most concern. This had been

[62] The Bersham lodge had recently been averse to any changes in the rules of the area union and increasingly felt that amalgamation would be the best option for the future security of the organization. The secretary, Jimmy Williams, was not close to McKay and became critical of the way the agent conducted himself at the national level.

[63] North Wales NUM special conference, 26 August 1975: CRO Flintshire D/NM/1133.

[64] In decisions made by the area, the Point of Ayr lodge would now wield the most power as the pit employed more members than Bersham. For the first time in the history of the union, Flintshire became the dominant force in decision-making as Wrexham could now only boast one pit.

[65] North Wales NUM annual delegate meeting minutes, 25 May 1976: CRO Flintshire D/NM/1153.

the case for a long time in Scotland and south Wales. But it was in Yorkshire that the alliance proved crucial both in terms of affecting the arithmetic of the NEC, and also the style of politics at area level. McKay saw himself as playing a central role in both the Labour Party and the union in neutralizing this advance by making his presence felt locally and nationally. In a speech to the delegates at Wrexham, he pressed his views further:

> It is important that we do not let these people, who for political reasons, want to wreck this country so they can rise from the ashes, but in doing this they will drag down every working family in Britain. As far as their power in the NUM is concerned, North Wales and Cumberland stand in their way.[66]

North Wales as an area was now clearly aligned with Cumberland and Lancashire, and on the NEC McKay became a staunch Gormley loyalist. In relation to the Labour Party, the left in the union was becoming increasingly sceptical about the pay guidelines announced by Wilson and about the emphasis on keeping the party in power at all costs. Scargill, now in control of the Yorkshire Area and supported by the left in Scotland, Kent and south Wales, made it clear that if the Labour government came into conflict with the trade unions, then they would be betraying 'socialism and working class principles'.[67] Gormley himself was aware of the developing tensions, and in his auto-biography he allocates a full chapter to those whom he calls 'wreckers' in the national union.

In 1975 the Yorkshire Area tabled a resolution claiming £100 a week for faceworkers. This was attacked by Gormley and a number of other Labour loyalists who were keen to dissociate themselves from the left. The factions were now clearly defined and the focus in the union shifted to the contrasting politics of Scargill and Gormley. Gormley was always quick to threaten a national ballot in order to provide a bulwark against the left, and was supported by McKay and others in the debate over pay in

---

[66] North Wales NUM annual delegate meeting, agent's report, 25 May 1976: CRO Flintshire D/NM/1153.
[67] Scargill, 'The new unionism', 24.

1976–7.[68] In a speech to a special national conference, McKay made his point about the need for democracy within the union:

> I reject the communist idea that the membership are not able to make their own minds up and should be led by those who know what is good for them. Miners are intelligent and sensible, they will balance the pros and cons, and I for one will abide by their decision, and if it is a strike I will be on the picket line with you.[69]

The issue of pay was clearly driving a wedge between factions on the NEC and straining the relationship between the NUM and the Labour Party. In a speech to the West Flintshire Labour Party in 1976, Gormley echoed the warnings of McKay about the recklessness of the left. He called on miners to show 'responsible action and sympathy for a government that has helped us'.[70]

Due to the tight structure of the North Wales Area, the leadership of McKay was secure and no factions existed on the AEC. In a speech to the annual delegate conference in 1977, the newly elected president William Jones expressed his admiration for the proselytizing approach of the agent:

> We feel as members at a disadvantage when meeting the bigger Areas, but I can assure you friends that it is not the case when we have our Area Agent present, for believe me he lets everyone know he is around and is respected by a lot of people for his forthright contribution he makes, even if it does embarrass others who don't like the truth anyway.[71]

McKay certainly was making his presence felt at the national level and an uneasy atmosphere was apparent at the Labour Party conference in 1976. He had objected to the fact that it was likely that Joe Whelan, a member of the CP, would lead the

---

[68] Gormley remained convinced that the wider membership had little time for the left and knew that, because of their belief in democracy, they would accept results that went against them. The defeat of the left in the EEC referendum in 1975 reinforced this view, but Gormley remained under constant attack on the conference floor, which was normally the preserve of the militants.

[69] Statement by Edward McKay to the NUM conference on the pay guidelines, 1976–7: NUM, Wrexham.

[70] *Wrexham Evening Leader*, 26 April 1976.

[71] North Wales NUM area annual delegate conference minutes, 4 April 1977: CRO Flintshire D/NM/1154.

delegation of the union at the conference. This approach by McKay stemmed from a motion from north Wales to the national conference in which the area wanted the union to adopt a policy whereby CP members would be excluded from meetings of the NUM delegations to the Labour conference.[72] McKay wanted delegation positions to be available only to those holding Labour Party membership cards. At the conference, Whelan verbally attacked the north Wales delegates and tried to provoke violence by taunting McKay. This issue was reported to the NEC and tensions remained high between particular areas over a whole range of issues.[73] In arguing against anti-Labour factions at successive NUM and Labour Party conferences, McKay claimed that the union's purpose was to 'curb the wrecking power of those who will use the union and its members to further the aims of the Communist Party'.[74]

In terms of a national and local profile, McKay was doing all he could to gain recognition on any issue relating to the trade unions or the Labour Party. He could be relied on to provide critiques of the left in the *Liverpool Daily Post*, *Wrexham Leader* and *Chester Chronicle*. McKay had little support in the area for his brand of factionalism, as most of the north Wales miners remained committed to the national union. Many miners did not really grasp the complexity of the rivalry between left and right, though he continued to make it the central plank of area policy. In another speech sprinkled with anti-Communist rhetoric reminiscent of the 1950s, he called for action from the wider membership to combat the Communist menace:

> I think it is time the rank and file of trade unionists and the public, if they want democracy and the right to free expression, should stand up and be counted. These people of the extreme Left stand for nobody. Their strength on the NEC is nowhere reflected in the coalfields or in any other industry. Democratic Socialists (and there is a vast difference) should not leave it to the Tories to oppose the communist menace.[75]

[72] Members of the Communist Party could not vote in the NUM delegation at the Labour conference. They could, however, attend the delegation meetings where decisions were taken, in order to give their views on the voting intentions of the NUM.

[73] Letter from North Wales NUM to Lawrence Daly, 4 October 1976: NUM, Wrexham.

[74] *Liverpool Daily Post*, 5 April 1977.

[75] North Wales NUM annual delegate conference, 4 April 1977: CRO Flintshire D/NM/1154.

To McKay, there was clearly a conspiracy at work to kill off the North Wales Area. He failed to acknowledge that on the left there were tensions and disputes over policy. Scargill himself was not a member of the CP and had faced criticism from the organization in his own coalfield during his campaign for the area presidency. The south Wales leadership, though a traditional standard-bearer of the left, was more concerned with the proposed large-scale run-down of the steel industry in the region than with the ideological purity of socialism on the NEC. In essence, the development of the left had little to do with political motivation but more to do with a pragmatic approach to the perceived inadequacies of the Labour government. Yet McKay continually claimed that 'people don't realise the pressure there is on us when you have big areas wanting to kill you off for political reasons'.[76]

The anti-communism of the area agent included an attack on the attempt of some Labour MPs who were pressurizing ministers into giving the *Morning Star* a regular share of the government's advertising budget. He declared to the *Liverpool Daily Post* that 'if ever the communists took over the country on the Russian model there would be no trade unions left in Britain'.[77] McKay also sent a warning to the Labour Party, claiming that the political levy would be withheld if the organization did not go some way towards expelling the extremists in its ranks. He claimed that the party owed its origins to the mining community and now was being destabilized by members who should be in other parties.[78] He felt strongly that contributions from trade union members should not go to support Communists and fellow travellers.[79] At the 1978 NUM annual conference, he warned that a resolution to introduce card voting rather than a show of hands at the NEC would mean that north Wales would be deprived of an effective voice.[80]

The level of factionalism between left and right dominated the 1978 conference and was epitomized by the clashes between

---

[76] *Liverpool Daily Post*, 19 May 1977.

[77] *Liverpool Daily Post*, 29 November 1976.

[78] The outburst of McKay concerning the MFGB and its commitment to the Labour Party from the early days exposes the level of area leadership acceptance of particular myths of labour history.

[79] *Liverpool Daily Post*, 20 January 1977.

[80] *Wrexham Leader*, 26 May 1978.

Yorkshire and Lancashire. On various occasions throughout the week, the Yorkshire delegates called for the resignation of Gormley. McKay and Les Kelly attended for north Wales, and the agent made his customary appeal for the protection of the autonomy of small areas.[81] McKay had become a figure on the national stage, a role that Ellis had earlier shunned, and the coal-field became firmly entrenched as part of the right-wing bloc masterminded by Gormley. The north Wales leaders were able to complement McKay's attacks on the left with rhetoric about representing 'real Labour' interests. This belief in socialism of a particular brand went some way towards preventing a backlash from the membership, for McKay never criticized the Labour Party in general. In an attack on Mick McGahey and the left in the NUM, he argued that

> The Socialism I was taught in North Wales was that everyone had the right to free expression, and that the big and powerful would protect the right of free expression of the small and the weak, but it would seem that in the NUM that is only true if the big and powerful agree with what the small say . . . I am not prepared to see all the struggles, the history and the tradition of North Wales and other small areas wiped out just because someone is seeking self-glory and personal power, or others who want to further a political ideology which is not acceptable to the majority of members and cannot get a mandate for such ideology through the ballot box . . . I asked Mick [McGahey] to stand down as Chairman of the NUM Delegation at the Labour Party Conference as he is leader of a Political Party who is in opposition to the Labour Party. He said 'I have a democratic right to be here. For that right I will fight and those who believe in democracy should fight with me'. Well Chairman, North Wales has a democratic right to have representation. For that right I will fight and I challenge Mick that if he believes in what he has said in the past to fight for that right with me.[82]

The proclaimed commitment to democracy, which was the foundation of the politics of the right, was soon to be tested with regard to the introduction of an incentive scheme to complement the existing system of payment in the industry. The debate about the reintroduction of incentives was to be a potent weapon of the

[81] Report by Les Kelly, Point of Ayr lodge re NUM annual conference 1978: CRO Flintshire D/NM/1133.
[82] NUM annual report, 1978: NUM, Wrexham.

left. Its success in using it in attacking the bankruptcy of the right was to pave the way for the ascendancy of the left culminating in the election of Scargill to the national presidency. The left claimed that, by the late 1970s, the union would finally break free from the shackles of the right, and the power of area fief-doms would eventually be eroded, paving the way for unity. Scargill himself had been clear about the negative effect that such an environment had had on the miners: 'if you have a right wing leadership in any union, the whole philosophy, the entire ideology, the notions of leadership will permeate through the union.'[83] The factionalism and personality clashes within the NUM were to tarnish the unity of the union down to the 1980s.

INCENTIVES, NORTH/SOUTH DIVISIONS, AND THE 'SCARGILL FACTOR'

With the introduction of the NPLA in 1966, it seemed as if the system of piecework had vanished from British mines for ever. The right within the union had been increasingly unhappy and felt that an incentive scheme would benefit the men in terms of wages and secure the future of the industry by pushing up production targets. The need for such a scheme was enshrined in the 1974 Plan for Coal, to which both the union and the Labour Party were com-mitted. However, the idea of incentives still angered the left, which saw the successful strikes of recent years and the concomitant unity as being the direct result of nationally directed wage agreements.[84] The debate around the issue of piecework was to be central to the dispute between the two opposing camps in the union.

In north Wales, discussion about such a scheme had been going on since the early 1970s. At a meeting of the union at Bersham, the men decided to reject the proposal for any system that would divide the membership and wanted a national ballot on any proposals.[85] When the scheme was initially rejected by

[83] Scargill, 'The new unionism', 7.
[84] The NCB was also in favour of incentives. First, they were seen as a way to increase production and profitability. Secondly, incentives would threaten the unity of the NUM as manifested in 1972 and 1974. The push for incentives had formed the basis of the Miron report on the future of the industry which had been prepared in 1973 as a solution to the growth of the left in the NUM. See Jonathan Winterton and Ruth Winterton, *Coal, Crisis and Conflict: The 1984–85 Miners' Strike in Yorkshire* (Manchester, 1989), pp.9–22.
[85] North Wales NUM Bersham colliery general meeting minutes, 28 September 1974: CRO Flintshire D/NM/1210.

the union in 1974, the men at Bersham welcomed the decision, but there were now signs of dissent among the general workforce. Cliff Rowlands of the lodge committee was worried about the influence of the left in determining people's thoughts on the scheme before they had been given the full facts. He thought that 'the future could be bleak if the militants continued to make progress'.[86]

The debate over incentives reappeared at the 1977 annual conference. A south Wales resolution calling for the maintenance of the present wages system was accepted very narrowly, but despite this the NEC debated the question again and decided to put the issue to a further ballot. Within particular coalfields, especially Lancashire and north Wales, the officials were busy mobilizing support for such a scheme. A number of Point of Ayr and Bersham miners wrote to the local press and *Coal News*, arguing in favour of incentives for all grades of workers.[87] At the annual delegate conference in the same year, McKay pointed out that

> one does not need to be clever to make popular demands, also you don't need to be very bright to find out that we must sell our product competitively, therefore, we must generate the wealth we need from the mining industry itself. This can only be done by a sensible incentive scheme.[88]

The men at both pits in the area were convinced that an incentive scheme would put more money in their pockets. They supported the south Wales resolution to the conference calling for £100 a week for faceworkers, but also made it clear that north Wales was in favour of incentives to supplement such a demand. In response to the threat of a strike over the issue in Yorkshire, McKay told the local press that 'there is no way that Scargill is going to tell us what to do'.[89] A pithead ballot, despite attempts by the left to challenge its legitimacy in court, was held in November of the same year, and the national membership

[86] *Liverpool Daily Post*, 19 November 1974.
[87] *Coal News*, June 1977.
[88] North Wales NUM annual delegate conference, 1977, agent's report: CRO Flintshire D/NM/1154.
[89] *Liverpool Daily Post*, 21 June and 16 September 1977.

rejected incentive schemes with 87,901 in favour and 110,634 against. In north Wales, the membership voted 67 per cent in favour of incentives. The hard work of McKay had been successful. In an attack on those who had campaigned against a vote in favour, he noted that 'sometime or other people must stop playing politics and realize the hard facts that no one owes us a living we must work for it'.[90] He quickly used the result in north Wales as an endorsement of his action and pledged to vote at the NEC for individual coalfields to negotiate their own system locally.

The right achieved success at the meeting of the NEC in December, when a Midlands resolution was passed, allowing the areas that had voted in favour of an incentive scheme to go it alone. McKay called a meeting in the coalfield to sanction his support for this resolution. The members requested an individual vote and they backed his stance with 620 votes in favour and 211 against.[91] The left retaliated quickly and, in January 1978, Yorkshire, Kent and south Wales took the national union to court to stop the independent action of the maverick coalfields. The High Court ruled that the result of the national ballot was not binding on the NEC and ruled in favour of the rogue areas. The flouting of union democracy was to have dramatic repercussions in 1984–5, when moderates claimed that the left had abandoned the sanctity of the ballot box. Striking miners responded to arguments about NUM democracy by recalling the incentives episode.[92] The vote on incentives was not forgotten by the left and the factionalism within the union reached a new peak as the two wings within the organization became increasingly estranged. Within eighteen months, all areas of the union had negotiated local schemes. The factionalism in the union went much deeper than the difference over the question of incentives, and it is hard to substantiate the view that if the scheme had not been introduced things might have worked out differently. Joe Gormley was seen as the villain of the piece by the left, but some areas were clearly in favour of increased earnings

[90] *Evening Leader*, 1 November 1977.

[91] North Wales NUM AEC minutes, 13 December 1977: CRO Flintshire D/NM/1133.

[92] Throughout this period, the national rulebook became a matter of factional warfare that was to reappear in 1984, leading to divisions within and between the federated areas of the NUM.

through piecework.[93] South Derbyshire, Lancashire and north Wales were able to justify their behaviour in flouting national decisions because of the federated nature of the union.

In north Wales, at the annual delegate conference in 1978, McKay welcomed the 'year of the incentive scheme'. He argued that, in view of falling productivity, the industry would never have reached the projections indicated in the Plan for Coal. Ironically, with the benefit of hindsight, the opposite turned out to be the case; pits closed as they were thrown into competition with each other. McKay, on numerous occasions, continued to berate the left and their support of industrial action. In a speech to delegates, he noted that it was 'strange that some members supported strikes yet they wanted to create a society where trade unions were illegal'.[94] This was an overt attack on the Communist members of the NEC, and McKay continued to be a critic of McGahey and others on the left.

Scargill, from his base in Yorkshire, continued his vocal opposition to the incentive scheme and claimed that the system of payment was costing lives. McKay contested this, maintaining that Scargill was using the deaths of miners to make a political point. In a powerful reply, Scargill challenged McKay to make use of the accident figures available to him and he would then see that the scheme was contributing to an increase in fatalities. McKay accepted the challenge with some gusto and claimed that he would never have supported the introduction of a scheme if it were at the expense of safety and that the accident rate had actually gone down.[95] Despite disputes about the actual figures, it is clear that the introduction of the incentive scheme led to greater risks being taken by the men. Increasingly, miners were being asked to speed up production, tempted by incentive payments. Some were also paid for working through their mealtimes. This led to developing tensions between faceworkers and general 'out-bye' workers. Young miners who worked as conveyor-belt attendants attracted increased criticism from senior workers for unnecessarily halting production, thereby driving a wedge between low- and high-paid miners who were

[93]   David Howell, *The Politics of the NUM: A Lancashire View* (Manchester, 1989), p.57.
[94]   North Wales NUM report of annual delegate conference, 10 April 1978: CRO Flintshire D/NM/1154.
[95]   *Wrexham Leader*, 31 March and 9 June 1978.

members of the same union. The area union had earlier been critical of the way contractors could break safety rules and take risks because of their system of payment. This was an environment that NCB miners now faced, which was sanctioned by the leadership of the union. Further, the incentive scheme did nothing to alter the balance of power within the division of labour, since the faceworkers still ruled supreme in terms of wage rates and domination of the union.

North Wales did not experience a challenge to the hegemony of the Wrexham leadership, and the furore over the issue of incentives did nothing to weaken the position of McKay. No major forces for change were forthcoming from either Bersham or Point of Ayr, and divisions in the union still concentrated on disputes between areas of the federation. The level of animosity at the national level became acute, and north Wales began to take issue with the dominance of south Wales in the industrial organizations of the Principality. Now that the incentive scheme had been settled, McKay chose the left in the south as the next target of his onslaught against those who he claimed were unrepresentative extremists tarnishing the traditions of the union.

In 1973, with the South Wales NUM at the helm, the Wales TUC was established. It seemed as though the north was playing an equal role in this development when Tom Jones, the ex-miner and veteran of the T&GWU, was made its first secretary. The South Wales NUM played a major part in the construction of the congress, with Dai Francis becoming chairman and the miners in the north showing little enthusiasm. A year later, McKay, reporting on his visit to the first conference, claimed that the body was dominated by the south.[96] This was obviously going to make the involvement of the north less likely, as McKay had been a vocal opponent of the call by leaders in the south for direct action in confronting government policy. In 1978, the area decided to challenge the fact that the south had two seats on the general council and the north had none. Cyril Gregory of Point of Ayr was chosen to challenge either Emlyn Williams or George Rees to take one of the seats. The issue quickly escalated, with both sides claiming that politics was playing a major role in the dispute. Emlyn Williams attacked McKay for raising the issue

[96] North Wales NUM AEC minutes, 7 May 1974: CRO Flintshire D/NM/1133.

and claimed that the north Wales leader was an 'extreme right-winger' who wanted to undermine the effectiveness of the organization.[97]

The factionalism of the NUM was now evidently spilling over into other labour organizations as the hostile camps locked themselves into a dispute over the broader politics of the movement. Ironically, most miners remained aloof as the congress was seen to have little power. The challenge of the north proved to be unsuccessful and the south retained its two seats on the general council. Still smarting from the challenge of the north, the south decided to counter-attack and it questioned the right of the area to have a significant vote on the NEC of the NUM. At their annual conference in Porthcawl in 1978, a number of delegates criticized the fact that the north had one vote and the south only two. McKay submitted a press release attacking the south Wales initiative: 'we in North Wales are an independent trade union . . . We have a democratic right to be represented. Look at the structure of the United Nations. Should it be only the powerful who have a say.'[98]

The federated structure of the NUM ensured that the level of factionalism would be maintained. The left was aware of this and pushed for the amalgamation of certain areas. Because of the crisis which beset the industry from the late 1960s onwards, factions developed in pursuit of particular strategies, and north Wales was swept along in the process. In 1979, moves were afoot again to challenge the autonomy of the area. Professor Vic Allen, who had been involved in the rise of the left in Yorkshire and was close to Scargill politically, called for amalgamation. McKay again could not see any benefit in the proposals, merely viewing them as a communist plot.[99]

The AEC also became involved in the developing tensions within the Labour Party and stressed that it would oppose the challenge of Tony Benn at the next conference, as it feared that the party was being transformed by the left. The dispute between south and north was temporarily suspended when Labour suffered a devastating defeat and the Conservatives were swept to power on a programme of trade union reform. McKay could

[97] *Western Mail*, 28 January 1978.
[98] *Wrexham Leader*, 12 May 1978.
[99] *Liverpool Daily Post*, 20 October 1979.

see parallels with the growth of the left in the union and the party, with south Wales and Yorkshire as prime movers in this process. In a statement to the *Daily Post* prior to the 1979 conference, the area claimed that 'the unions have a vital part to play in ensuring that the policies of the Left are defeated, the Party must not become dominated by a group that is not representative of the Labour Movement'.[100] In his report on the conference, Gregory, the north Wales president, noted that it was 'more of a communist get together than that of a Labour party conference'.[101]

In 1980 the South Wales NUM had become increasingly alarmed at the rising level of the importation of cheap coking coal into the region which would inevitably threaten jobs in the mining industry. The Bersham lodge immediately pledged support for any south Wales initiatives and called on the AEC to call a meeting between the two bodies to discuss future policy.[102] McKay was not as enthusiastic as the miners at Bersham and quickly poured cold water on the likelihood of joint action by claiming that a call for a ban on imports would damage the future of the industry.[103] Meanwhile, the South Wales Area was hoping to initiate a national strike in combination with the steelworkers, who were already about to embark on a dispute which they were to lose. The NEC refused to sanction the call for a national strike. The Wales TUC then took it on itself to call for a day of action to send a message of warning to the Conservative government. The North Wales AEC met to discuss what their role should be in the action because of the confusion between the South Wales Area and the NEC. They decided to advise members not to cross picket lines and gave each lodge the power to decide its own course of action.[104] This abdication of leadership further antagonized the relationship between north and south and was to have devastating repercussions in the events of 1984. The Point of Ayr lodge only went as far as sanctioning an

[100] *Liverpool Daily Post*, 28 September 1979.
[101] North Wales NUM report on Labour Party conference, Brighton, 1979: CRO Flintshire D/NM/1133.
[102] NUM Bersham lodge committee minutes, 25 January 1980: CRO Flintshire D/NM/1211.
[103] North Wales NUM report of annual delegate conference, 9 April 1980: CRO Flintshire D/NM/1155.
[104] North Wales NUM minutes of special AEC, 25 January 1980: CRO Flintshire D/NM/1133.

overtime ban for the day, and Bersham was given 'special dispensation' and allowed to work because of its precarious economic position.

In south Wales, the strike was solid, and pits, steel plants and docks were all brought to a halt. Bill Sirs[105] of the ISTC (Iron and Steel Trades Federation) claimed that the protest was a 'revolution against a reactionary government's policy which threatened to destroy industry in Wales and cripple the nation'.[106] After the bout of direct action led by the south Wales miners, the North Wales Area wanted any future course of action sanctioned under rule 43 of the national union, which stated that strikes must be validated by the consent of the majority of the membership through a national ballot. The Bersham lodge saw nothing positive in the action of the south and claimed that 'there had been a lack of positive leadership throughout the campaign and that the timing of the demonstration . . . only resulted in an unnecessary loss of earnings by our members'.[107]

Both George Rees and Emlyn Williams, as leaders of the south Wales miners, continued to press for concerted action. A meeting was arranged between the executives of the North and South Wales Areas that appeared to be quite constructive. McKay made it clear that he would support his colleagues in the south with 100 per cent commitment, but he remained critical of the Wales TUC in its call for industrial action.[108] The AEC then summoned a special delegate conference and argued that the matter should be handled by the national union since a policy of 'go it alone' could only lead to disaster. A resolution was passed supporting the south in its call for a national delegate conference to discuss the problems of coal imports and pit closures.[109] Meanwhile, south Wales continued its push for action but was quickly rebuked by a coalfield ballot when the membership voted massively against strike action.

---

[105] Ironically, Sirs was to move rapidly away from his militant rhetoric in 1984 when he castigated Scargill for his tactics in the strike. See Bill Sirs, *Hard Labour* (London, 1985), pp.1–42.

[106] *Financial Times*, 29 January 1980.

[107] NUM Bersham lodge committee minutes of special meeting, 30 April 1980: CRO Flintshire D/NM/1211.

[108] *Wrexham Leader*, 8 February 1980.

The pessimism concerning the industry's future that coursed through the union was confirmed in 1981. The NCB announced that output would be reduced, which meant the closure of pits. The national union responded immediately, and on 12 February threatened a national strike to protect specific pits earmarked for closure. A number of area unions took matters into their own hands. The case of south Wales again exposed fractures within the NUM. McKay was to be cast as a villain by the left for seeking to stop a push towards concerted action. South Wales pickets were mobilized and they entered the north Wales coal-field on 19 February, much to the dismay of McKay and the AEC. The agent immediately attacked the action and claimed that it would be better for everyone concerned if the south Wales men returned to their own coalfield, 'stopped playing politics and dug a bit of coal'.[110] Point of Ayr was the scene of a mass picket which disturbed those on the lodge who were in favour of the protest. The action was unofficial, but the secretary, Les Kelly, was adamant that he would not advocate crossing the picket line. He called for a national ballot on the course of future action and felt that the members picketing local pits should be from the north Wales coalfield to avoid any unnecessary tensions.[111] The relationship between north and south now reached crisis point, with McKay referring to the pickets as 'bully boys' and 'yobbos' and claiming that they were an unofficial group forcing their demands without validation by a national ballot.[112] George Rees immediately responded and condemned the statements that McKay was frequently making to the press inviting him to meet the south Wales executive to discuss the issues involved. In characteristic fashion, McKay replied indignantly that he would never justify himself to the south, as he was only concerned with explaining himself to miners in the north.[113]

At a special conference of the north Wales miners on 20 February 1981, the membership discussed the problem and

[109] North Wales NUM special delegate conference, 11 February 1980: CRO Flintshire D/NM/1155.

[110] Daily Telegraph, 21 February 1981.

[111] Letter from Les Kelly, Point of Ayr lodge, to Ted McKay, 23 February 1981: NUM, Wrexham.

[112] Letter from Ted McKay to Lawrence Daly, 23 February 1981: NUM, Wrexham.

[113] Letter from George Rees to Ted McKay, 23February 1981, and reply, 3 March 1981: NUM, Wrexham.

generally deplored the action of the south Wales pickets. None-theless, they were in agreement with the call for action from the NEC and argued that a nationally directed plan would be acceptable to the area. The escalation of action was abruptly halted when the government announced a dramatic U-turn on the planned closures. This caused confusion in many coalfields and a significant number of miners remained on strike while awaiting directions from their own leaderships. An area delegate conference was subsequently called in south Wales and it was recommended that the miners return to work. The NEC did not drop its decision to call a strike in the future, but it was put on hold in order to see what negotiations with the government could bring. However, the days of consensus had long gone.

In north Wales, as in other areas, the U-turn was treated with scepticism, and many felt that this was merely a stay of execu-tion. Speaking at the annual delegate conference in April 1981, McKay voiced a concern that would prove to be prophetic.

> I cannot with the best will in the world see how this government can go back on a policy it was so committed to, but the real tragedy of the U-turn is that the government changed only by the threat of muscle power and not by the logic of the miners' unanswerable case, so therefore, the government basically does not believe in what they are doing, and I firmly believe that those pits are still on the closure list.[114]

The issues of cheap imports, the rationalization of the steel industry and the announcement of pit closures had further estranged the north Wales miners from their counterparts in the south. With the defeat of James Callaghan in 1979, many miners felt that the union should adopt a more militant strategy to combat the excesses of the economic policy of the Conservatives. Nonetheless, they rejected calls for strike action on three occasions prior to 1984.

The level of factionalism that had reached a peak in the late 1970s was to leave the union divided, with devastating con-sequences for the future. The election of Scargill in 1981 totally demoralized the right, and the left held the main positions of

---

[114] North Wales NUM report of annual delegate conference, 13 April 1981: CRO Flintshire D/NM/1155.

authority within the hierarchy of the national union. McKay, however, remained convinced of his mission to save the union from communists and militants. In his agent's report for 1981, he directed criticism at Scargill and the advocates of militancy:

> Leadership is getting the best for the members with the least amount of hurt to them or the community. The miners are not, and must not be used as shock troops for someone's private army to fight political battles which have no connection to the mining industry.[115]

The conflict between north and south Wales exposed the problems inherent in the structure of the national union and also the question of democratic legitimacy. McKay might have seen his position as being apolitical save for a commitment to the Labour Party, so long as it was not in the hands of the left, but his approach was ideologically charged, and he attacked the left with gusto, raising tensions within his own coalfield with his style of leadership. Belief in the sanctity of the ballot box had been previously overshadowed by the issue of incentives and the rights of majorities in terms of NEC representation. Nevertheless, the north Wales leadership did have a limited case in justification of its position, as there was a contradiction between the politics of particular leaders and the views of the wider membership. This was clear in the ballots against strike action, especially in a left-wing coalfield such as south Wales. The presidential campaign of Scargill in the winter of 1981 and his subsequent election highlighted some of the ambiguities in the political culture of the British coalfields. Even a politically cautious area such as north Wales was not immune to the attractions of his leadership.

Scargill had formed part of the left faction on his election to the area presidency in 1973, though his style differed from the leadership in south Wales and Scotland.[116] He was to bring to the NUM left an iconoclasm that some members of the

---

[115] North Wales NUM report of annual delegate conference, 13 April 1981: CRO Flintshire D/NM/1155.

[116] As an official of the Yorkshire Area, Scargill's experience of industrial relations had not depended on the ability to bargain and compromise. The job of compensation agent had a more adversarial role bereft of complex negotiating strategies. When Gormley retired, Scargill became the only viable candidate of the left, as McGahey was ineligible because he was too old. This was something that Gormley had been aware of, and he hung on until the last to prevent the Scottish Communist from succeeding him.

Communist Party found disconcerting. The power of his forceful personality was apparent during the NUM conferences of the 1970s. With the retirement of Gormley imminent in the late 1970s, his path to the leadership seemed to be clear, and he even gained the support of areas such as north Wales. Scargill was himself aware that there was a level of discontent in particular coalfields due to the inaction of certain officials. In his *New Left Review* article of 1975, he outlined his thoughts on union leadership:

> I believe you've got to win the rank and file and you've got to show people by example. I believe that far too often we've had leadership in the union that has been a bit remote from the everyday problems of the members.[117]

In 1979 at the north Wales annual delegate conference, McKay predicted that a leadership contest would soon emerge because of the retirement of the president. He offered a word of advice to the candidate, though this was clearly aimed at the left. 'The miners of Britain will not take kindly to anyone using that position in the furtherance of personal ambition, or a political ideology that would not get past the ballot box.'[118] A year later, the AEC was in dispute with Scargill over his view that more than 100,000 miners would lose their jobs through pit closures. The area sent a resolution to the NEC warning against the predictions of Scargill and noting that any rash actions over closures would be disastrous for the union.[119]

It became clear that the north Wales leadership would not support Scargill in the forthcoming election, but McKay was worried about the outcome, as voices of support were already emerging from both Bersham and Point of Ayr. The right was rapidly losing ground, and its inability to agree on a suitable candidate to stand against Scargill was a symptom of its decline. Trevor Bell of the white-collar section COSA was one nomination, along with Ray Chadburn of Nottinghamshire, who did not even get the nomination of his own area. The Lancashire Area, hoping to uphold the mantle of Gormley, selected Bernard

---

[117] Scargill, 'The new unionism', 28.
[118] North Wales NUM Annual Delegate Meeting Minutes, 1979: CRO Flintshire D/NM/1154.
[119] *Evening Leader*, 24 June 1980.

Donaghy, though Scargill himself commanded support at some pits.[120] In some areas, there was a clear move away from the recommendations of officials. In north Wales, both Point of Ayr and Bersham swung behind Scargill, thereby securing his nomination from the coalfield. This suggests that the leadership of McKay was not secure and that there had been an apparent radicalization of the workforce at both pits. Subsequent events proved that this was not the case and show that when trade unionists cast their votes for particular candidates they are not always politically motivated.

Scargill toured the coalfields and was well received in Denbighshire and Flintshire, where he addressed large meetings, making the prospect of pit closures the central plank of his policy. This forthright approach was particularly appealing to north Wales. The miners of Wrexham had seen pits closing, causing disillusionment within the coalfield from nationalization on-wards. Further, Scargill's emphasis on the expansion of the industry raised hopes in the former mining communities. In a visit to the area, Scargill, was commended for calling for the sinking of six new pits.[121] Both the NCB and his opponents were quick to seize on this, claiming that there was no hope of future investment in new collieries. John Northard of the NCB wrote to McKay in October 1981, attacking Scargill for promoting this view at a time when the industry was at a crossroads. He told McKay that there were reserves in the coalfield, but that they were sharply inclined and heavily faulted.[122] Trevor Bell, who was close to McKay politically, challenged the claims of Scargill by making representations to the NCB concerning new pits. Bell claimed that the comments of Scargill should be put down to 'blatant electioneering with no regard for the sensitivities of his audience living in an area of high unemployment'.[123]

McKay, Bell and Sid Vincent of Lancashire had, for some time, been part of a so-called 'progressive group' which had

---

[120] For a discussion of the leadership contest in terms of the Lancashire Area, see David Howell, *The Politics of the NUM: A Lancashire View* (Manchester, 1989), pp.70–3.

[121] North Wales NUM AEC minutes, 12 October 1981: CRO Flintshire D/NM/1133.

[122] Letter from John Northard, NCB, to Ted McKay, 7 October 1981: NUM, Wrexham.

[123] Letter from Trevor Bell to Ted McKay and Sid Vincent, 13 October 1981: NUM, Wrexham.

worked to undermine the development of the left in the union.[124] The members of the group were finding that they were unable to construct a realistic strategy.[125] They failed to develop a coherent campaign around one particular candidate to challenge Scargill, and they were increasingly finding themselves at odds with the views of the membership. Their political commitment to each other was not strong enough to overcome the pressures of area parochialism. Early in 1981, Vincent had tried to make McKay and others understand the enormity of the challenge now facing the right.

> There are two power bases within this National Union and what any person thinks or otherwise, you have got to accept this as a fact, they are Yorkshire and Nottinghamshire. The only way that the Yorkshire vote can be defeated is for the whole of the Progressive Areas to vote together and yet this has never happened. The Yorkshire Area vote along with the rest of the left wing area votes at the last Annual Conference totalled 126. The Nottinghamshire Area has got to be the power base for the Progressive Group.[126]

With the ballot for the presidency imminent, the 'progressive group' was almost powerless, as they could not even count on support from their own areas. On the day before the result, McKay admitted that Scargill would probably win: 'he went

[124] McKay was close to Roy Ottey who represented the Power Group on the NUM NEC. Ottey provided McKay with details of comments that left-wingers had made to the press and in various meetings. For example, in a Russian trade union publication, McGahey allegedly claimed that Soviet workers enjoyed democratic rights and freedoms, and determined the nature of Soviet democracy. Letter from Roy Ottey, Power Group, to Ted McKay, 22 June 1978. Like McKay, Ottey eventually ended up as an employee of British Coal after the strike of 1984–5. Details of his union career can be found in his autobiography, Roy Ottey, *The Strike: An Insider's Story* (London, 1985). A more critical account of his role in the strike can be found in Roger Seifert and John Unwin, *Struggle without End: The 1984/85 Miners' Strike in North Staffordshire* (Newcastle under Lyme, 1988).
[125] Although there are no details of specific areas in the correspondence of the 'progressive group', the names of the 'usual suspects' appear: Vincent of Lancashire, Toon of south Derbyshire, McKay of north Wales, Ottey of the Power Group, Hanlon of Cumberland and Bell of COSA.
[126] Letter from Sid Vincent to all members of the 'progressive group', 5 January 1981. The problem for the right in its wish to mobilize the votes of Nottinghamshire was that political change had affected the balance of power within the area union. From the late 1970s, the Nottinghamshire Area council was becoming more radical, taking up positions far in front of the membership. This had potentially catastrophic consequences for the union in the strike of 1984–5. A background to the politics of the Nottinghamshire miners in the 1980s can be found in W. John Morgan and Ken Coates, *The Nottinghamshire Coalfield and the British Miners' Strike, 1984–85* (Derby, n.d.).

down so well when he visited the coalfield that our lads thought he was the second messiah.'[127] He stressed that as a member of the NEC he would stand by the result, adding that 'Scargill must remember that he represents the whole union and not just the militants'. As predicted, Scargill took over 70 per cent of the vote, with his nearest rival, Trevor Bell, taking a mere 17.3 per cent. Donaghy in Lancashire had proved to be a disaster and the reluctance of the 'progressive group' to rally behind Chadburn in Nottinghamshire resulted in his taking only 9.1 per cent of the vote.

On the surface, it looked as if Scargill had a clear mandate for industrial action to oppose closures and that the union had firmly rejected the traditional politics that had restrained militancy. However, the optimism that greeted the success of Scargill in north Wales and other coalfields was transient, as the events of the next four years were to prove. The union was to suffer a massive defeat at the hands of a ruthless Conservative government, and the formation of a breakaway organization, complemented by the rapid run-down of the industry. The north Wales coalfield was again faced with a crisis in which the political culture of the region would expose the fragility of working-class unity.

With the election of Thatcher, many activists in the union felt that a positive lead in terms of opposition was the only answer to combating the anti-union stance of the government. The north Wales miners had reacted to this by nominating Scargill for president against the advice of McKay. The latter was still far from sharing the politics of the new president, but he had to play a delicate balancing act, for he knew that there was considerable support for Scargill at both pits. There was a marked leftward shift in terms of resolutions passed at the annual delegate conference from 1982 onwards. Les Kelly at Point of Ayr called for the establishment of a strike fund. He felt that it was likely that the government would press ahead with pit closures in the near future. John Alan Jones, also from Point of Ayr, stressed that he was in favour of the increasingly political role that the union was taking, in terms of resisting the plans of the Conservatives.

[127] *Evening Leader*, 7 December 1981.

As a union we must protect our own industry by exerting pressure in the right quarters. If it cannot be done with this Government we should pursue objectives as relentlessly as positively and with as much cunning and force as capitalists pursue theirs . . . if you think that these words smack of politics, then you are right. If you think that Trade Unionism and Politics are separate issues you are naïve. If you think that Trade Unionism and Politics should never be associated then we will never win our struggle.[128]

The speech by Jones was a thinly veiled attack on the role that McKay had been playing in opposing the politics of Scargill. McKay continued his crusade, challenging through the local press every prediction of Scargill. He described the president's supposed 'hit list' of pits to close as a myth. Tom Ellis, who had now left the Labour Party and joined the Social Democratic Party (SDP), was increasingly critical of the role of the trade unions and supported McKay in his view. The MP and the union leader formed a strange alliance. McKay had earlier labelled Ellis a hypocrite for supporting the proposals of the Conservative Trade Union Bill. McKay himself was not a thorough opponent of all the legislation. He had castigated Scargill in 1980 for advocating non-compliance: 'our point of view in North Wales is to change the law and not to break it . . . we want changes and not breakages of law in a democratic society.'[129]

In 1982 the north Wales union was in a state of flux which was to have a weakening effect on the union over the next few years. McKay was unhappy about the changing industrial relations climate and longed for the relatively cosy consensus of the early Callaghan years. The lodges at both pits contained a mixture of 'old school' pragmatists and a number of recent converts to the cause of the left. The wider membership remained largely immune to the politics of the union, save for a commitment to the politics of Labourism. General meetings attracted little attention and members only used the union when they had specific grievances. This relationship between the official and the member has been lost sight of in romantic accounts of the all-embracing presence of the union in the workplace. The majority

[128] North Wales NUM report of annual delegate conference, 19 April 1982: CRO Flintshire D/NM/1155.
[129] *Wrexham Leader*, 5 September 1980.

of men in north Wales had little experience of conversing with elected officials or of the practice of industrial relations, with 'charge hands' and prominent faceworkers leading delegations to the union office. Surprisingly, miners were content to deal with their own problems in terms of pay or disputes with deputies. But none of them would visit the manager's office without union representation. However, the election of Scargill had brought more miners into the culture of activism and a restless minority increasingly questioned the role of the area union.

Between 1982 and late 1983 the climate was marked by a short period of calm before the storm, and the miners were content to carry on with daily routines, thinking little about the bombshell that was to be dropped on them by a massive pit closure programme. The 1979 election and the defeat of Callaghan had represented a shattering of the post-war consensus which was to have a dramatic impact on the mining industry, the wider trade union movement and the Labour Party. With the appointment of Ian MacGregor to the chairmanship of the NCB in 1983 and a massive Conservative majority from its electoral landslide in the same year, the scene was set for one of Britain's most dramatic industrial struggles of the twentieth century. The culture of the coalfields was to be changed for ever, and north Wales was to suffer a split in the union and a level of animosity that still affects groups of former miners. The area union became a focus for a rank-and-file revolt of both members who were on strike and those who continued to work, with Ted McKay playing the role of villain in both camps.

IV
THE FRAGMENTATION OF UNITY, 1983–1988

There's an eerie silence over the old pit site,
Where once wheels wound by day and by night.

When we fought for our pits, we were labelled as yobs,
Now Wrexham has lost nearly six hundred jobs.[1]

The 1980s were a most painful experience for British miners, their families and communities. The pit closures of the Wilson period were to pale into insignificance alongside the Conservative closure programme and the twelve-month dispute which followed. Miners were to see their union divided, their pits closed and the destruction of the way of life which had shaped their political consciousness and their cultural affiliations. The strategies and institutions which they had traditionally used to provide a barrier against the excesses of the market, such as union solidarity and a powerful Labour Party, were no longer effective weapons against the politics of Thatcherism.

Although this chapter is entitled 'The Fragmentation of Unity', this characterization should be used cautiously, as already, in 1983, the tensions within the union were beginning to intensify as the left became increasingly confident following the election of Arthur Scargill. In terms of the North Wales Area, an emphasis on unity became even more problematic. The AEC was showing signs of division as a number of critics emerged to question the role of Ted McKay. At Point of Ayr, unity certainly existed, but at its most potent level it was only applicable to certain groups of miners. The Wrexham miners generally worked together and benefited from the galvanizing role of Ithel Kelly, an under-manager from Ifton who had the reputation of a tyrant in some quarters. Kelly clearly favoured Wrexham miners, creating divisions between union members. His favouritism led to petty squabbles over the allocation of overtime and

---

[1] Extract from 'Lament for Bersham' by Keith Hett, from *Bersham Pit Bottom and Other Poems* (private publication, 1986).

this had an impact on unity underground. In the most extreme cases overtime tickets would be sold between miners, emphasizing the individualism of the Point of Ayr men and the inability of the union to interfere in all aspects of the labour process. The Lancashire contingent seemed to have assimilated more completely than the Wrexham men, though this was offset when over thirty miners entered the colliery from Burnley in 1982 after the closure of Hapton Valley.[2]

At Bersham, the workforce was more settled as most miners were drawn from villages around Wrexham. The last major influx had been from Gresford in 1973, though many already knew a number of workers at Bersham because the coalfield had always been small, with families switching from pit to pit at times of closure. The majority of the workforce was concentrated in the villages of Rhostyllen, Rhosllannerchrugog, Gwersyllt and Llay. However, a number of men who had entered from other pits outside north Wales felt that the union was weak in terms of its approach to the management and totally bereft of a militant strand. Keith Hett from Cronton colliery in Lancashire became the only lodge member who had a background in the CP; he was to emerge as one of the most committed strikers at the pit.

The countdown to the strike seemed to be programmed by some sense of inevitability. Peter Walker recalls that the day after the Conservative election victory in 1983, Margaret Thatcher wanted him to move to the Department of Energy as she felt that the government would soon be challenged by Scargill.[3] In north Wales, only a minority viewed the situation with some alarm. Within the coalfield, the union had not formerly acted as an educative institution. There was very little political education available to the wider membership in terms of either day-release courses or a culture of campaigning that reached beyond the personnel of the respective lodges. This was to have a significant outcome as the dispute intensified and the union found it difficult to argue its case when most sections of the media solidly backed

---

[2] By the early 1980s, the management culture of the NCB began to change, with a significant impact on work relationships. The introduction of incentives prevented unity by playing miners off against each other. The craftsmen were often angry, as they made less money than faceworkers owing to the 'bonus system'. Deputies and overmen, often favouring friends and neighbours, distributed in an *ad hoc* manner the allocation of overtime on which miners increasingly relied.

[3] Peter Walker, *Trust the People* (London, 1987), p.92.

the claims of the NCB. During 1984 every member of the union was to become overtly politicized and forced to take sides in an industrial battle which was to prove to be the most divisive in the history of the union.

To understand the position of both the union and the Conservative government in the early 1980s one must not lose sight of recent history. The defeat of Edward Heath in 1974 had left scars on the right of the party, and the infamous Ridley Plan, leaked to *The Economist* in 1978, was to form the basis of contingency plans for conflict in the coal industry.[4] The Conservatives were keen to use the 'tyranny of the left' argument to justify their approach to industrial relations. This seemed strange to many miners, particularly in north Wales, as both pits had been strike-free for some time and the level of political activism stretched no further than a vote for Labour in local and general elections.

In March 1983, the government announced that Ian Mac-Gregor, who had recently presided over a programme of rationalization in the steel industry, was to be appointed chairman of the NCB. With the backing of a massive electoral mandate the following June for the Conservatives, the scene for confrontation was set. The subsequent strike exposed the full weight of the state and its ability to suppress dissent, highlighting the weakness of Labour and trade union solidarity in providing an alternative to Thatcherism. The media, the courts, the police and the very welfare system that the miners had helped to construct were all used against mining communities in the most sophisticated manner. Miners were shocked at the way in which the various institutions turned against them and provided justification for the politics of the government and the economic case of the NCB. Before the strike, not even the most politically enlightened miners envisaged the mobilization of the state on such a level.

After 1982, the left in the NUM was firmly in control at national level and the NEC pledged to fight pit closures with direct action supported by all areas of the union. But the left suffered a major setback when the call for action was dismissed in a series of national ballots. The first occasion came in January

---

[4] For a detailed analysis of the Conservative preparation, see John Saville, 'An open conspiracy: Conservative politics and the miners' strike', *Socialist Register* (1985–6), 295–329.

1982, when 55 per cent voted against a strike. In October of the same year, the miners voted 60 per cent against and, in 1983, the call for action was again rejected. The pattern emerged of the most threatened areas responding with votes in favour of a strike and the more secure areas voting against.[5] However, this does not tell the whole story, as coalfields such as Leicestershire and north Wales were far from secure and both areas had tiny memberships.

In north Wales the vote in the 1983 ballot was only 23 per cent in favour of striking, and it seemed increasingly likely that each area was going to pursue an autonomous path in defending jobs and communities.[6] This path was sanctioned by rule 41 of the national rulebook, which gave authority for action by individual areas. Provision for national strike action was normally justified by rule 43, which maintained that a national ballot had to be held before a national strike. Many viewed this shift as a manœuvre by the left, as it was apparent that it would not get a positive national vote for a strike over the issue of closures. This was clearly the case, but rather than it being a sinister plot, it was merely one way out of a problem of representation in the context of defending the jobs of union members.

The south Wales miners again took up the role of persuaders in north Wales.[7] Before the ballot in 1983, they had lobbied members at both Point of Ayr and Bersham, receiving a mixed response that was to become increasingly hostile as the events of 1984 unfolded. Members at Bersham were quick to point out that nobody rushed to the defence of the coalfield when Gresford was closed ten years earlier. Nonetheless, it was generally felt that the appointment of MacGregor would lead to further closures. Keith Hett informed the *Daily Post* that the only chance for the survival of the coal industry in north Wales would be through trade union solidarity: 'if not the industry would be massacred.'[8]

---

[5] Many miners were unhappy that the ballots combined the two issues of pit closures and action over wages. This was seen by some as a deliberate ploy by the left to get members to act over pit closures, using a pay claim as the vehicle for militancy.

[6] David Howell, 'The miners' strike of 1984–85 in north Wales', *Contemporary Wales*, 4 (1991), 73.

[7] At the end of February 1983, the NCB had announced the closure of Lewis Merthyr Tymawr and a sit-in at the pit was followed by a strike throughout the south Wales coalfield. See David Howell, *The Politics of the NUM: A Lancashire View* (Manchester, 1989), pp.85–7.

[8] *Daily Post*, 9 March 1983.

The AEC reaffirmed its opposition to closures, but stressed that it would first seek a ballot on the question.[9] Again, the coalfield sought direct action through the national union and believed that the fact that some areas were going it alone could only lead to confusion and division. This scepticism on the part of north Wales activists was to prove prophetic a year later as the coalfield divided. At the 1983 NUM annual conference, an emergency resolution opposing the predicted run-down of the industry was carried unanimously. The conference voted heavily in favour of an overtime ban against the NCB's proposed pay offer and on the issue of closures. The policy of banning overtime had usually been a first step to a strike, as in 1972 and 1974, although this was becoming problematic as miners increasingly worked extra shifts to supplement earnings. Amongst the lower-paid workers at Point of Ayr, there was often a daily scramble for overtime. The wider political culture, affected by rising unemployment and the push for home ownership, played a significant part in fostering this attitude.[10]

The changing culture of NCB management ensured that the ban would lead to lockout situations at particular pits, exacerbating the antagonistic relationship between pit deputies and NUM members. It was crucial that, in case of a strike, the pit deputies' union[11] was kept from aiding the NUM by sympathetic action. The higher echelons of management were undergoing a transformation owing to the 'MacGregor effect'. In his memoirs of the period, the NCB chairman recalls that he 'took steps very early on to streamline the board and bring in some outside non-executive directors, who . . . would be more sympathetic with the changes that had to be made than were some existing

[9] North Wales NUM minutes of special meeting of lodge officials, March 1983: CRO Flintshire D/NM/1483.
[10] Discussions with miners in the coalfield suggest that there was a changing culture from the late 1970s onwards as workers increasingly moved into home ownership and took holidays abroad, and there seemed a shift away from the archetypal pattern of colliery settlement and character.
[11] Much has been made of the relationship between the NUM and NACODS and how this fragmented during the strike. In the case of north Wales this animosity was absent. Although NACODS members represented the first line of management underground, their role was primarily one of safety. All NACODS members had previously been NUM members, retaining their commitment to the politics of the union and to the TUC and the Labour Party. Interviews with Brian Gildart and Don Partington, December 1997.

members'.[12] The attempt to challenge the existing consensual relations between sections of the NCB and the NUM soon proved successful. At Point of Ayr, the men found that they had been locked out on a number of shifts. This raised tensions and the lodge was shocked by the attitude that the manager was taking.[13] At Bersham, the attitude of the management was not quite as stark, but it tried to persuade the union that industrial action would seriously damage future prospects.[14] Meanwhile, McKay remained sceptical of the effectiveness of industrial action and kept up his vocal criticism of the left in the national union.

At the AEC meeting in November 1983, McKay stated that north Wales was totally in support of the overtime ban but doubted that it would change the energy policy of the government. Further, continuation of the action would eventually cause disunity amongst the men: 'to be beaten by the Board would be bad enough, but to be beaten by the members would be a disaster if, through the failure of the tactics we were not able to carry the majority of the membership with us'.[15] In contrast to the position in north Wales, the ban was having a radicalizing effect in other areas. In Yorkshire at Cortonwood, a pit traditionally associated with moderation, men pressing the lodge for an intensification of action became a regular feature of general meetings.[16]

The situation in north Wales at the beginning of 1984 was reaching crisis point as miners going to work on the Sunday nightshift were sent home on a number of occasions.[17] McKay complained to the NCB and claimed that the policy was one of extreme provocation promoted by the management. The whole situation was escalating when the NCB dropped a bombshell, announcing the closure of Cortonwood. This was certainly a messy start to a national mobilization with the absence of a national ballot, and with a number of coalfields solidly opposed

[12] Ian MacGregor with Rodney Tyler, *The Enemies Within: The Story of the Miners' Strike, 1984–85* (Glasgow, 1986), p.139.
[13] NCB minutes of stage-one meeting re Point of Ayr and overtime ban, 29 November 1983: CRO Flintshire D/NM/1350.
[14] Letter from Bersham manager Mike Owens to Jimmy Williams, lodge secretary, 2 March 1983: NUM, Wrexham.
[15] North Wales NUM AEC minutes, 23 November 1983: NUM, Wrexham.
[16] Interview with Mick Carter, Cortonwood NUM, May 1997.
[17] North Wales NUM AEC minutes, 16 January 1984: NUM, Wrexham.

to strike action over closures. The union was still having difficulty at the national level in bringing everyone round to a militant approach. The left might have been in the ascendant, but a number of important critics remained on the NEC. In the twelve months before the dispute, the right was down but not totally out, and McKay, along with Sid Vincent, tried in vain to counteract the dominance of the pro-Scargill members. Previously Vincent had been trying to fill the shoes of Gormley in busying himself in the affairs of the Labour Party. In a letter to McKay in 1982, he stressed that it was important that the NUM support the attacks on Militant, as it was clear that some members of the NEC were sympathetic to the policies of the revolutionary group.[18] However, the likes of Vincent and McKay were becoming increasingly marginalized and found that, despite their good intentions, they were unable to alter the balance of power at national level.[19]

The last chance of recreating political balance at the top of the union came in 1983 when Lawrence Daly announced his retirement from the post of general secretary. The candidate of the left had already been established as Peter Heathfield from north Derbyshire; he seemed the most likely contender, given the success of the Scargill platform two years earlier. Heathfield represented the recent tradition of fusion of Labour left-wingers with members of the CP. He was a member of the Labour Party and shared the position of Scargill on the question of closures. Roy Lynk, the financial secretary from Nottinghamshire who went on to become the figurehead of the breakaway union in 1985, initially touted for support in moderate areas of the union. In a letter to McKay he stressed that he was seeking the nomination, as Scargill only ever gave a one-sided view of the issues.[20] The north Wales leadership was not yet ready to commit itself to a particular candidate, though it shared the views of other areas in sensing that the retirement of Daly before he was

[18] Letter from Sid Vincent, Lancashire NUM, to Ted McKay, 10 August 1982: CRO Flintshire D/NM/1195.
[19] Although Vincent worked with McKay on the NEC, he still wanted to promote a centrist strand by often using the rhetoric of unity to defend his position. For details of Vincent and his attempts to balance opposing forces in his own coalfield, see Howell, *The Politics of the NUM*, pp. 118–20.
[20] Letter from Roy Lynk to Ted McKay, 24 November 1983: CRO Flintshire D/NM/1195.

sixty was induced by the national officials. This was an attempt to get Heathfield elected before he reached fifty-five, an age at which he would have been ineligible for the position. Two eventual challengers emerged, John Walsh of Yorkshire and, surprisingly, Les Kelly, the lodge secretary from Point of Ayr who was still a working miner.

Heathfield made it clear that he was a supporter of the present leadership and was adamant in his resistance to closures on economic grounds. From the number of nominations that he received it seemed clear that he would be the eventual victor. However, Walsh was to run him close and this was to be a warning to the optimists of the left who felt that the union now had a leadership that reflected the feelings of the wider membership. Walsh himself had been a critic of the left in his own coalfield and bluntly stated that he was in favour of 'less aggro and more results'. He also maintained that in 'a truly democratic union the members should always be consulted before industrial action to preserve the organization's unity and strength'.[21] This was his attack on the failure of the leadership to sanction a ballot on the overtime ban. Walsh and others were aware of the plans of the left to push for industrial action through rule 41.

Les Kelly aimed to promote a centrist position between Heathfield and Walsh, who seemed to be occupying antagonistic positions on the issue of closures. Kelly was certainly distanced from the politics of McKay and his attacks on the national leadership, but he felt that he could go some way to foster unity. The north Wales candidate fought a low-key campaign, though he too was critical of the left and the fact that their exaggerated claims were now being pressed with more certainty. In a statement to the local press, Kelly warned that 'if the present style of leadership was allowed to continue or even reinforced by the appointment of a left-wing General Secretary then the union's decline would go unchecked and would probably accelerate'.[22] He promoted himself as a pragmatist and a Labour loyalist with no commitments to any particular fringe groups, but he only managed to secure the nomination of his own area. Kelly was not opposed to the principles behind the overtime ban, but

---

[21] John Walsh, election pamphlet, 1983: David Howell collection.
[22] *Daily Post*, 9 January 1984.

rather to the tactics of its implementation. He called for an immediate ballot on the issue in order to gauge the support of the men and preserve the unity of the union.[23]

Clearly, Kelly had a keen understanding of the economic and political situation before the initiation of the strike in March 1984. This could no doubt be ascribed to the fact that he was still working at the point of production and was in contact with the workforce on a day-to-day basis. Commenting on the importance of democracy in his campaign literature, he was acutely aware of the fragile solidarity that held the national union together:

> We are in danger of losing the acclaimed strength, authority and dignity of the NUM . . . we must realise that we can no longer just rely on the traditional 'head to head' conflicts, we must develop new strategies to combat the management of 1984.[24]

The contest was decided by the single transferable vote system. Kelly was eliminated in the first ballot, securing only 13,547 votes, though Walsh ran Heathfield close with 70,571 against the left candidate's 74,186. It is evident that, if Kelly had not stood, Walsh might well have taken the position and provided the union with a counterbalance to the policies of Scargill. With the victory of Heathfield, the NUM nationally was firmly in the grip of the left, and the dissenters who formed the rump of the so-called 'progressive group' found themselves in a position of insignificance on the NEC and on the conference floor on issues that divided the factions.

On 5 March 1984, the Yorkshire NUM met to discuss the closure of Cortonwood and announced that a strike throughout the coalfield would commence a week later. At the NEC meeting on 8 March, Scargill announced that the strikes taking place in Yorkshire and Scotland (over the closure of Polmaise colliery) were official, in accordance with rule 41, and he called on other areas of the union to support these initiatives. The strike was now under way without the sanction of a national ballot and the pickets mobilized themselves to pursue the so-called 'domino

---

[23] *Evening Leader*, 11 January 1984.
[24] Les Kelly, election pamphlet, 1984: NUM, Wrexham.

strategy' of bringing each coalfield out in turn. They were helped by the ringing endorsement of the vice-president, Mick McGahey, who in answer to calls for a ballot proclaimed that miners on strike would not be 'constitutionalized' out of taking action.[25] The situation in north Wales over the subsequent weeks was to be one of chaos, with the AEC and the lodges along with the wider membership fragmenting over a number of issues relating to the strike.

Within a week of the announcement that the area strikes were official, pickets entered the north Wales coalfield. Again, activists from south Wales headed north but were met with confusion at both Bersham and Point of Ayr. There had been an initially ambiguous response in south Wales, but the work of pickets quickly led to total support. The lodge officials and McKay were still trying to piece together a policy now that the NEC had thrown the ball into the court of the individual areas. Some miners honoured the picket line, others crossed it. A number of union loyalists wanted to wait for the direction of the lodge officials owing to the initial state of confusion concerning the legitimacy of the action. A special conference of the area was quickly convened on 14 March to assess the situation and pro-vide a united front. A few weeks earlier, McKay had been aware that any hopes of a settlement to the overtime ban seemed futile, as the attitude of the management was going to lead to a strike that the union did not want.[26] Nonetheless, with miners now on the streets, both the agent and the AEC had to make a decision that was to be of immense importance to the future strategy of the union.

The atmosphere at the conference was intense; many viewed the situation with exasperation, as this was a new situation for the north Wales miners who were being asked to strike without a national mandate.[27] The outcome of the meeting was to call an area ballot for the sake of unity. Those in favour of strike action

[25] See Martin Adeney and John Lloyd, *The Miners' Strike, 1984/85: Loss without Limit* (London, 1986), p.196.

[26] *Daily Post*, 16 January 1984.

[27] The call to strike without a ballot left some areas in an unfamiliar position of having to direct action by their own initiative; this seriously weakened co-ordination from the outset. For example, Lancashire had an admirable record in responding to strike calls from both the MFGB and the NUM, but with the confusion of 1984 support became increasingly erratic and this led to eventual fragmentation. See Howell, *The Politics of the NUM*, pp.105–40.

viewed this decision as a defeat; the result would be a foregone conclusion given the vote against strikes in previous ballots. The lodge officials were in the dubious position of having the ability to sanction an area strike through the rulebook, but also knowing that the majority of the workforce would, in all probability, be against such a policy. This raised the important issue of union representation: was the job of the official to lead or to represent the majority view? Because this question was never addressed the relationship between the agent, the AEC and the wider membership rapidly deteriorated.

The membership was informed that the area ballot result would be binding and the national officials would be consulted if a strike was rejected. McKay added a rejoinder that the AEC totally deplored the NEC's decision not to call a national ballot. In the event of strike action, safety cover would be withdrawn temporarily, though apprentices would be left to continue with their education.[28] Picket line activity would operate within the law and would be directed by the lodge members. The crucial statement emerging from the meeting was that the AEC endorsed the NEC's decision to make the strikes official in Yorkshire and Scotland and recommended that the membership in north Wales vote for strike action.[29]

The north Wales ballot was held within days and McKay made it clear that he wanted no influence exerted by outside bodies, including pickets from other coalfields. At Bersham, attitudes were already hardening with a sign hung from one of the office windows reading 'No ballot, no strike'.[30] The south Wales picket at Point of Ayr was creating tension and McKay reported the situation to Peter Heathfield, the new general secretary. He also attacked Terry Thomas, a union official from south Wales, for raising concerns about the future of Bersham in an attempt to influence the ballot.[31] Already, the role of McKay was that of opposition to the so-called 'domino strategy' and he

---

[28] After six months of strike, Point of Ayr seemed unaffected. Apprentices continued with their training and recruitment was maintained throughout the dispute. Interestingly the management did not take an arbitrary view in recruiting the sons of existing miners. The sons of both strikers and workers were shortlisted for interview, though the bulk of them took up their positions once the strike was over.

[29] North Wales NUM minutes of special conference, 14 March 1984: CRO Flintshire D/NM/1133.

[30] *Liverpool Daily Post*, 15 March 1984.

[31] *Evening Leader*, 16 March 1984.

did not hide his hostility to the role of flying pickets. The ballot went ahead with a large majority voting against strike action. This was to undermine the prospects of unity and the difficult job of the AEC was even more problematic now that miners could argue that they could legitimately cross picket lines.

NUM NORTH WALES AREA BALLOT RESULT, 16 MARCH 1984

	Point of Ayr	Bersham	Total
Voting Yes	170	106	276
Voting No	356	239	595
Spoilt Votes	2	1	3

The pattern of voting is important and is not really a true indication of the support that was to materialize. For example, at Point of Ayr, once the strike was into its sixth month, fewer than one hundred men remained out. Therefore, over eighty members had voted in favour of strike but felt a greater allegiance to the feeling of the coalfield and the sanctity of the area ballot. At Bersham, fewer had voted in favour of a stoppage but all heeded the strike call owing to local activists urging support for the cause. It was initially believed – mistakenly – by those opposed to a strike, that the area rules meant that a ballot had to be taken before such action. In reality, the rules only required a strike to be reported to the AEC and then to be sanctioned by the NEC:

National Union of Mineworkers (North Wales Area) Rules
29. In the event of a dispute arising in any Area or applying to the workers in any Branch likely or possible to lead to a stoppage of work or any other industrial action short of a strike the questions involved must be immediately reported by the Appropriate official of the Area in question to the NEC which shall deal with the matter forthwith, and in no case shall a cessation of work or other form of industrial action short of a strike take place by the workers without the previous sanction of the NEC.

McKay knew that the result of the ballot and the power of the picket line would lead to a divisive situation in the coalfield. He again contacted Heathfield, asking him to respect the democratic decision of the area. The agent proposed that a cooling-off period would be beneficial in order for the constituent bodies of the NUM to assess the situation. Further, the national officials should lead a campaign against pit closures as a prelude to a national ballot that would unify the workforce and the country around the case for coal.[32] However, events nationally were rapidly overtaking the sentiments of the officials in those areas that were initially not committed to the strike.

At a special meeting of Point of Ayr miners at the Gronant institute on 17 March, Jack Walsh, one of the Burnley miners, proposed that no members should cross the picket line. The proposal was seconded by John Morris and went to a vote. It was carried by the floor, 196 to 133. At the same meeting, it was demanded that the union should immediately hold a national ballot. The decision to respect the picket line taken at the meeting was not accepted by a number of members and the situation at the pit was still unsure, as around half the workforce remained on strike and the other half went in. Five days later a further meeting was called, which again was well attended. McKay spoke at some length, defending the importance of democracy and speaking on behalf of those who were arguing for a national ballot to promote unity. John Morris called for a cooling-off period of one week and proposed that if a national ballot was not called during this time a final decision should be taken as to whether to stay out or return. This proposal was seconded and had support from the floor. John Harper then moved an amendment that the men should stand by the area ballot and return to work. The amendment was carried by 140 votes to 115.[33] This was decisive, as many at Point of Ayr now felt that the area ballot and the subsequent vote of the general meeting legitimized opposing strike action. This decision went against the policy of the AEC which had held a special conference three days earlier. Although there were reservations about the route to the dispute and the absence of a national ballot, the conference passed a clear resolution that upheld the legitimacy of the picket line:

---

[32] Letter from Ted McKay to Peter Heathfield, 19 March 1984: CRO Flintshire D/NM/1195.
[33] North Wales NUM minutes of special meeting, Gronant institute, 24 March 1984: CRO Flintshire D/NM/1133.

In full recognition of the North Wales Area ballot result, but because of the very divisive and confused situation the North Wales Area Special Conference held today 21 March 1984 in Flint have unanimously agreed; with the intention of bringing unity and stability within the Area; to recommend that no members in the North Wales Area should pass an official picket line.[34]

This was the crucial point in the developments when the agent could have gone to the members and argued the case for a strike with the full backing of the AEC. Both lodge committees did this, most notably at Point of Ayr where the officials faced a great deal of animosity from those who were to go on to form the eventual breakaway. McKay played a Machiavellian role, stressing that he supported the views of the area, but at the same time undermining the legitimacy of the strike in the pages of the local press. On 22 March he gained a favourable editorial comment in the *Evening Leader* when it reported that there was no future for democracy in the NUM. McKay added that he was 'concerned that people who don't believe in the ballot box can overturn the democratic decisions of those who do'.[35] Four days later, commenting on the situation at Point of Ayr where miners continued to cross picket lines, he called for the NEC to take control and criticized NUM leaders for siding with those on strike and disregarding the views of those remaining in work.[36]

Desperate to resolve the escalating crisis, McKay attempted to group together the remaining moderates on the NEC in order to counteract the effectiveness of picketing in areas that had voted against the strike. He contacted Roy Ottey of the Power Group on 26 March and stressed that something had to be done about the escalation of the conflict. Ottey agreed and contacted Sid Vincent of Lancashire. The remnants of the 'progressive group' met at the Brant Inn in Leicestershire and discussed ways of forcing a national ballot. They had expected more to attend, but the important Nottinghamshire representatives were tied up in meetings in London. This seriously weakened the impact of the meeting and, on the whole, it was an

---

[34] North Wales NUM minutes of special conference, 21 March 1984: CRO Flintshire D/NM/1133.
[35] *Evening Leader*, 22 March 1984.
[36] *Daily Post*, 26 March 1984.

exercise that was welcomed by the press and the NCB, but did little to change the attitudes of the majority of miners who were on strike. The group released a press statement calling for a national ballot and advised members already working in areas that had voted against the strike, to continue working, while sticking to the overtime ban.[37] McKay stressed that unless there was an immediate national ballot, the union would tear itself apart. In an interview with the *Evening Leader,* he attacked the leadership: 'they seem to be able to find time to meet Ray Buckton [leader of ASLEF (Associated Society of Locomotive Engineers and Firemen)] but not us. Our Areas have voted not to strike and nothing but a national ballot can overturn that decision.'[38]

Members of the AEC now found themselves at odds with McKay and his support for those who were continuing to cross picket lines. At a special conference on 30 March, there was a heated discussion of the Brant Inn meeting and the part that McKay had played in the release of the subsequent press statement. The members rejected the document in its entirety by a vote of ten to six and McKay left the meeting further isolated from those adhering to the proposals of the NEC.[39] Miners on strike and those continuing to work were still looking to the agent for guidance and, while he continued to pursue his own agenda, the rank and file began to organize themselves amongst both workers and strikers. McKay was aware of this and warned that, if the ballot was not forthcoming, the miners would rebel against the national leadership.

With the majority of Bersham miners already out, the strike was to be total in Wrexham in a matter of weeks. At Point of Ayr, men continued to work, with some boasting that they had not lost a shift. To make the divisions more concrete, the pickets reported that the overtime ban that remained in place was breached.[40] The south Wales miners intensified their picketing

[37] For details of the meeting by one of the main critics of Scargill and the left, see Roy Ottey, *The Strike: An Insider's Story* (London, 1985), pp.79–92.

[38] *Evening Leader,* 28 March 1984.

[39] North Wales NUM special area conference minutes, 30 March 1984: CRO Flintshire D/NM/1133.

[40] Mark Wilkes, a strike loyalist at Point of Ayr, busied himself in recording the shift patterns of members who were breaking the overtime ban, though his efforts were quickly thwarted by the police. Interview with author, December 1997.

and the Vale of Clwyd Trades Council abandoned their April monthly meeting to attend the picket line and give support to those who were committed to the strike.[41] Sympathetic Labour councils throughout the country did their best to provide for the children in what was increasingly likely to be a lengthy dispute. The Conservatives, bolstered by their massive electoral victory, seemed indifferent to the level of distress.[42] In most coalfields the strike was taking root as an organizational pattern emerged in which a number of bodies worked to provide a significant level of support throughout the twelve months. North Wales remained in a state of confusion, especially at Point of Ayr, where the position of those on strike and those working reached a stalemate.

To settle the question of the ballot, the NEC called a special delegate conference on 19 April. It was felt by many that this was the defining moment in terms of an attempt to challenge the legitimacy of the strike.[43] North Wales was split on the issue of altering the rules of the union so that a simple majority could sanction strike action, rather than the existing rule of a 55 per cent majority. It was decided that this should be left to the two delegates to decide.[44] Les Kelly of Point of Ayr and Raymond Ellis of Bersham represented north Wales. Ellis argued vociferously for a national ballot, especially because of the situation in the coalfield, with Bersham at a standstill and over 70 per cent of Point of Ayr men continuing to work.[45] The conference rejected calls for a national ballot and voted to carry on with the present policy of area strikes. Scargill called for those continuing to work to stop immediately and support the 80 per cent of members who were already out. This was the last chance for a national ballot and many on the right knew that their efforts were futile. They resigned themselves to defeat and concentrated on minimizing divisions in their own coalfields. Back in north Wales, the criticism of McKay and the call for a ballot by Ellis at the conference altered little. Bersham remained solid, while the series of

[41] *Rhyl Journal*, 12 April 1984.

[42] Matthew Parris, the political journalist and then a Conservative MP protested to the district auditor at the decision of Derbyshire County Council to provide food for the children of strikers. *Miner*, 16 April 1984.

[43] At a meeting of the NEC on 12 April, the right had already suffered a defeat when it failed to persuade the committee to order a national ballot.

[44] *Western Mail*, 18 April 1984.

[45] NUM report of reconvened special delegate conference, Sheffield, 19 April 1984: NUM, Wrexham.

meetings held at Point of Ayr consistently reached an impasse because of the presumed legitimacy of the area ballot. The AEC called a special delegate conference on 24 April to clarify again the position of the coalfield. The meeting fully endorsed the decision made at the special delegate conference in Sheffield, and consequently the North Wales Area was on official strike: it ordered those going to work to cease doing so immediately. The picket line at Point of Ayr was now official.[46] The AEC issued a statement to every member stating that the action was official under rule 29 of the area rulebook. Further, the committee explained that members who continued to work would be liable for disciplinary action against them under rule 9, which could be used to expel members for breaking the rules of the union.

On 1 May, McKay tried to redirect the action of the area in order to gain control of the deteriorating situation between strikers and workers. In a letter to Peter McNestry of NACODS, he stressed that the strike in the coalfield was official and he wanted deputies to respect picket lines.[47] This was a hypocritical appeal, as McKay was not condemning his own members who were crossing the line. A number of miners interviewed, both strikers and workers, claim that McKay was meeting with pickets and then addressing those who were working, allegedly talking to the latter in the colliery canteen.[48] McKay was in an unenviable position of having to represent all members on both sides of the divide, a dilemma that many other officials did not have to face in their own coalfields. Nonetheless, his strategy did not heal the divide and in many ways exacerbated an already difficult situation.

The major trade unions in north Wales supported those on strike and the T&GWU, ASLEF, NUR, NALGO (National and Local Government Officers Association) and NUPE (National Union of Public Employees) all pledged financial support to strikers at both collieries. On this occasion McKay played the role of union loyalist, accepting the solidarity of other unions and asking those working to examine their consciences.[49] The AEC

[46] North Wales NUM minutes of special delegate conference, Flint, 24 April 1984: CRO Flintshire D/NM/1133.
[47] Letter from Ted McKay to Peter McNestry, 1 May 1984: CRO Flintshire D/NM/1195.
[48] Interviews with Point of Ayr miners, 1996–7, at the Red Lion Inn, Llanasa.
[49] *Evening Leader*, 10 May 1984.

met again and agreed that the union must remain fully committed to the dispute by showing firm leadership to those on strike. Nonetheless, the leadership at both pits was aware of the damaging impact of outside pickets entering the coalfield. They felt that the picket line at Point of Ayr should be manned by local miners, though it was accepted that this could not be enforced.[50] McKay again called for national direction, stressing that personalities on both sides were doing nothing to seek an agreement to settle the conflict. The Social Democratic Party (SDP)/Alliance candidate for the European Parliament elections, Tom Ellis, backed the agent. He claimed that if more men on the NEC were like McKay, 'Scargill would not have succeeded in leading the union towards the greatest disaster for the miners since 1926'.[51]

At the end of May, the AEC could at least feel that it had some control over the situation, although McKay often adopted a hysterical tone in his comments to the local press. However, the situation at Point of Ayr was to take a sinister turn when the working miners threatened the lodge officials with legal action. On 2 June, the union was served with an injunction from three members, Jim McKay, John Harper and David Kenny. The subsequent court case caused further divisions at the colliery. John Harper, who had at the beginning of March written a letter to Scargill claiming that as president he was the only hope that miners had, was a constant thorn in the side of the lodge.[52] Throughout the dispute, he attempted to cajole men into returning and forged links with working miners in other areas. The group who were emerging as representatives of the working miners saw themselves as a lodge committee in waiting, hoping to overturn the existing officials as a result of legal action.

The High Court ruled in favour of the litigants as the north Wales decision to strike had been in response to a Kent resolution, which gave it a national dimension. The call for a strike had not originated in the area, thus negating the validity of action under rule 41. Consequently, the lodge could no longer refer to the strike as official, or threaten those at work with disciplinary

[50] North Wales NUM minutes of special AEC, 15 May 1984: CRO Flintshire D/NM/1133.
[51] *Evening Leader*, 22 May 1984.
[52] Letter from John Harper to Scargill, 2 March 1984: NUM, Wrexham.

action. The legal challenge had been given financial impetus by miners who were opposed to the strike.[53] A thousand pounds came into the fund for legal action during the first week of its establishment; this was organized by Harper and others including Ken Payne. Jim McKay stressed that most of the men had given £5 each to meet the legal bill. As a rejoinder, he stated that there was no animosity between him and his brother Ted, although they were on different sides of the fence. Ted McKay had himself attacked the threat of disciplinary action against working miners emanating from his own AEC.[54] This sent out mixed messages to those who continued to work, as the comments of McKay seemed to justify the action of the litigants. The agent was becoming increasingly estranged from all sections of the membership, and he was jeered by north and south Wales miners when he spoke at a rally in Wrexham on 12 June.

Harper was now confident that he could make a difference to the situation at Bersham. This pit had not mounted a picket as all members were on strike. Harper offered to meet anyone who wished to return to work in order to co-ordinate a movement within the coalfield. Jim McKay had been mandated from a meeting of working miners held in the Midlands to do what he could to break the strike in his own area.[55] The men at Bersham nonetheless remained solid, and it was to be some four months before cracks emerged in this solidarity. The AEC still maintained its precarious grip on the strike, but the situation at Point of Ayr was now viewed as a lost cause, especially as the injunction added further legitimacy to the actions of those still working.

By August, the AEC was aware that the Point of Ayr lodge was in danger of being deposed because it only represented a minority. It was eventually agreed that elections for positions should be postponed for six months in order to assess the situation.[56] This led to a spate of letters in the local press from Harper and others, accusing the union of again running scared

---

[53] *Daily Post*, 25 June 1984. Nonetheless, many working miners resisted contributing to action against their own union, often taking advice from a deputy or a member more committed to the broader ideals of the union. Some felt that the NUM meant more than just a vehicle for justifying strike action.

[54] *Daily Post*, 25 June 1984.

[55] *Evening Leader*, 16 July 1984.

[56] North Wales NUM AEC minutes, 15 August 1984: CRO Flintshire D/NM/1133.

of democracy. Ironically, a number of working miners maintained their support for the lodge throughout the duration of the
strike, emphasizing that Harper and McKay themselves were not
highly regarded by the bulk of the workforce. With the strike
now in its sixth month, a stable pattern emerged in the coalfield.
At Point of Ayr, men continued to cross picket lines, using the
argument of the result of the area ballot and the subsequent
injunction to justify their actions. At Bersham, the strike remained solid with little need for picketing, as all members
remained committed to the action. The AEC throughout was in
a precarious position at each pit, as rank-and-file members were
directing the strike away from the officials, especially at Bersham.

THE STRIKE AT BERSHAM

The recent history of Bersham had been a chequered one, with a
number of threats to its existence from the 1960s onwards. The
industrial relations climate at the pit had been consensual, and
before 1984 the relationship between the lodge committee and
the management had been one of mutual respect. The politics of
the lodge had also been relatively static with Jimmy Williams, the
long-serving secretary, secure in his position. The committee had
supported Scargill in 1981, though no significant left force
existed among the wider membership. One exception was Keith
Hett, who was to play an essential leadership role during the
strike, directing operations outside the structure of the lodge.
This caused concern amongst other committee members who
wanted to retain some control over developments once the strike
was under way.

Hett had been a member of the CP and a trade union activist
on Merseyside before moving to Bersham. He was initially
shocked at the low level of political awareness at the pit, in that
there were no pressures from the membership to direct the policy
of the lodge. Nonetheless, as the events of 1984 unfolded, he
noticed a rising level of optimism amongst the workforce, signifying growing resistance to the pit closure programme. The first
influx of pickets after the March announcement of a strike
gained a favourable reception, though there was some confusion.
A series of meetings advocated a cooling-off period with steps
taken to push for a national ballot, but other members pressed

for respect for picket lines. The lodge seemed to be unable to formulate a clear policy on a course of action and others were already filling the vacuum. Hett immediately set up a miners' support group (MSG), which took the initiative away from the officials. A situation developed in which both were operating separately and, at times, in conflict.

On 23 March 1984 the lodge met and decided that, in order to avoid chaos, it should recommend that all members stop work for a week in order to seek advice from the AEC concerning the question of the national ballot.[57] The atmosphere between management and men had by this time still not deteriorated as it had in many other pits throughout the coalfields. This relationship remained throughout the strike, with lodge officials attending meetings with the manager and involving themselves in the bureaucratic procedures that had been in place before the strike. After the national delegate conference, the lodge immediately pledged support for strike action under rule 41.[58] This was a decisive moment and, from this point onwards, the strike at the pit was solid. The lodge found that events had overtaken them as the MSG began conducting the strike. The officials contacted the group, pledging their support in terms of raising funds and rooms were allocated in the area office. This did not lead to any weakening of the autonomy of the MSG, and the rank and file remained in firm control. Members organized the collection and distribution of funds and forged links with other trade unionists in north Wales.

Scargill visited the coalfield in the first month of the strike and spoke to packed audiences. The president claimed that Bersham was on the hit list of closures and was supported in his claim by the future North Wales Euro-MP, Joe Wilson. The NCB responded quickly and stressed that the pit had a secure future and that the corporation was spending half a million pounds to develop access to future reserves. Keith Raffan, the Conservative MP for Delyn, also entered the fray, calling for MacGregor to invoke a High Court injunction to stop secondary picketing. A number of Bersham miners were now focusing on the situation at Point of Ayr, and many were calling for a mass picket to halt

---

[57] NUM Bersham lodge minutes, 23 March 1984: CRO Flintshire D/NM/1212.
[58] Letter from Jimmy Williams to Ted McKay, 25 April 1984: NUM, Wrexham.

production. McKay meanwhile was still urging the national officials to seek a dialogue with the NCB because the dispute was turning into a war of attrition.[59]

Keith and Ann Hett busied themselves in forging significant links with trade unionists on Merseyside. This was designed to form a transmission belt of support in terms of food, money and labour, which was sustained to the end of the strike. The MSG itself involved women who had full voting rights. It was felt from the start that the committee should not be amalgamated with the lodge. Hett felt that this might weaken the militancy of the group. He had experienced the frustration of 'entrenched moderation' when he was the lone voice of the left on the lodge before the strike. The MSG met regularly, and the occasions were often rowdy owing to the informal structures that were adopted. Wrexham Labour Party gave significant support, with local councillors playing a prominent role in fund-raising. Throughout the summer, the MSG operated successfully outside the lodge, though Hett still attended meetings. He felt that the officials were attempting to marginalize him because of his activity in the coalfield and his reputation as a Communist. The activists had almost no contact with McKay and, from the outset, had been highly critical of his role in attacking the leadership of Scargill. This represented something new in terms of the activity of the NUM locally. The union leadership in north Wales had always maintained tight control over the membership, and there had not been a recent rank-and-file mobilization.

Ann Hett focused on setting up a miners' wives support group that would act as another forum for discussion and a channel for receiving donations. Women soon were involved and visited the picket line at Point of Ayr where they were given a hostile reception. The Bersham women forged links with the women at Point of Ayr, who had been relatively isolated from the outset. This was an attempt to bring both sets of strikers together and was welcomed by the women. Both Point of Ayr and Bersham women attended the massive Women Against Pit Closures (WAPC) rally in Barnsley on 12 May 1984. In a speech at Gronant a week earlier, Scargill had pledged that he would pay for the coaches personally and called on them to keep up their

---

[59] *Evening Leader*, 1 May 1984.

picket at Point of Ayr.[60] Ann Hett had been a Labour Party member, trade union activist and experienced in local politics, so she was well versed in the issues at stake. A number of other women were certainly politicized by the dispute, but many remained hostile to attempts to involve them at a more overtly political level. For most women the whole dispute was about preserving a world they were losing, not the promotion of a world that would herald a new division of labour along feminist lines. The dispute was based around this defence of a working-class way of life which was being eroded by the excesses of Thatcherism.

Throughout the strike both men and women worked together and reported their activities in the *Bersham Star*, a newsletter which the MSG printed to keep sympathizers informed. A number of local groups were set up in Oswestry, Mold and Chester, providing a system of support for all those on strike.[61] The whole operation was a great success, and it was felt that the strike at Bersham could go on for some time, given its significant level of support. However, owing to the tensions between the constituent bodies of the union, it was apparent that an atmosphere of suspicion was bound to emerge. This later created ruptures in the solidarity of the strikers. The MSG and the lodge committee felt that McKay was still playing a duplicitous role. Williams wrote to the agent in order to question him about rumours that he was about to start a 'back to work' movement in the middle of October. McKay maintained that he would continue to represent those men who were still at work: 'Jim, you represent Bersham who are total in this dispute and can speak out for Bersham. I must represent the total viewpoint.'[62] In the same month, the lodge was adopting a more militant approach, withdrawing safety cover as a consequence of stockpiles of coal being moved from the old Hafod site. The management warned

[60]   A significant body of literature is building up on women and the strike. See Vicky Seddon (ed.), *The Cutting Edge: Women and the Pit Strike* (London, 1986); Lynn Beaton, *Shifting Horizons* (London, 1985); Jill Miller, *You Can't Kill the Spirit: Women in a Welsh Mining Valley* (London, 1986); Jean Stead, *Never the Same Again: Women and the Miners' Strike* (London, 1987).

[61]   *Bersham Star* (for striking miners and supporters), 1984: CRO Flintshire D/NM/1306.

[62]   Letter from Ted McKay to Jimmy Williams, 18 October 1984: NUM, Wrexham.

that this would lead to some rapid deterioration, especially with regard to the two main shafts.[63]

The first week in November saw the first men return at Bersham, a development that led to the opening of the floodgates with only sixteen members remaining on strike until March 1985.[64] Three surface workers broke ranks and entered the colliery; this led to an immediate walkout by members of COSA and NACODS. The lodge could see that this movement could escalate and immediately called a general meeting.[65] A proposal from the floor called for a ballot to gauge once again the opinion of the men. An amendment was also moved that pledged support for the strike to continue without such a vote. The proposal got 140 votes and the amendment 90; a ballot was organized for 8 November.[66] On the day of the ballot more strikers returned to work and the pit became a focus of media attention, with a large number of supporters hoping to lobby the lodge and enforce a positive vote for continued action.[67] Pickets from Point of Ayr, Leicestershire, Lancashire, south Wales and Durham flocked to the colliery, realizing that it would be a bad day for the strike if a previously solid pit returned. The vote went 154 to 145 in favour of staying out; the strikers were jubilant, but within days the strike crumbled as the majority returned. Alf Jones of the lodge committee was sad that the men were returning but claimed that they had been literally starved back through poverty.

Jimmy Williams knew that the strike was over despite the ballot result, and he wanted the men to go back together as they

---

[63] *Daily Post*, 25 October 1984.

[64] One young member of the strikers returned one week before the March return but did not receive any bad feeling from those that remained out. Interview with Keith Hett, August 1997.

[65] The return of Bersham miners occurred in the context of the NCB Western Area drive to tempt men back. A week earlier more men had returned in the neighbouring north Staffordshire coalfield giving the NCB the upper hand in the propaganda war. For details of the collapse of the strike in Staffordshire, see Roger Seifert and John Unwin, *Struggle without End: The 1984/85 Miners' Strike in North Staffordshire* (Newcastle under Lyme, 1988), pp.80–95.

[66] North Wales NUM minutes of special general meeting of Bersham lodge, 6 November 1984: CRO Flintshire D/NM/1212.

[67] Throughout the British coalfields, Bersham became a symbol of how far the strike enjoyed support when numbers returning to work were increasing. With the pit previously solid, developments in Wrexham had far-reaching implications for militant pits in other areas.

had all suffered together.[68] He was convinced that initiatives had been taken earlier, with McKay playing a role in advising small groups who wished to return.[69] Hett remained unrepentant and claimed that lack of leadership from the lodge and especially the agent had contributed to the collapse of the strike. He was convinced that both the lodge and the agent had wanted the strike to end, hoping that a ballot could be held earlier in order to initiate a return.[70] After the ballot result, Scargill came to Wrexham to rally those who were working to maintain the strike, but not even the passionate pleas of the president could prevent the collapse. During this period, McKay fled the area office, claiming that he had been intimidated when a noose was placed in the office window. The agent had also been receiving letters criticizing him for his role in the strike: many of an obscene nature and some, allegedly coming from the Liverpool Support Group, advising him to commit suicide. After the ballot result the office was occupied by Lancashire and Point of Ayr miners, though they were quickly advised against action because of the legal implications for those AEC members who remained on strike.

The remaining strikers carried on the dispute but found themselves isolated from the lodge. The MSG had to find new premises as they were moved from the area office, a decision that the strikers viewed as the final act of betrayal. The strikers called for the dismissal of the president, Raymond Ellis, because he was now crossing picket lines at Bersham. Ellis resisted requests to resign, claiming that he represented the majority of the men and not the sixteen who were still on strike. Now in self-imposed exile, McKay kept up his attacks on the NUM leadership, claiming that eventually it would have to listen to the membership and not just the activists. He warned that 'God will never forgive Arthur Scargill for what he had done to mining communities'. Once the bulk of the Bersham membership had returned and the majority in north Wales were back at work, he felt more confident in his attacks and McKay hit the headlines in response to Scargill's

---

[68] The case of Bersham again highlights the strength of localism in mining communities. The miners who returned paid little attention to the broader picture, and many felt as if they were no longer strike-breakers. To some, the fight had been a local one; Bersham had given its best shot and now reluctantly admitted defeat.
[69] Jimmy Williams, Interview, August 1997.
[70] Keith Hett, Interview, August 1997.

claim that Bersham would close, stressing that 'the future of Bersham will not be settled by shouting political slogans from a platform'.[71]

The new situation at Bersham had implications for the constitutionality of the strike in north Wales. The AEC met on 19 November to discuss the issue and there was a heated debate between the Bersham officials who had returned to work and Point of Ayr representatives who were still committed to the strike. It was decided that, in view of the situation, the AEC would have to inform the NEC that it could no longer give a commitment to industrial action under rule 41. It was also agreed that a letter of complaint should be sent to Heathfield concerning the absence of the agent from his duties. One of the trustees, Percy Jones, was approached to play a caretaker role in order to allow the union to continue to function adequately.[72] The strikers at Point of Ayr remained out and Les Kelly informed the national union that the position at his pit remained unchanged. The collapse of support for the strike at Bersham did not lead to bitterness within the workforce as between those who had returned and those who had remained on the picket line. In fact, the men working at Bersham still referred to the men at Point of Ayr as 'scabs' and felt that they had given their all in being on strike for eight months. Fifteen miners remained on strike until the end and returned after 5 March – the last miners in Wales to end the strike.

The case of Bersham is an interesting one in terms of the relationship between union leaders, the wider membership and the broader structure of NUM area politics. From the outset, the lodge was indecisive owing to the lack of direction that would normally have come from a national ballot before strike action. The parochialism of the lodge had not prepared the members for autonomous political action, as strikes at the pit were a relatively rare occurrence. The activities of McKay did not help and the elected officials found that events, both locally and nationally, were rapidly overtaking them. Only one member, Keith Hett, had the experience of militant trade unionism and he, almost on

---

[71] *Daily Post*, 23 November 1984. McKay had earlier condemned Scargill for the acceptance of money from Libya in the wake of the murder of Police Constable Yvonne Fletcher.
[72] North Wales NUM minutes of AEC, 19 November 1984: CRO Flintshire D/NM/1133.

his own initiative, organized the MSG that became a more dominant force than the lodge. The membership felt comfortable with this form of organization but, as the strike dragged on, many looked to the familiar formality of the lodge as a way out of the deadlock. With the holding of the November ballot, the bulk of the men returned and Hett and the other strikers became isolated. Initiatives had swung back to the elected officials, and they were firmly in the driving seat once the men were back in work.

Once the strike was over, the atmosphere at the colliery reverted to the pre-strike climate of joviality and comradeship, and the sense was widespread that all had contributed to the fight, though some more than others. The story was very different at Point of Ayr, where, from the outset, unity was completely absent and a striking minority faced a hostile environment. An important difference with the Point of Ayr strikers was that there the lodge was able to direct the action and remained committed to the struggle for the full twelve months. Nonetheless, attempts at rank-and-file organization and autonomy were apparent, and the Trotskyist groups, Workers Revolutionary Party (WRP) and Militant, played a part in pushing for a more concerted effort in mobilizing rank-and-file militancy.

THE STRIKE AT POINT OF AYR

Point of Ayr had been the most successful colliery in north Wales for a number of years and investment was focused on developing reserves for the future. From the 1960s through to the late 1970s, the NCB had difficulty with local recruitment owing to competition from British Steel at Shotton and the Courtaulds plants in Greenfield and Flint. Thus, the pit developed a cosmopolitan workforce, including the contingent of around thirty miners who had moved from Burnley in 1983. The lodge was of a similar political complexion to that of Bersham, but there was a growing level of dissent focused on the leadership of McKay from about 1981 onwards. No Communists worked at the pit, though the Burnley men and a small number of the indigenous workers were acknowledged militants. Other strong individual characters had knowledge of the trade union movement and took an interest in political affairs. These anti-strike activists were to form the nucleus of the working miners who had been able to gain support for their impassioned pleas at a series of meetings that preceded the strike in 1984.

From 1981 onwards, tensions had been raised at the pit owing to numerous visits by south Wales miners, though, at this time, relations were not as bad as they would later become. Some of those who remained on strike for twelve months point out that several of those who established the breakaway at the pit often spoke in favour of the stance that the south was taking. It is clear that an aversion to the strike was not inevitable, even after the area ballot result against such a course of action. Paul Parry remembers that communications between the AEC, the lodge and the wider membership were poor.[73] Depending on the nature of the picket, the strikers were successful on some shifts in the early stages. Problems were more evident when outside groups became involved and antagonism spread throughout the union. As at Bersham, some members sought to bypass the lodge, causing resentment between the committee and the activists. This did not go as far as Bersham, as the lodge was able to establish unity by giving total support to the striking minority through to 1985.

At the end of the first month of the strike, the pickets at the pit gained a substantial advantage when the T&GWU members driving the Crosville buses refused to go through the picket lines. The workers then had to face the indignity of walking through the line and down the long colliery road with their heads down, but this did not alter their attitudes. They were also aided by McKay who, although stressing his support for the strikers, backed the claims of those working for a national ballot. He also went out of his way to condemn outside bodies on the picket line and criticized the NUM leadership for siding with those who were already on strike.[74]

The police presence at the pit was crucial in keeping the pit working, especially as the strike at Bersham was solid. A number of plain-clothes officers were used to infiltrate the pickets at the pit, a tactic justified by chief constable David Owen as the best

---

[73] Interview with Paul Parry, Point of Ayr miner, August 1997.

[74] *Rhyl Journal*, 29 March 1984. McKay warned NUPE that they should desist from sending more of their members to the pit and that they should stay out of the affairs of the NUM in north Wales.

way of catching members committing offences.[75] Ironically, the colliery saw little violence, and north Wales generally was trouble-free. Miners from Bersham attended the picket line but were largely unsuccessful in attempting to promote north Walian solidarity. The lodge itself, and especially Les Kelly, came under increasing criticism from those who continued to work, and certain members argued that it should be representing the majority. Kelly invited Scargill to address the membership at Gronant in order to try to bolster support, but this seemed to have little effect on those crossing picket lines.[76] Scargill claimed that the dispute would be over in weeks if Point of Ayr and Nottinghamshire joined the action.[77]

The problem with the meetings and rallies that were held once the strike was under way was that the speakers were preaching to the converted. The meeting at Gronant gave impetus to those on strike and to the wider labour movement in the region, but it did little to get the message across to those in work. In fact, the men still working were receiving mixed messages in the crucial early weeks of the strike: one from the lodge urging support and one from McKay arguing for unity through a national ballot and respect for the area vote. This was read as a justification for those crossing picket lines.[78] Within two months, the working miners began to organize themselves, though no more than half a dozen were actually involved in pressing for the injunction against the lodge officials. They released a number of press statements and leaflets justifying their course of action. Most of these were compiled by the troika of Jim McKay, John Harper and Ken Payne, who were to go on to lead the moves for the break from the NUM in 1986. The forthright nature of their pronouncements exposed the fragility of trade union unity. In a powerful statement to the press and the membership in May 1984, they expressed their view of the action being taken:

> If there are those in North Wales who do not have the courage to stand and fight for democracy and the right to participate in our union and

---

[75] *Evening Leader*, 10 April 1984.
[76] *Prestatyn Visitor*, 10 May 1984.
[77] *Daily Post*, 7 May 1984.
[78] Outside influence was having a dramatic impact at the pit. In the crucial early weeks of the strike, the picket line was dominated by people not associated with the union. This provoked a counter-solidarity whereby working miners collectively rejected the pleas of strike supporters from Liverpool and other towns.

cannot look intimidators in the eye, let them slink off to the South Wales Area, where their officials have openly said that the day of the ballot box is over.[79]

The question of the ballot was also troubling some of the lodge members who were committed to the struggle. Elwyn Williams had initially argued for a national ballot but refused to cross the picket line for the duration of the strike. The more militant activists were critical of the pragmatism of the lodge and there was an early call for the resignation of the chairman, Les Hughes, who remained on strike but declined to play an active role. A small core of activists thought that the lodge was not doing enough to forge a more resolute commitment to the use of the mass picket.[80] The lodge itself was trying to come to terms with a rapidly worsening situation as the strike continued with only around 100 members in support at the pit. Furthermore, Les Kelly and the delegate Vic Roberts were busy trying to secure help for the strikers from the wider movement and working to pull the area in a particular direction which might minimize McKay's criticism of the national leadership. The officials had enough problems with those who were working; they did not want a further division amongst those who were meant to be committed to the actions of the union. At the same time the police were continually aiming to frustrate the effectiveness of picketing, and two coaches from Liverpool at the end of June were turned back from the pit at Bagillt six miles away, even though they contained a Euro-MP and a number of city councillors.[81]

Local Labour activists pledged support, but particular branches were in a delicate position, as some contained party officials and councillors who were continuing to work. Barry Jones, Labour MP for Alyn and Deeside, found that the situation at the pit was used against him when he called for government intervention to end the dispute. The Welsh secretary, Nicholas Edwards, replied to Jones and expressed the fragility of solidarity in some of the coalfields: 'the most decisive intervention is being

[79] Printed statement by working miners of Point of Ayr, May 1984: CRO Flintshire D/NM/1514.

[80] Discussion with Paul Winter, a Point of Ayr striking miner, August 1997.

[81] *Daily Post*, 22 June 1984.

provided by miners in your part of Wales. I am glad to see an increasing number at work there.'[82] The situation at the pit certainly impeded the role of the constituency Labour parties, leaving a vacuum that was only partially filled by the revolutionary left. From the outset, the WRP and Militant sent full-time organizers into the coalfield to recruit members amongst the strikers.[83] Once at Point of Ayr, they became regular features on the picket line. Three miners joined the WRP, and a branch of the Young Socialists (WRP) was set up in Rhyl. Point of Ayr featured prominently in the party newspaper, and WRP leaders such as the Redgraves attended strike meetings in Prestatyn. The strikers were glad to see as much support as possible because of their isolation and welcomed the fund-raising activities of the party. However, they remained unconvinced by WRP politics, and miners who joined quickly became disillusioned.

Militant had a similar impact on the strikers. They provided food and donations but were unable to recruit more than one member. The entryist sect had no base in north Wales despite its proximity to Liverpool, where the group had significant support. Most members of the union saw them as a pest and became increasingly critical of the role that they were playing in the dispute. Again, the language of revolution fell on deaf ears as the pragmatic strikers continued to view the dispute through the traditional lens of Labourist politics. They regarded their trade union as a vehicle for forcing economic and political change on a particular government, but not one that reached beyond a commitment to parliamentary politics.[84] The perceptions of both sides in the dispute at Point of Ayr were coloured by the depth of Labourist hegemony. Both strikers and workers could use the rhetoric of trade union democracy to justify their respective positions. No shift away from a commitment to Labour occurred amongst the miners at any stage in the strike, though some wanted more support from the leadership of Kinnock and Hattersley. The revolutionary left, once again, misjudged the

---

[82] *Rhyl Journal*, 28 June 1984.

[83] Most members of the WRP and Militant did not even know where the pit was as the left had never had a base in north Wales; they arrived in Wrexham and were informed by Keith Hett that they were at the wrong pit.

[84] This view was shared by both strikers and workers and proved difficult for the revolutionary left to grasp. Both the WRP and Militant merely dismissed Labourism as a process of 'false consciousness'.

politics of the dispute in that it was primarily defer
wholly devoid of any radical political objectives.

The management at Point of Ayr took a less sympat   ___.
compared with their counterparts at Bersham. They continued
to publish an information sheet, *Point of Ayr Pioneer*, which kept
workers informed of the situation at other pits and stressed that
the strike was not having the effect that the union claimed. Once
the injunction had been served on the lodge from Harper,
McKay and Kenny, the move gained the support of the management. The *Pioneer* claimed that this was also happening in Lancashire, Staffordshire, the Midlands and south Derbyshire.[85] The
strikers hoped to counteract this with the work of the support
groups. Committees were set up in Flint, Connah's Quay,
Queensferry and Rhyl. Members raised funds in Liverpool,
London, Ireland and, through a regular pub collection, in the
Deeside area.

The women's support group at the pit was quickly organized
and was to play a prominent role in the strike both nationally
and locally. After the initial rally, when Scargill spoke at
Gronant, the group was set up with Lynne Cheetham as chair,
Sue Sutcliffe as secretary and Heather Parry as treasurer. Initial
problems occurred because the women did not really know each
other owing to the geographical distance between the various
villages that provided the pit with labour. The majority of the
wives had husbands in work, and hence local initiatives seemed
futile to some. The group operated for fund-raising in Liverpool,
where trade unionists sent regular food parcels to the coalfield.
Cheetham travelled to Brussels to address the European Parliament and Parry spoke at the Plaid Cymru conference in the
same year.[86] The women quickly became politicized and were
angered at the stance of the TUC and those who continued to
work. However, this did not represent a shift towards feminist
politics. Once again there was an appreciation of the work that
the left was doing but there was still an aversion to what seemed
to be an alien political culture.

For some women, even the formal organization of a women's
group seemed to be a significant leap into the unknown, away

[85] *Point of Ayr Pioneer*, 3 (July 1984): NUM, Wrexham.
[86] Notes from an unpublished essay by Heather Parry, 'Women and the strike': Paul
Parry collection.

from their traditional lifestyle. A number of wives stayed home as much as possible, owing to the fact that they had lost friends because of the situation at the pit. One woman interviewed claims that most women in her village ignored her until the strike was over. Another striker's wife was reported by a neighbour for working in the local post office while claiming benefit to supplement the family income.[87]

Some writing on the dispute has overplayed the change in the role of women. Penny Green claims that their involvement 'broke down traditional notions of the "women's place" in a very traditional community'.[88] In fact, many women did not take part in activities that had a perceived political dimension. Most were content to support the strike in traditional ways that reflected the dominant division of labour in the mining family. This is not to suggest that women were content in the home, as for many years most miners' wives had had to work to supplement the family income and many were themselves trade unionists. But for many women in the villages, familiar experiences remained apparent – infidelity, divorce, domestic violence. This was situated in a working-class culture that generally meant more freedom for the male and a restricted sphere of domesticity for the female. Nonetheless, the support of the women informally and formally in terms of organization was to be one of the main factors in ensuring that the strike lasted so long.

Six months into the strike it was obvious to all those concerned that the 600 workers at Point of Ayr would continue to cross the picket line. John Mannion, a rank-and-file activist, thought this was down to the fact that the pit had always been moderate. Mannion was to become a thorn in the side of the lodge, playing a similar role to that of Keith Hett at Bersham in directing the strike away from the control of the officials. Mannion ran the strike office in the NUPE building in Rhyl and stated to the press that 'the level of support locally for the strike was disgusting, which was not surprising, as it was a Tory constituency'. Strikers and supporters had already criticized the ban placed on them for making collections at Theatre Clwyd and in Mold town centre.[89]

[87] Interview with a Point of Ayr striking miner's wife, May 1997.
[88] Penny Green, *The Enemy Without: Policing and Class Consciousness in the Miners' Strike* (Buckingham, 1990), p.189.
[89] *Chester Chronicle*, 15 February 1985.

The colliery was now being referred to as the 'Point of Shame' by local trade unionists, and the strikers totalled fewer than 100 as Christmas approached. The role of Mannion and others was causing concern for the lodge as it was aware of the events in Wrexham where the officials were playing a secondary role to the MSG. The revolutionary left had instilled in the minds of a small number of strikers that 'bureaucracy' was bad and they became critics of the officials. However, the lodge was able to maintain its credibility owing to the work that it was doing in relieving distress. Mel Williams was delivering the food parcels, Les Kelly was negotiating with the building societies to prevent strikers losing their homes, and Vic Roberts was fund-raising with the members on Merseyside. The behind-the-scenes work of the lodge was immense, and almost all its members carried out their duties under pressure from a large majority who continued to break the strike. To make matters worse, there was a small, determined group aiming to overthrow the officials and to elect working miners.

With the lodge officials constrained by the injunction, they pressed McKay to play a more active role. A delegate at the AEC strongly criticized the agent for his continuing attacks on Scargill in the local press.[90] The committee also dismissed his claims of intimidation and stressed that the agent's view of the events concerning the occupation of the headquarters by strikers was inaccurate. The lodge felt that they had no NEC representation as McKay had gone into hiding and could not be contacted. Kelly wrote to the agent asking him to clarify his position on the strike. In his reply, McKay stressed that he had always stood by the decisions of the area but that he had never made it a secret that a national strike under rule 41 was a mistake.

> As far as North Wales is concerned your Lodge know what the position is. We had a secret Area ballot to take strike action in support of Yorkshire and Scotland which was defeated. After the National Special Conference which supported strike action under Rule 41 we applied to have an Area strike under that Rule. Members of this Area subsequently applied to have this decision overturned, and were successful in that action.[91]

[90] North Wales NUM minutes of AEC, 21 December 1984: CRO Flintshire D/NM/1133.
[91] Letter from Les Kelly to Ted McKay and reply, 28 November 1984: Les Kelly collection.

Throughout the strike, McKay had been receiving letters concerning the Point of Ayr lodge. The pressure intensified after the committee postponed elections because of the general situation in the coalfield. One letter alleged that the strikers were out to 'get' the agent because of his criticisms of Scargill: 'I guess you already know that the Lodge is gunning for you so take care.' Another personal letter from a working miner stated: 'I am fed up at commies from Shotton, Chester and Rhyl running our Lodge and our Lodge agreeing with them.'[92] Throughout the strike the lodge continued to hold meetings open to all members, but normally only a few working miners attended. At a special general meeting on 9 December 1984, those present reiterated their commitment to the strike and vowed to fight on irrespective of Bersham.

> We recognise that there is some deep dissatisfaction as to the manner in which the strike developed. But because of the Lodge Committee's awareness of the issues and the repercussions of the NCB closure programme and its effects on thousands of jobs of our colleagues in other Areas, the Lodge Committee had no alternative, because of our principles – but to follow our instincts, and take action we are currently involved in.[93]

After the failure of the proposed NACODS action in October 1984, the climate at Point of Ayr was one of demoralization; this was compounded in November when the great majority of Bersham strikers returned. Eighty-three Point of Ayr miners remained out until the end of the dispute in March 1985 and the return to work was difficult, the strikers being jeered as they approached the colliery. Unlike in other coalfields, there was no colliery band to lead the Point of Ayr men back. The strikers were divided across different shifts. A number of men never wanted to return owing to their feeling of immense disappointment. Two members, Alan Jones and Eddie O'Grady, could not accept the way that the manager and others treated them in the initial meeting and promptly turned round and walked back down the pit road. Both miners had played a significant role in the strike, and the strength of their convictions led them to refuse the redundancy pay on offer.

---

[92] Letters to Ted McKay, December 1984: CRO Flintshire D/NM/1513.
[93] NUM Point of Ayr minutes of lodge committee, special annual general meeting, 9 December 1984: NUM, Wrexham.

Paul Parry and John Alan Jones, two Point of Ayr strikers, had been aware of the moves in south Wales in arguing for a return to work without an agreement, for they had been in the coalfield when the proposal was under discussion. They were both opposed to returning without an agreement but acknowledged that, nationally, the strike was over.[94] The lodge officials had proved to be adept in handling the delicate situation and maintained their positions, and no members were sacked as a result of the dispute. Lodge members quickly settled back into the everyday pattern of union business but soon found that they had a further problem owing to the formation of the breakaway Union of Democratic Mineworkers (UDM).

DEFEAT AND DEMORALIZATION

As in 1926, the organization of a breakaway originated in the Nottinghamshire coalfield, where the majority of the miners had worked throughout the dispute. The anti-strike delegates from the coalfield were bolstered in their actions by the announcement that the NCB would now recognize any organization that was formed, irrespective of the wishes of the NUM. At the grassroots level, the right-wing businessman David Hart had financially supported strike-breakers and paid for representatives to tour the coalfields in order to undermine support for Scargill. In July 1985, the Nottinghamshire Area voted to leave the national union and the UDM was officially established the following October, seeking recruits in all coalfields.[95]

At Point of Ayr, a group of working miners emerged led by John Harper, Norman Walker and several others. This group became the representatives of those who had rejected the call for

---

[94] Interviews with around thirty strikers indicate that many retained mixed emotions about the strike. Most had no regrets about taking action. Some felt the strike should have ended in November and some remained critical of the eventual return without a settlement.

[95] There is some debate as to whether the Nottinghamshire miners jumped or were pushed. Some argue that the proposed rule changes that the NUM was seeking to implement in 1985 placed officials of working areas in a difficult position with regard to the wishes of the rank and file in their own coalfields. The Nottinghamshire delegation faced hostility at the annual conference in July. On returning to Nottinghamshire, delegates voted by 228 to 20 to leave the NUM. In October, Leicestershire, south Derbyshire and Nottinghamshire voted on whether to form a new union. south Derbyshire voted narrowly in favour but Leicestershire voted against the breakaway.

a strike. It is unlikely that, in the middle of the strike, they had plans for a break with the NUM. The injunction was expected to have been enough to facilitate the transfer of power from the lodge to a new group of officials who would take over once the strike ended. After the success of the injunction, the working miners' leadership focused on the annual general meeting of the lodge in December, which the officials were required to hold in order to take nominations for elections to the committee. They planned to pack this meeting with working miners in order to overthrow the existing members, thus further legitimizing the position that they were taking with regard to the constitutional nature of the dispute.

The lodge was aware of this move and announced that, because of the divisions, it would be unwise to hold elections, and that these would be postponed for six months.[96] Harper and Jim McKay were furious at what they saw as another attempt to curtail the democratic processes that had previously existed in the union. The lodge officials contacted Ted McKay, but he felt that it was a matter for Point of Ayr to sort out and gave them no advice or support. Ironically, the lodge had consulted working miners, and 240 members turned up at the meeting. A vote of confidence in the position of the lodge was passed by 140 to 96. From this stage onwards, it seemed likely that there would be a break with the NUM if similar moves were made in other coalfields. The north Wales men met miners from other pits, and when the return to work was announced in March 1985, they again focused on transforming the lodge, which was still dominated by strikers. However, most of those who had worked through the strike re-elected the existing officials, which came as a great surprise to Harper, Jim McKay and their close associates. Those who had refused to strike wanted to forget the whole episode and were averse to getting involved with the political wrangling in the union.

Once the Nottinghamshire leaders had decided in mid-1985 to set up the UDM, the hard core of those in favour of splitting the union in north Wales had another chance to test the opinions of the workers. A number of men put their energies into

[96] North Wales NUM minutes of Point of Ayr special annual general meeting, 9 December 1984: NUM, Wrexham.

investigating the possibility of a breakaway at Bersham, though it was thought to be imperative to establish an initial base at Point of Ayr. Both lodges and the AEC sought to prevent this action by campaigning for unity. Ted McKay criticized the NUM leadership, but pleaded with the men to stay in the union. He may have been aware of the insecurity of his position, especially if a moderate section of the workforce was to split with the NUM, leaving it in the hands of the strikers.

> Decisions at national level, attitudes during the dispute, ill thought out tactics etc. All these have had a detrimental effect on the NUM. But we cannot keep looking back, we must now try to put the dispute firmly behind us . . . the North Wales leadership (including both Lodge Committees) completely disassociate themselves from any irresponsible acts by groups or individuals.[97]

Strikers at Point of Ayr were aware that such a move by the UDM to organize in the coalfield would lead to disaster as it was the biggest pit, thus guaranteeing negotiating rights with the NCB to the breakaway.[98] The only way out of this was to play the promoters of the split at their own game and use the argument of the ballot box. To make a positive vote for unity more likely, the AEC agreed to a series of rule changes which emphasized the need for a coalfield ballot before any strike action was taken that would be binding on all members. The first ballot went ahead in December 1985 and Bersham members voted to stay in the NUM by 327 to 43. Two months later the crucial Point of Ayr ballot was held and the membership voted for unity by 498 to 63. In analysing the outcome of this result, it is clear that only a minority had been vocal in proposing a breakaway. From the end of the strike through to 1992, strikers continued to be voted onto the lodge and Les Kelly and Vic Roberts remained secure. They faced a greater struggle against members in the ranks of the strikers, as around half a dozen escalated their criticisms of the union leadership from 1986 onwards.

[97] North Wales NUM leaflet by Ted McKay, December 1985: NUM, Wrexham.
[98] After the strike, the NCB granted negotiating rights to the largest union in each coalfield. In Nottingham, rights went to the UDM, and the NUM wanted to avoid a similar situation arising in north Wales.

For Jim McKay, Norman Walker, John Harper and Ken Payne the battle was still not lost. They were not prisoners of the ballot box as they had claimed in 1984. Despite the ballot result for unity and the wishes of the membership to remain in the NUM, they busily worked to construct a branch of the UDM. In December 1985, they claimed that 200 had applied for UDM cards.[99] Their initial projections seemed way off the mark, since only around seventy people attended the first meeting of the branch. Norman Walker had initial success in terms of surface recruitment, but there was little support underground where work relations were slowly getting back to normal. The national leadership of the UDM spoke at Gronant in a further attempt to promote membership but, as in Lancashire, the north Wales coalfield failed to be convinced of the need for a new organization to represent miners.[100] By mid-March 1986, the UDM North Wales president, Norman Walker, rejected allegations that the union was crumbling, though he did admit that the membership had fallen from 150 to 67.[101] In the same month, Ted McKay reported to the NEC that UDM membership at Point of Ayr was now below fifty.

In terms of the politics of the UDM in north Wales, there was still clearly a Labourist tinge to the 'business unionism' of the leadership. Most of the hard core remained Labour voters and campaigned accordingly in the 1987 general election. John Harper went on to be an organizer for one of the anti-poll tax groups in the area. The politics of the 500 or so who had broken the strike remained static and they moved neither left nor right as a result of the traumatic twelve months. This was also the case with the strikers, who remained committed to the Labour leadership of Kinnock and Hattersley, whom the lodge continued to nominate for leadership positions. The few who had become involved in the politics of the 'far left' repeatedly voiced their concerns, expressing disquiet at the role that the lodge was playing in trying to promote the election of a number of non-strikers to the committee. The UDM retained a rump branch after 1987 though it continually lost members. This was largely due to the number of miners who were opting to finish on

[99] *Prestatyn Visitor*, 12 December 1985.
[100] *Rhyl Journal*, 22 January 1986.
[101] *Prestatyn Visitor*, 13 March 1986.

redundancy terms, with new recruits overwhelmingly joining the NUM.

Defeat intensified divisions on the NUM NEC. A process of de-alignment occurred as the traditional left/right factions became increasingly blurred. First, there was the facilitation of the breakaway in a number of coalfields. Secondly, there was the complete intransigence of the officials in their articulation of a policy for preventing such a split. The rules revision conference of 1985 was crucial in that it codified the aversion of the union to the situation in Nottinghamshire and lacked any sense of conciliation. Thirdly, the left caucus began to disintegrate and one section realigned itself alongside some areas that had questioned its politics in the pre-strike period. Both south Wales and Scotland moved away from Scargill's leadership, articulating criticisms of his position on industrial relations and the question of the breakaway.

Officials in south Wales became increasingly hostile to the direction that the strike was taking at the behest of the national officials. The South Wales Area in the last quarter of the strike had been pursuing an autonomous path to develop its own strategy.[102] At the rules revision conference, they opposed the proposal that would allow the NEC to call other federated areas out on strike. The eventual detachment of Nottinghamshire or, at least, of the greater part of it, had a further impact on the politics of the NEC. The exodus of members from a traditionally moderate coalfield undermined the strength of what was left of the old-style moderates. Fissures even began to appear in the leadership troika of Scargill, Heathfield and McGahey.[103]

In north Wales the factionalism of the national union contaminated area politics. Two months before the end of the strike the NEC discussed future organization. It was felt that north Wales should amalgamate with Lancashire to become the NUM western division with an office based in Bolton.[104] McKay once more resisted this with the backing of the AEC. However, the agent was having problems in his own coalfield, as moves were

[102] Interview with Kim Howells MP, former research officer of the NUM South Wales, January 1995.
[103] McGahey raised criticisms of Scargill at the Lancashire miners' annual conference in 1987 over the issue of flexible working. See Howell, *The Politics of the NUM*, p.206.
[104] NUM Minutes of NEC, 10 January 1985: NUM, Wrexham.

afoot amongst the Point of Ayr membership to displace him from his seat on the NEC. It was decided to propose Elwyn Williams for the position. Williams had been on strike but was not seen as one of the prominent leaders: this would help in garnering support from those who had resisted the strike call. Amazingly, once this was leaked to the press he was described as a left-wing Marxist who was seeking to push the north Wales union towards a closer relationship with Yorkshire. Williams was far from being on the left and was merely a Labour loyalist who had never been associated with other organizations. He wanted a more resolute approach to the ongoing problem of pit closures and the plight of sacked miners. The north Wales rulebook quickly halted the move by the Point of Ayr lodge and the area president ruled – wrongly – that the move was out of order.[105]

While the politics of the union both nationally and locally were in a state of flux, the coalfield was delivered a further devastating blow when it was announced that Bersham would close. Men would be offered transfers to Point of Ayr and the pit would cease production in March 1987.[106] In order to protect the maximum redundancy payments of the miners, there was no fight to oppose the closure, with only the indefatigable Keith Hett a voice of opposition in the wilderness. The Bersham lodge wanted as many men as possible to transfer to Point of Ayr. Around sixty members moved and quickly settled in, as there were already a number of Wrexham miners from Gresford, Hafod and Ifton. Many renewed old friendships and found the transition relatively smooth. The biggest obstacle was the settlement of the families. A number of Bersham miners moved to Prestatyn and various villages surrounding the pit but the majority moved back to Wrexham because their families could not adjust.

Two coaches of Wrexham miners now complemented the workforce at the colliery, bringing miners from Chirk, Rhos, Gwersyllt and Llay. Some miners found that they had to rise at three-thirty in the morning in order to make it for the early shift at six. None of the transferees involved themselves in the politics of the union and many were totally demoralized due to the scale

[105] *Daily Post*, 22 April 1985.
[106] North Wales NUM minutes of AEC, 19 May 1986: CRO Flintshire D/NM/1483.

of the recent defeat. Keith Hett was one of the last to leave Bersham, but on arrival at Point of Ayr he quickly carried on his educative duties in encouraging the sale of the *Morning Star* and the distribution of the *Miner*. He steadily built up a small left-wing grouping based on a number of young trainees. The group consisted of mainly Labour left activists and a CP presence that carried on the arguments for socialism and militancy at the point of production.

More than a year after the dispute, the climate at the pit was returning to pre-strike joviality, thus expressing a fragile unity. There had been initial tensions on both sides between strikers and workers. One unrepentant striker quickly vetted new trainees to find out if their fathers had 'scabbed' and refused to associate with them if the answer was positive. John Alan Jones, a lodge member, faced a barrage of hostility owing to his fund-raising trips to Ireland during the strike. Underground a number of slogans were daubed on mine cars and roadways associating him with Irish terrorism. At a general meeting where he raised a point, someone shouted that he should 'get back to the IRA'.[107] The lodge retained its pro-strike balance throughout the succeeding years. The greatest divisions were to come when the UDM established its branch at the pit. The bulk of the miners who had worked through the strike surprisingly expressed bitterness at the breakaway. In a number of districts, UDM members were attacked and a war of words between the two sides appeared on roadways underground.

This raises the important issue of the perceptions of strikers and workers. The dispute had thrown up a third group towards whom animosity could be directed. The pit had around fifty members of the UDM, about the same number who had stayed out at Bersham until November, and around seventy members who had been solid at Point of Ayr. It is surprising that this did not lead to an explosion of hostility and violence and an unworkable environment underground. Surprisingly, the pattern of camaraderie and occupational unity persisted, though this did not fully extend to the leaders of the UDM. Workers and strikers

---

[107] *Chester Chronicle*, 19 April 1985.

continued to socialize together and maintained an acceptable relationship in the workplace.[108]

With the closure of Bersham, the north Wales coalfield consisted of one pit, forcing further changes on the union. The AEC agreed that the area structure should now consist only of three senior officials and the three trustees.[109] On 16 February 1987, the union bade farewell to the Bersham delegation. This was quickly followed by the announcement that Ted McKay was to take voluntary redundancy from the NUM to become an employee of British Coal. In his last address he criticized the role that the union was taking in respect of the UDM: ' I pray that the NUM will not have to wait too long for the men big enough to make small decisions needed to bring unity to all miners.'[110] In his pronouncements to the press, he claimed that Scargill could not see him go quickly enough. McKay accused the president of being 'a Walter Mitty type character who had let the miners down and used the union to boost his own ego'. He felt that the failure to hold a ballot was the reason why the strike was lost and why the union was now divided.[111]

In a complete turnaround, McKay praised his old adversaries in south Wales for their attacks on the president and added that the future of the union was dependent on their leadership.[112] Kim Howells, who was sorry to see McKay go, stressed that the union would be the poorer.[113] The *Evening Leader* also praised McKay: 'he may not be missed by Mr Scargill, but he certainly would be by rank and file members.'[114] McKay had failed to play a coherent role throughout the twelve months of the dispute and found himself the villain in a Greek tragedy since all sides remained critical of his approach. Even after his retirement,

[108] The relationship between strikers, workers and UDM members exposes the difficulty in accounting for the nature of collective identity. Apart from the link of occupation and a loose commitment to Labour politics, identity was not static but was adaptable to changing circumstances. After the strike the collective identity of workers and strikers merged to construct UDM members as an 'outsider group'.
[109] North Wales NUM minutes of AEC, 12 January 1987: CRO Flintshire D/NM/1483.
[110] Last address by Ted McKay to the north Wales miners, 27 March 1987: CRO Flintshire D/NM/1483.
[111] *Daily Post*, 27 March 1987.
[112] *Western Mail*, 27 March 1987.
[113] Letter from Kim Howells to Ted McKay, 25 February 1987: CRO Flintshire D/NM/1195.
[114] *Evening Leader*, 27 March 1987.

there was opposition to moves to award him an honorarium of £10,000, a decision sanctioned by the Point of Ayr lodge. Underground he became known as 'Ten Grand Ted' and was regarded with contempt by those who had been committed to the strike.

Les Kelly replaced McKay as the NEC representative and it was felt by some that he would take on the former agent's right-wing mantle. Trevor Bell, a traditional moderate, was surprised when this did not occur since he was hoping to revive and unify resistance to Scargill.[115] The uncertainties within the NEC did not facilitate an effective union response to the post-strike onslaught by British Coal, which had adopted a more resolute approach to industrial relations. One major issue that they were hoping to promote was that of flexible working. Many miners saw this as a non-issue, since most were working a massive amount of overtime to supplement their income. Flexible working sparked controversy at successive NUM conferences, which usually divided between the views of the south Wales leadership and those close to Scargill. The issue came to a head when British Coal announced that the proposed development of the Margam super pit in south Wales was to be conditional on the acceptance of flexible working patterns. The south Wales delegation broke with the national union and agreed to discuss the issue in principle. On 7 March 1987, Des Dutfield, the area president, announced that the leadership in south Wales was willing to negotiate on a local basis. This issue also exposed the growing rift between Scargill and McGahey. At the Lancashire Area conference in 1987 McGahey claimed that 'what the Welsh miners have agreed to is a concept but not to any specific details of this concept'.[116] In an interview with *Marxism Today*, he also warned that the union could not leave the UDM to negotiate agreements for all British miners. The NUM was rapidly losing its credibility because of its refusal to sit with the breakaway in negotiations with British Coal. McGahey reminded the members that 'if you never move an inch, that is not a movement that's a

---

[115] Les Kelly was sceptical of any form of caucusing during this period when the union needed unity, not division. Interview with the author, May 1997.

[116] Lancashire NUM minutes of annual conference, 6–9 May 1987: David Howell collection.

monument'.[117] Scargill attacked this view and stressed that any attempt to negotiate alongside the breakaway would be a betrayal of NUM members in Nottinghamshire. At successive NUM conferences, the vote went against any moves to sit with the UDM, though north Wales normally voted with south Wales for a more pragmatic approach.

The union was also split over the overtime ban that was introduced in 1987 in response to a disciplinary code that the management had introduced after the strike. Under the code, a miner could be sacked for acts away from the workplace and for conducting political affairs on the property of British Coal.[118] In north Wales the ban was maintained, but the lodge was critical of its ineffectiveness and wanted the national union to call a halt to the action before the men started to turn their backs on the union.[119]

The major issue concerning the north Wales miners was the position of the UDM and the NUM's inability to negotiate on behalf of the members, unless they accepted the place of the breakaway at the negotiating table. Les Kelly saw this as highly damaging to the union. The issue caused ructions at successive conferences, but the pro-leadership majority was always able to secure a policy of not sitting with the breakaway, despite the problems that this caused in coalfields where the membership was split. The national union seemed to be locked in a dispute between pragmatism – advocated by north Wales, south Wales and Scotland – and principle – advocated by Yorkshire, Nottinghamshire and the north-east. Some felt that a challenge to the position of Scargill was the only way out of the impasse. This would give the membership a chance to voice their criticisms directly and hopefully to go some way towards reunifying the British miners, as they were becoming an endangered species owing to the rapid rate of colliery closures.[120]

The level of factionalism at the national level suggested that the leadership of Scargill could be in serious jeopardy. To

---

[117] *Marxism Today* (July 1987), 25.

[118] At some collieries in other coalfields, miners had been sacked for distributing copies of the *Miner* and Labour Party material.

[119] Interview with Les Kelly, May 1997.

[120] Between 1983 and 1990, the number of British pits fell from 170 to 73. More importantly, resistance to closure even at previously militant pits was minimal. *British Coal Annual Report*, 1993.

pre-empt the straitjacket of the Conservative trade union legislation, which would have forced the president to seek re-election,
he resigned in 1987, immediately announcing that he would be
standing again. The contest refocused attention on the politics
and perceptions of the British miners, with many commentators
relishing the prospect of a defeat for Scargill. The presidential
election campaign of 1988 was to raise debate within the
membership and provide some interesting insights into the
political consciousness of the miners at Point of Ayr. Both candidates for the position of president were from Yorkshire, but
representing two very different traditions in the union. John
Walsh, the challenger, wanted a quick return to the pre-strike
days of consensus. He saw himself in the mould of Joe Gormley,
negotiating primarily in terms of increasing wages and improving
conditions. In contrast, Scargill wanted to maintain a militant
approach to the UDM and pit closures.[121]

With the NEC already racked by tensions and its current
divisions, the areas that had been most vocal in opposition to
Scargill, particularly south Wales and Scotland, were unsure how
to respond. Certain members of the NEC thought that these
areas would put up a candidate, hoping to split what was
remaining of the left vote and carrying the rest, but ideological
divisions and alliances were difficult to assess. Walsh still had an
ambiguous relationship with south Wales. He remained bitter
about its support for Scargill in promoting national action under
rule 41 in 1984.[122] Les Kelly was sure that George Rees of south
Wales would stand; that might have led to a significant joint
approach in Wales which would have healed the rifts of the past.
But the Point of Ayr lodge had already nominated Scargill.
Walsh himself would have preferred an individual from south
Wales to stand, though Dutfield felt that the whole exercise was a
waste of money in a period of escalating crisis for the industry.[123]
Critics outside the NUM were quick to congratulate Walsh in
challenging Scargill. The bulk of the PLP were keen to see
Scargill ousted as he was regarded as a continuing electoral

---

[121] Scargill and his supporters referred to the strike in all their policy proposals. This
call for loyalty to the president relied on the threat of claims of betrayal that would be
directed at strike loyalists if they chose to act against the politics of Scargill.
[122] Interview with John Walsh, NUM Yorkshire, March 1995.
[123] Interview with Les Kelly, January 1995.

liability.[124] Neil Kinnock was quick to snipe at Scargill when unveiling a statue of Aneurin Bevan in Cardiff. When asked about Scargill and the election, he replied that he was meant to be answering questions on Bevan – 'a real socialist'.[125]

From the moment that nominations came in from the areas, it was evident that the odds favoured Scargill. Walsh only secured nominations from Leicestershire, COSA and the Power Group. Scargill secured Durham, Kent, the Midlands, North Wales, Lancashire, Cokemen's, Derbyshire, Northumberland, Nottinghamshire, South Derbyshire, Yorkshire and Power Group No 1.[126] Early predictions were that the result was going to be close but that Scargill would probably win. In fact, he claimed 54 per cent of the vote, with Walsh returning 46 per cent.[127] The election revealed a clear division within the NUM nationally and in each coalfield. The defeated Walsh claimed that 'the vote shows Mr Scargill has no mandate for his confrontational style. Since I was nominated by three Areas, and won in ten of them, some members of the NEC are not reflecting their members' views.'[128] This was the case in north Wales, where the lodge had nominated Scargill but the membership had favoured Walsh. However, Scargill secured a respectable 40 per cent of the vote at Point of Ayr, which shows that a number of miners who had worked through the strike favoured Scargill. The official leadership in north Wales did not explicitly campaign for Scargill; if they had, the vote might well have been higher.

The presidential election of 1988 clearly shows that the majority of miners still felt a loyalty to the leadership of Scargill, notably in south Wales where the officials had made no secret of their aversion to his policies. Miners across the coalfield confounded commentators by failing to endorse their critique of Scargill. There was, however, a problem with representation, as the nomination in particular coalfields did not reflect the voting patterns that showed support for Walsh. The outcome of the election proved that the miners were blessed with independent

[124] Interview with Kevin Barron MP, March 1995.
[125] *Guardian*, 17 November 1987.
[126] South Wales had been against the contest from the outset and decided against nominating a candidate. The South Wales Area was now firmly anti-Scargill but felt that any challenge would be a futile exercise.
[127] *Miner*, January 1988.
[128] *Coal News*, February 1988.

thought and loyalty to each other irrespective of the views of the media and other trade unions that were calling for the defeat of Scargill.

Three years after the dispute, in 1988, the north Wales miners concentrated at Point of Ayr continued to work hard in a hostile environment and maintained their commitment to the NUM. In the 1987 general election, they again voted heavily in favour of Labour, though the Conservatives continued to hold Delyn, to the dismay of the union.[129] The events of the twelve-month strike had not shattered the commitment that men had to the politics of Labourism, and recruitment to the party actually increased during this period. The fragile unity slowly strengthened, and miners worked hard to maintain a specific north Wales identity. The replacement of Ted McKay by Les Kelly went a long way towards developing this revised identity, and the area no longer vociferously promoted a 'right caucus' within the national union. In many ways, Kelly's leadership represented a return to the pre-Mackay days, but in a radically different context. Some younger miners became more active in the union, and the area maintained its presence at national demonstrations. The strike had been a body blow to most of those committed to the dispute, and for many it affected their perceptions of the Point of Ayr work-force for some time. Nevertheless, former strikers were to regain their activism in the next crisis that was to face the coalfield when John Major and the Conservatives won the general election of 1992 and privatization became a matter of practical politics.

---

[129] Labour Party membership increased in the workplace branch and in local branches that contained significant numbers of miners. These included Mostyn, Ffynnongroyw, Holywell and Prestatyn. (Membership details from Patrick Heesom collection.)

V

THE END OF AN ERA, 1989–1996

Thousands of ex-miners
Are drawing the dole,
People are dying, because
They can't afford coal.[1]

The defeat of the Labour Party in the 1987 general election intensified the fatalism of British miners concerning the future prospects for coal, as the Conservatives maintained their commitment to other sources of energy and to the privatization of electricity.[2] From the end of the strike in March 1985, the position of the coalfields had been further eroded as, week by week, increasing numbers of miners opted for redundancy whilst recruitment in the remaining pits was negligible. The 1990s were to witness the end of mining in north Wales with the closure of Point of Ayr in 1996 and the end of an era for the NUM in Denbighshire and Flintshire.

In the closing months of 1989, Point of Ayr experienced difficulties in terms of profitability, even though the number of workers had decreased and productivity had improved. British Coal progressively raised output targets and the climate on the surface and underground was one of permanent crisis and impending doom. Nonetheless, neither the management nor the trade unions felt that there was an immediate possibility of closure as development prospects were good in terms of future reserves and their extraction. The pit had been recently modernized with the opening of a state-of-the-art drift mine.[3]

On the national scale, developments were more worrying. In the five years since the strike ended, over one hundred pits had

---

[1] Extract from 'The price of coal' by Keith Hett, from *Bersham Pit Bottom and Other Poems* (private publication, 1986).
[2] For a critical analysis of Conservative plans for the privatization of the electricity industry and the devastating impact that this would have on coal, see Ben Fine, *The Coal Question: Political Economy and Industrial Change from the Nineteenth Century to the Present Day* (London, 1990), pp.143–72.
[3] *Rhyl Journal*, 6 July 1988.

closed, with the loss of over 100,000 jobs. The NUM had lost half its membership and was rapidly losing its wider influence in the TUC and the Labour Party.[4] Robert Haslam, who had replaced MacGregor as chairman of the NCB, stressed that further closures would go ahead as the market for coal continued to be squeezed. Arthur Scargill continued to peddle his consistent line of opposition to contraction by use of the strike weapon, though clearly the wider membership was in no mood for another fight.

In all areas of the NUM, an increasing number of activists continued to opt for redundancy rather than gamble on an uncertain future. In contrast, Scargill promoted a more up-beat view of the strength of the union: 'in 1990 we have more economic power in stopping one pit than we did stopping fifteen pits in 1984 because of the concentration of capital. I think it's time for miners to recognize their potential strength.'[5] In north Wales, the union officials were aware of the feelings of the membership and they trod a delicate line between accepting the decisions of the national union and being mindful of the pragmatism of the workforce. It was clear to Les Kelly and the president, Vic Roberts, that the union's refusal to negotiate with the UDM was harming its ability to campaign effectively for decent pay rises, as all pay deals were merely imposed on the NUM by British Coal.[6] Lodge officials attempted to involve the wider membership in the affairs of the union, but general meetings attracted only a handful of members beyond the lodge. Competition for lodge positions had also subsided, and Kelly was worried that it would be difficult to maintain a viable committee if the number of workers continued to fall.

Within the local labour movement, many felt that the pit had an uncertain future, and a local councillor, Barbara Roberts, announced in late 1989 that the pit would probably soon close. British Coal rejected this claim but stressed that the colliery would have to maintain its competitiveness in an increasingly hostile economic environment.[7] Major developments at the pit

[4] *Guardian*, 6 March 1990.
[5] *Guardian*, 23 May 1990.
[6] In response to the formation of the UDM, British Coal dissolved the 1946 conciliation scheme, extending recognition to the breakaway as part of a new joint scheme.
[7] *Daily Post*, 26 July 1989.

were now primarily geared towards a new system of mining using American techniques that would reduce further the number of workers. This move was to raise questions about health and safety, since miners would now be forced to work under roof bolts as a means of primary support in roadways and headings.[8] The end of 1992 saw the end of traditional coalface working at Point of Ayr much to the distress of the union. The 'continuous mining' machines which had been tested at Asfordby colliery in Leicestershire were to be used as the sole method of coal extraction. Les Kelly was adamant that this rapid conversion was not promising with regard to a long-term future, especially as the large development project in the giant North Seam had been abandoned as a costly exercise. The pit manager, Peter Redford, writing in *Coal News*, was clear that American methods were the only means of improving profitability: 'if we can't roof bolt it we won't mine it.'[9]

The incremental privatization of the industry was becoming a reality, although British Coal claimed the opposite. Between 1988 and 1990, Point of Ayr lost 150 jobs, with many of the positions being filled by outside contractors, some of them employed by RJB Mining which was to buy the bulk of the remaining industry under formal privatization.[10] This caused further tensions within the workforce, especially on the surface. A number of men had accepted redundancy on a particular Friday from British Coal and then accepted their jobs back with contractors on the following Monday. The union was powerless to stop this, but could recruit them into the membership, which they did. Vic Roberts attacked British Coal for seriously damaging the long-term future of the pit. The increased number of contractors reached embarrassing proportions and Roberts claimed: 'They [British Coal] were beginning to realize that they had in fact, let too many men go out of the industry and that this was having an adverse effect on the industry as a whole.'[11]

---

[8] Roof bolting was an experimental technique opposed by the NUM, who felt that the system was not suitable for the geological conditions of the British coalfields. Miners no longer had the security of metal supports and now had to rely on what appeared to be flimsy bolts that were inserted into the roof and sides of underground roadways.

[9] *Coal News*, December 1991.

[10] North Wales NUM minutes of annual delegate conference, 15 September 1990: NUM, Wrexham.

[11] North Wales NUM minutes of annual delegate conference, 18 May 1991: NUM, Wrexham.

At the monthly consultative meetings, representatives of all the trade unions pleaded with the management to recruit juveniles rather than rely on private companies. The utilization of contract labour was less expensive for British Coal as it could rely on outside companies to regulate the labour supply and dilute the effectiveness of the union at colliery level. Week after week, men as young as thirty were arranging interviews with the personnel manager to inquire whether redundancy would be available. The union was caught up in a pessimistic climate and could realistically only do a 'holding job' in keeping the membership on board. Once the American system of mining was in place, with the use of 'continuous miners', the workforce was slashed from over 600 in 1985 to fewer than 200 in 1994. When the north Wales delegate conference assembled in 1992 it was felt that Point of Ayr was now merely an experimental pit to be used as a testing ground for the rest of the industry.[12]

The structure of the north Wales union was maintained with an office and a place for the area on the NEC. Les Kelly had been voted on to the committee in 1987 and was asked by the national officials to run the area office on a lay basis. In 1989, Kelly was re-elected on a full-time basis, retaining the position in 1992. Rosemarie Williams was also re-employed as an administrative assistant. Williams had worked in the office since the late 1950s; she was advised wrongly that her position was being made redundant at the end of the McKay period. Both Kelly and Williams ensured that retired miners and the members at Point of Ayr continued to be adequately represented. The politics and the high drama of the pre-strike period and the tensions that had emerged during the dispute had almost disappeared, as it was felt that any day could bring the announcement of closure.

FACTIONALISM: LOCAL AND NATIONAL

The day after the 1987 general election an atmosphere of gloom descended on Point of Ayr. As miners sat in the canteen prior to the afternoon shift, many sipped their tea silently as it began to

---

[12] North Wales NUM minutes of annual delegate conference, 16 May 1992: NUM, Wrexham.

sink in that the Conservatives would have another five years to dilute the coal industry and the NUM in the process. The modernizing zeal of Neil Kinnock had not been enough to transform the massive Tory majority of 1983 into a victory for the Labour Party.[13] Miners on both sides of the fence in terms of their positions during the strike all felt that Kinnock was the best leader available and were critical of Scargill's attacks on him. There was some debate in 1988 when Tony Benn and Eric Heffer had challenged the leadership to a contest, but even Andy Hutchinson, who was seen as a Scargill loyalist, cast his vote for Kinnock at a general meeting.

The aftermath of the election led to a post-mortem as to why Labour lost, and the NUM in north Wales became embroiled in the internal politics of the Delyn Constituency Labour Party (DCLP) over the selection of a future parliamentary candidate. David Hanson, who did not come from an industrial background but had fought a good campaign in 1987, was touted as the best person by leading lights in the party.[14] On the whole there was support for the changes that Kinnock had made, particularly over the expulsion of Militant. Party activists at Point of Ayr were not identifiable in terms of previous support for, or aversion to, the strike. Some strikers could loosely be defined as on the right of the party and some of those who had worked were more sympathetic to the left. This raised tensions in the workplace branch that could not easily be located on a left/right spectrum.

The DCLP itself found that there was a developing 'awkward squad' which was increasingly critical of the way the party leadership seemed to be dictating to the constituencies. Point of Ayr miners were concentrated primarily in four branches: Prestatyn, Ffynnongroyw, Mostyn, and their own workplace branch. The Prestatyn branch was growing rapidly and was crucial in working to slim down the Conservative majority of Keith Raffan, the MP for Delyn. Mostyn and Ffynnongroyw had

[13] Labour Party members at Point of Ayr and the surrounding villages had worked hard to unseat the Conservative MP, Keith Raffan. However, the resilience of north Wales Liberalism again deprived Labour of the seat. David Hanson ran Raffan close, leaving Delyn with a Conservative majority of 1,224. The Liberal Alliance garnered 8,913 votes to ensure that for another five years the miners would remain trapped in a Conservative enclave.

[14] David Hanson was originally from Cheshire and had worked for a national charity before becoming an MP. From the outset, he gained the backing of the non-industrial branches in the constituency, the largest being at Mold.

had branches for many years but the former had recently been re-established after a period of decline. A number of activists in Mostyn placed themselves firmly on the left of the party and were constant critics of some of the national policy shifts and the deference that the DCLP showed to the national leadership. As the 1992 general election approached, a rift developed in the constituency over the selection of the candidate to fight the Conservatives. The Mold branch was influential and from the outset favoured the candidacy of Hanson.

Hanson was a pragmatist committed to the cause of modernization and was able to promote himself as a candidate untainted by factionalism. However, a number of miners in the constituency were influenced by the appearance of John McDonnell, formerly of the Greater London Council (GLC), who was viewed, inside the party, as further to the left than Ken Livingstone. He failed to be nominated but eventually found a seat in Hayes and was a successful candidate in the 1997 general election.[15] The Mostyn branch was critical of Hanson because of his firm embrace of modernization, and he received a frosty reception when he spoke in the local community centre at the selection meeting. McDonnell went down well and received the nomination of the branch. Prestatyn soon followed suit, and the mining activists were pleased with the radicalism to which McDonnell seemed to be committed. The Point of Ayr workplace branch also endorsed McDonnell, though this caused tensions in the union. Les Kelly was critical of his reputation, arguing that this could lead to an aversion to Labour, especially in a marginal seat like Delyn. Kelly favoured a more cautious candidate and felt that members outside the NUM were working to influence the decision of the workplace branch.

After some debate, the constituency finally opted to give Hanson another chance and he duly won the seat in 1992, the first Labour victory that the area had experienced. What the episode shows is that politically active miners were still to the left of the regional Labour movement but were pragmatic enough to see the credibility of the Kinnock leadership. They opposed the

---

[15] For an account of John McDonnell and his relationship with Livingstone, see Ken Livingstone, *If Voting Changed Anything, They'd Abolish It* (London, 1987).

tactics of the entryists, but once a radical candidate was offered they looked upon him favourably.[16] An activist minority continued to press for left policies within both the union and the local labour movement. Once the poll tax had been introduced, a minority on the Point of Ayr lodge argued for non-payment and affiliation to the campaign. This was voted down as it was felt that it would undermine the role of the Labour Party once it was in power.

Although the union membership at Point of Ayr was shrinking, the miners maintained their presence and influence in local politics. Overall, the workforce felt that the only hope was for a Labour victory in 1992 with everything else viewed as a costly distraction. The lodge worked hard throughout north Wales but specifically focused on Delyn, a seat that was fast becoming an important marginal.

With the resignation of Thatcher and the election of John Major, the Conservatives created a lifeline for themselves, winning the election of 1992 with a much reduced majority. The north Wales miners now felt that the battle was probably over in terms of a long-term future for the industry, though they gained some consolation from Labour's victory in Delyn. The party and the union still shared the same core values and the miners firmly committed themselves to the cause of 'democratic socialism'. The wounds that had been opened up during the miners' strike had started to heal as many of the older miners accepted redundancy, and Point of Ayr was now blessed with a young workforce committed to the industry. The lodge retained its familiar structure as the pattern of deference that had been a tradition in north Wales continued. David Edwards challenged the president in February 1992, though the contest was bereft of politics. Edwards was viewed by the men as an inexperienced maverick seeking glory. He only managed to attract thirty-nine votes, and Vic Roberts was again secure at the helm of the union. Les Kelly was also re-elected unopposed.[17]

---

[16] This had also been the case in the 1930s when north Wales miners had welcomed the intention of S. O. Davies to stand in Flintshire. Davies was well to the left of mainstream Labour, remaining a constant critic of the leadership until the 1970s. See Robert Griffiths, *S. O. Davies: A Socialist Faith* (Llandysul, 1983).

[17] North Wales NUM minutes of special AEC, 12 February 1992: NUM, Wrexham.

Internally the NUM was in a position of stalemate as Scargill's leadership was protected by the increased rate of pit closures in areas traditionally opposed to his approach. Negotiations with British Coal were non-existent owing to the problem of the UDM. Each area merely turned in on itself and was concerned with the welfare of its own members. This was a return to the days before reorganization in 1945 as area autonomy reached a new peak with the annual conference as the only symbol of the solidarity of British miners. This process of autonomy and estrangement had been intensified in 1990, when claims about the financial dealings of the national officials caused an explosion of accusatory bitterness within the NUM and its constituent areas. Old wounds were reopened and old enemies took up earlier positions in order to attack the leadership and its tactics in the 1984–5 strike.

The allegations published by the *Mirror* newspaper in March 1990 again brought the British miners to the centre of media and political attention. Since the end of the strike reporters had left the coalfields, and the plight of mining communities went largely unreported as pits continued to close and union membership plummeted. The *Mirror* alleged that the national officials had received money from Libya and the Soviet Union during the twelve-month dispute, claiming that Scargill and Heathfield had used some of this money to pay off private debts.[18] The bulk of the membership was immediately exposed to these allegations, as the *Mirror* was the most popular newspaper amongst miners. The issue dominated discussion within the Labour Party, with some feeling that Scargill was finally getting his deserts for his role in the dispute, which some party members viewed as having damaged electoral prospects. Kinnock was quick to call for a public inquiry, suggesting that miners needed an explanation of the conduct of their president. Scargill claimed that an inquiry would clear him and Heathfield, but that the basis of such an inquiry should be decided by the NEC.[19]

The whole system of collecting funds during the dispute had developed in a chaotic way, with each area of the union responsible for its own system of distribution. At the national level the

---

[18] NUM: report of Gavin Lightman QC to the NEC, 3 July 1990: David Howell collection.
[19] *The Independent*, 7 March 1990.

officials worked hard to evade the consequences of sequestration through opening bank accounts overseas to maintain the union's viability in a period of financial crisis.[20] To most miners the issue of the system of collecting and depositing funds was not a matter of concern; the important point was the allegations of financial impropriety levelled at the officials by the media. In north Wales both critics and supporters of Scargill rushed to his defence and felt that the president had sound principles, even if these at times prevented constructive negotiation with British Coal.

The NEC immediately announced that there would be an inquiry led by Gavin Lightman QC, a member of the Haldane Society of Lawyers. The tabloid press thought that this would ensure a whitewash and that the left would close ranks and clear Scargill and Heathfield of any wrongdoing.[21] Once again the press overplayed the power that Scargill purportedly had over his own executive. In fact, the NEC made it clear from the outset that they would not use the union finances to fund a libel action and were adamant that the inquiry would be wide-ranging. The inquiry subsequently completely cleared the two officials of financial impropriety and the use of funds to pay off their mortgages and home loans. This satisfied the membership and silenced the tabloids, but it still left a big question mark over the internal workings of the union and the relationship between the NUM and its constituent areas.

The report of Gavin Lightman was immediately criticized by Scargill and Heathfield because its conclusion suggested that there was a series of 'misapplications' of funds, which were meant to relieve the hardship of striking miners and their families. Lightman was concerned with the existence of unofficial accounts which were not disclosed to the NEC and which were continued once the strike was over.[22] In defence of the secrecy surrounding the accounts, Scargill claimed that the NEC contained individuals who could not be trusted as several of them had opposed the strike from the outset. This was certainly true of Ted McKay, who had attacked Scargill throughout the dispute

---

[20] For an account of financial contributions given to the NUM by other countries, see Jonathan Saunders, *Across Frontiers: International Support for the Miners' Strike, 1984/85* (London, 1989).

[21] Paul Routledge, *Scargill: The Unauthorised Biography* (London, 1994), p.211.

[22] Lightman, report, p.46.

and was critical of the tactics employed by the national leadership. At the time of the visit of the NUM's chief executive, Roger Windsor, to Libya, McKay openly attacked the move in the local press and continued to argue for a ballot and settlement of the strike. Thus, the actions of the officials were comprehensible in working to maintain a fund that would be kept from sequestration. Nonetheless, this raised an important issue concerning the democratic deficit that may have existed in the national union since the NEC was meant to be the governing body of an organization carrying out the policy of the national conference.[23]

Lightman went further and thought that money raised by Russian miners in 1984–5 was probably meant for the relief of striking miners in Britain and not for international purposes channelled through the International Miners' Organization (IMO),[24] as Scargill and Heathfield maintained. Lightman claimed that this was a breach of duty, which was not reported or explained to the NEC. In general, the report was critical of the role of the IMO. Lightman felt that it was a shadowy organization of which most miners had not even heard. In north Wales, most members of the lodge were unaware of its existence until the whole affair appeared in the press. The IMO secretary, Alan Simon, would not co-operate with Lightman's investigations, and members of the NEC had little knowledge of the organization until it was implicated in the allegations printed in the *Mirror*.[25] In his conclusions, Lightman urged the NUM to consider seriously its future affiliation to the IMO and found the attitude of Simon to an investigation backed by one of its affiliates to be a serious abrogation of responsibility.

---

[23] The structure of the union ensured that there would always be a clash of interest between areas and the national union. This allowed for differing interpretations of the majoritarian principle. In the post-strike period, this became explicit and pronounced, as a minority on the NEC remained cross-pressured by the legitimacy of national decisions and majorities against national decisions in their respective areas.

[24] The IMO brought together miners who had previously been divided by the Cold War. Miners in the West had been affiliated to the Miners' International Federation. Eastern bloc countries sent their representatives to the World Federation of Trade Unions. Scargill led the calls for unity in a meeting in 1983 backed by the French CGT, leading to the founding conference of the IMO. Nonetheless, mining unions in a number of countries stood aloof from the organization due to its support of communist-dominated unions from the East. See Paul Routledge, *Scargill*, pp.267–8.

[25] Kevin Barron, Labour MP for Rother Valley and NEC member, viewed the IMO as Scargill's 'baby' and was largely critical of its existence. Interview with the author, March 1995.

The Lightman report concluded, firstly, that the NUM probably did seek financial support from Libya in 1984. Secondly, money raised in the Soviet Union did not benefit the NUM in Britain and was used for the IMO. This was a mis-application of funds as it was apparent that Russian miners felt that they were contributing to the strike. Thirdly, it was wrong for the officials to obtain loans from a number of funds without the prior consent of the NEC or at least of the Finance and General Purposes Committee that contained NEC members. Both Scargill and Heathfield rejected the claims of the Lightman report and undertook a lengthy tour of the coalfields to set out their case. In north Wales, Heathfield addressed a large meeting in Wrexham and was given an enthusiastic reception by both strikers and workers and won the full backing of the area union. McKay once again made his presence felt in the local press, castigating Scargill but declining an invitation to attend the meeting to press his arguments in person.[26] Kevin Barron and Kim Howells, two ex-NUM employees and subsequently Labour MPs, attacked Scargill in Parliament, with others forming a queue to criticize the union leadership. McKay took the advice of the commissioner for the rights of trade union members seeking financial backing to prosecute Scargill and Heathfield.[27] This move came to nothing, as he had no support amongst the NUM officials in north Wales.

In the meantime, the four-man investigating team appointed by the NEC set off for Paris to question the officials of the IMO. As a result, Scargill and Heathfield were exonerated of any wrongdoing, though some NEC members felt that there had been a misapplication of funds because certain decisions on distribution had not been made by the committee. There was concern about the role of outside individuals in influencing

[26] McKay now pulled no influence in the union in north Wales due to his becoming an employee of British Coal Enterprise (BCE) after the closure of Bersham. BCE had been set up by British Coal in 1984 in anticipation of the large-scale contraction of the industry. It had the power to offer loans to small businesses, provide workspace and help with the training and placement of former miners. BCE in north Wales based itself on the site of Bersham colliery after closure, with McKay taking the helm. For a critical survey of BCE and its allocation of funds, see Ken Coates and Michael Barratt Brown, *Community under Attack: The Struggle for Survival in the Coalfield Communities of Britain* (Nottingham, 1997), pp.73–8.
[27] Seamus Milne, *The Enemy Within: The Secret War against the Miners* (London, 1994), p.96.

decisions at national level. Both the south Wales and Scottish representatives felt that the NEC was increasingly powerless to oppose the policies of Scargill owing to the dominance of his supporters on the committee. At a special delegate conference on 10 October 1990, the leadership received a vote of confidence, although the South Wales Area called for resignations. The matter was finally settled when a motion was passed to endorse all financial dealings since 1985 and a large majority confirmed reaffiliation to the IMO.

In north Wales the issue had quickly blown over, and the union was clear in its support for the two officials. The whole episode made little impact on the membership, and there was no exodus to the UDM. Vic Roberts defended the system of collecting funds during the strike and the way in which the union allocated monies. The Point of Ayr lodge on a number of occasions had helped members financially in times of hardship or in cases related to wage disputes.[28] In general, miners in all areas of the coalfields still opted to support one of their own against outside intervention, even if allegations had come from a Labour-supporting newspaper like the *Mirror*. However, this did not always suggest a political response in defence of union leaders, as there was still an aversion to the 'far left'. During the period of the Lightman inquiry, members of the Trotskyist group associated with the American newspaper, the *Militant*, visited Point of Ayr to defend Scargill and to sell their paper. The lodge secretary, Bernie Haniewicz, reported their presence to the personnel manager, and they were forced to leave the entrance of the colliery.[29]

The *Guardian* reporter, Seamus Milne, in his book, *The Enemy Within*, subsequently challenged the Lightman report. He argued that the smearing of Scargill was just one episode in a large-scale conspiracy against British miners in general and the NUM in particular. Milne supported the view of Scargill that he had no knowledge of Roger Windsor's visit to Libya and that the Russian money was indeed meant for international purposes.

---

[28] Interview with Vic Roberts, February 1997.
[29] Here again we see the resilience of Labourism and the inability of outside groups trying to help the miners' cause to penetrate the collective consciousness of the workforce. The concept of 'them and us' remained occupationally defined, thus inhibiting the unity of the diverse organizations committed to the goals of the union and the case for coal.

Further, he concluded that it was justifiable for the officials to keep certain funds secret from the NEC because this money was not meant for the union.[30] *The Enemy Within* is clearly the case for the defence of the two national officials, and it exposes the weaknesses of the Lightman report, giving a sophisticated account of MI5 involvement in undermining the effectiveness of the NUM. However, there was a changing culture within the higher echelons of the union from the strike period onwards and at times this resulted in what might be termed a democratic deficit between the officials and the NEC. Mick Clapham, industrial relations officer and subsequently Labour MP for Barnsley West and Penistone, claimed that the atmosphere in the Sheffield office increasingly became clouded by suspicion. Scargill went out of his way to monitor all developments amongst the staff because he felt that some of them were working to undermine his policies towards the UDM, and his negotiations with British Coal.[31] Les Kelly also felt that the NEC was at a stalemate because of the union's inability or unwillingness to negotiate in a rapidly deteriorating environment for the future of the industry.[32]

The allegations of the *Mirror* and the subsequent inquiry dogged the NUM in a period of developing crisis as the industry continued to decline rapidly. The miners themselves still had a sense of collective identity and worked to maintain a united stand in terms of loyalty to the union, and this secured the position of Scargill. Even after the demoralization of the defeat in 1985 they sought to maintain a sense of dignity and continued to press for a future for coal. Nonetheless, factionalism both locally and nationally remained a feature of labour politics. The next eighteen months were to send more shock waves through the coalfields following the Conservatives' re-election in 1992. They were soon to announce that a further wave of pit closures would be implemented; these would almost totally destroy the remnants of the coal industry.[33] North Wales was to take centre stage in the

---

[30] Milne, *The Enemy Within*, p.420.
[31] Interview with Mick Clapham MP, March 1995.
[32] Interview with Les Kelly, May 1997.
[33] The scale of the decline of the industry through the 1980s is significant in terms of the speed of the devastation. When Labour left office in 1979 there had been 235,000 miners; in 1992, before the next bout of closures, the number stood at 32,000. Figures taken from Mike Parker, *The Politics of Coal's Decline: The Industry in Western Europe* (London, 1994), p.49.

battle to save British pits, and the area union proved to be resilient and united in campaigning for the retention of mining in Wales.

THE 1992 COAL CRISIS

The Conservative election victories in 1987 and 1992 and the subsequent privatization of the electricity industry sealed the fate of British miners and of deep-mined coal. Politically, the miners knew that coal could not be given a secure future by an administration hostile to the industry. Economically, the privatization of electricity and the subsequent 'dash for gas' created an uneven playing field for coal, no matter how economically it was produced; the market for the product was rapidly shrinking. Most miners at Point of Ayr knew that an announcement on further closures would soon emerge, but the union was optimistic that the pit would escape the first wave of job losses owing to its recent success.

In October 1992, when British Coal announced that thirty-one of the remaining fifty pits would be closed, Point of Ayr completed its best weekly production record in the history of the colliery. Only 429 miners produced a record 20,137 tonnes, smashing the tonnage per man-shift record that it had set only two weeks previously.[34] When the announcement was made that the pit would be one of the thirty-one to close the union was left in a state of shock. The only ray of hope which the miners had was that Point of Ayr was one of the ten where production would not be immediately halted. The American mining techniques were showing initial success, and the management and the men had worked comfortably together on a training programme which saw a number of miners and the union president travelling to the United States to familiarize themselves with the new methods of extraction. *Coal News* regretted the series of closures but stressed that there was no market for the coal from the thirty-one pits. Deep mining activities would be brought to an end in Lancashire, north Staffordshire, north Wales, Durham and north Derbyshire.[35]

[34] *Liverpool Daily Post*, 13 October 1992.
[35] *Coal News*, October 1992.

Both management and men in north Wales criticized the decision and argued that Point of Ayr should never have been on the list for closure. Les Kelly claimed that the pit was producing coal cheaper than any that was imported from other countries. Peter Redford, the colliery manager, added that 'the men had worked tremendously hard to turn out excellent performances in a very difficult climate'. The union had heard a few weeks earlier that a closure announcement of a number of pits was imminent following the leaking of a document from British Coal. The document had suggested that only thirty pits would close and Point of Ayr would survive. Initially the corporation had refused to confirm or deny the report and had claimed that the view of the union was mere speculation. Nevertheless, the remaining miners in north Wales had been relieved to hear that for the moment they still had jobs.[36]

Once the closures were confirmed shock waves were sent through the coalfields, even reverberating in 'middle England' where support for the cause of the miners had been very limited during the strike of 1984–5. The miners, their union, their communities and Scargill were once again thrust into the spotlight by the media, and the world of mining was exposed to the population at large. Popular resistance to the policies of an increasingly unpopular government had been given initial impetus by the furore surrounding 'Black Wednesday' and the forced withdrawal of Britain from the Exchange Rate Mechanism (ERM), leading to further divisions within the Conservative Party. The impact of mass demonstrations and public opinion forced a significant rethink by the government, which led to an initial U-turn on the closures. The united response of the public to the plight of the miners reached epic proportions, in contrast to the 1984–5 strike.

The NUM held a special delegate conference soon after the announcement of the planned closures, though the atmosphere was more cautious than it had been eight years earlier when a similar programme of closures had been declared. Miners were still accepting redundancy in droves and there was little talk amongst delegates of the strike weapon as a means of protest. After some debate, the union cautiously accepted the need for a

[36] *Liverpool Daily Post*, 9 and 13 October 1992.

strike ballot, but this would be of secondary importance to taking the issue to the wider public, in order to force a reversal of policy.[37] British Coal would have been largely unconcerned about a strike in the pits, as the problem was one of markets and there was no danger of the lights going out, as electricity was increasingly generated by gas. In terms of numbers, the miners could not muster the industrial strength that they once had in promoting the effectiveness of mass picketing. This was recognized by most union activists, and many felt that it was now left to the British public to salvage what remained of the coal industry.

Due to the level of hostility to the closures, the government quickly moved to dispel the threat to its energy policy. Michael Heseltine, as president of the Board of Trade, announced that twenty-one of the collieries would be given a reprieve while the prospect of market viability was further investigated. This would be carried out by the Commons Select Committee on Trade and Industry, which included critics of the government's energy policy from inside the Conservative Party. Nonetheless, ten of the thirty-one pits were regarded as lost causes in terms of profitability and could not escape the immediate axe. The two massive demonstrations in London in support of the miners seemed to suggest that the government could have been pushed further in backing down.

Again, the TUC and the Labour Party sought to attack the government through existing structures of negotiation. This took a number of months as the union was aided by the High Court ruling that maintained that British Coal had acted unlawfully in the pursuit of closures.[38] A number of NUM delegates felt that the report of the Select Committee would merely dilute the severity and the speed of the closure programme but would do nothing to prevent closures in the future. The Select Committee duly reported that a subsidy should be made available to the electricity-generating companies to burn additional tonnes of coal for five years. This would by no means protect all the pits

[37] For details of the delegate conference, see David Howell, *The British Coal Crisis, 1992–93* (York Papers in Politics and Policy, no. 2), pp.5–7.
[38] This ruling came towards the end of December when a climate of despondency had already descended on the coalfields and some miners resigned themselves to the fact that the industry was in its death throes.

earmarked for closure, but would provide a breathing space for further developments. In essence, the report promised little in the way of preventing the 'dash for gas' or the cutting back on coal imports and opencast mining.[39]

The acceptance of the report by the Labour MPs close to the NUM led to further rifts in a deteriorating relationship between the party and the union leadership. Mick Clapham felt that Scargill was not aware of the constraints that could be imposed by the structures of power in Westminster. He felt that it was a completely different playing field once a decision was taken to accept the role of a Select Committee and the pursuit of an agreed report.[40] The feeling of powerlessness was reflected in the views of those working at the point of production. A number of miners felt that the fight was now out of their hands, and only public opinion and pressure in Westminster could force a dramatic change in policy.

Heseltine invited Boyds, an American mining consultancy company, to report to him on the future viability of the thirty-one pits including Point of Ayr. There would be no compulsory redundancies in north Wales during this review period, though voluntary redundancies would still be offered.[41] The Boyds Report was predictably pessimistic and argued for changed working practices, though even this would not guarantee a viable future for most of the pits, especially the ten of the thirty-one that were seen as beyond help.[42] At the end of January 1993, the *Guardian* reported the findings of the Select Committee, endorsing its call for £500 million of subsidies and an expansion of the existing market to create a promising future for the remaining pits. The NUM and a number of Labour MPs attacked the report and stressed that it did not go any significant way to

---

[39]   Nonetheless, Labour members viewed a unanimous report as providing a platform of influence over government policy as some Conservative members remained critical of the scale of pit closures.

[40]   Mick Clapham MP, interview with the author, May 1995.

[41]   *DTI Coal Review* (November 1992): Patrick Heesom collection.

[42]   Boyds was an American organization that promoted flexible working practices as the only way forward, although even this would mean closures and job losses to sustain profitability. The United Mineworkers of America had found its position undermined from the 1960s onwards owing to the new culture of industrial relations that swept the coalfields. For details, see David Brody, 'Labour relations in American coal mining: an industry perspective', in Gerald D. Feldman and Klaus Tenfelde (eds.), *Workers, Owners and Politics in Coal Mining: An International Comparison of Industrial Relations* (Oxford, 1990), pp.74–117.

protect jobs and did nothing to address the problems of a rigged energy market.

A more positive report was produced by McCloskey Information Services, which placed the problem in the context of the Conservative Party's privatization of electricity.[43] Writing in the *New Statesman* in February 1993, Gerard McCloskey merely reiterated the argument which the NUM themselves had put forward against coal imports.

> The moral must surely be that relying on imports for more than a small proportion of UK coal supplies is a much less sure policy than supporting the domestic industry. Currency fluctuations, uncertain markets, and even strikes – the US producer Peabody is currently strike bound – could put doubts over imports, whereas British coal can now be delivered at close to world contract prices, with the additional benefit of being quoted in sterling.[44]

The NUM kept up the arguments for a British coal industry both nationally and locally, but the leadership was somewhat constrained by the pragmatism of the Labour Party and the demoralization of the workforce. Scargill met the leaders of the rail unions and planned a series of joint initiatives that would give some industrial muscle to the public opinion forming in opposition to the government. An NUM delegate conference in February 1993 backed a series of one-day strikes as part of the fight against pit closures. The membership voted in favour of stoppages along with NACODS and the Rail, Maritime and Transport Union (RMT).[45] The first strike took place on 2 April and the coalfields were stopped save for the pits dominated by

[43] McCloskey Coal Information Services Ltd was set up in 1988 to provide research and analysis of energy markets in relation to coal. Its consultancy division, Coal Ink Consultancy Ltd, provided commercial consultancy support to the world coal industry. This included supply, demand, price forecasting and advice to projects concerning coal supply programmes. Power Ink Ltd. is the sister company of McCloskey Coal Information Services, established in 1995 as an information company specializing in electricity markets. The leading figure in all these ventures is Gerard McCloskey, who has been the managing director of MCIS since its formation. During the coal crisis of 1992 local authorities called on the consultany expertise of McCloskey in order to develop strategies to counter the arguments of the government.

[44] Gerard McCloskey and Pat Coyne on the Select Committee for the Coal Industry, *New Statesman and Society*, 5 February 1993.

[45] This was not overtly sympathy action on behalf of the RMT as they had their own grievance over plans for privatization of the railways. Also, the miners at the ten pits that were to close immediately were unaffected, as production had already stopped.

the UDM, which had declined to take part in the action. Another strike followed, but once the RMT settled, there seemed little likelihood of the miners going it alone. Miners continued to take redundancy, which in all but name was compulsory, as payment figures could be reduced if the membership voted to delay a closure decision.

Within a year of the crisis most of the pits on the original list had closed or were earmarked for closure. It was predicted that only around fifteen pits would remain in Britain, as opposed to around 200 that had existed ten years earlier. Once again miners felt let down by the wider Labour movement and increasingly powerless economically and politically in a hostile environment. The miners in north Wales had won a temporary reprieve but Point of Ayr continued to shed its workforce, and to many the 1992 crisis merely signalled the postponement of the inevitable.

In contrast to 1984–5, the public viewed miners as victims of circumstances that were largely beyond their control. The failure of the Conservative government after 1992 to address the problems of de-industrialization, rising crime, inner-city deprivation and political sleaze was seen through the lens of a particular way of life that once represented the essence of 'Britishness'. The 'class element' of the miners' struggle was diluted and replaced by the notion of a 'national interest' which seriously challenged the legitimacy of a government that seemed increasingly out of touch with the feelings of the British people.[46] Within the space of a week, over 200,000 people twice marched through London, clearly opposed to the closure of pits and the destruction of mining communities. Two Conservative MPs supported Roy Lynk, the moderate leader of the UDM in Nottinghamshire, as he imprisoned himself down a pit on the closure list. In Lancashire at Parkside colliery, a women's camp was established that came to symbolize the fight to maintain the industry. The camp was visited by thousands of people from all parts of the country representing a multiplicity of social backgrounds.[47]

[46] This was recognized by emerging stars in the Labour Party and laid the foundation of New Labour in terms of its commitment to the notion of 'one nation' that sought to break with the class-ridden disputes and policies of the past.

[47] Women's Pit Camps signalled the re-emergence of women's groups that had formed the basis of support for miners in 1984–5. Most coalfields witnessed the activity of women, and the camps became potent symbols of protest once the public furore over closures had subsided. See Sylvia Pye, 'The great British miners' strike of 1984–85', in Marat Moore (ed.), *Women in the Mines: Stories of Life and Work* (New York, 1996), pp.245–66.

What was left of the British 'revolutionary tradition' claimed that the protests represented a shift in the attitudes of the population and that the militancy showed that there was support for a general strike and widespread civil disobedience. Once again, the 'far left' misjudged the significance of the events surrounding the furore over the closure programme. The Conservatives also misjudged the mood of the people and continued to mould their arguments around a view of 'economic orthodoxy' that was rapidly losing ground as the government began to slide down in the opinion polls. The demonstrations to save the pits were again based on a campaign involving the construction of 'community' and did not represent the emergence of something new in terms of radical politics.[48] The miners were seen as part of the history and tradition of archetypal British workers who remained rooted in the popular perceptions of the British people. A feeling of outrage emerged to question the excesses of Thatcherism even though Cecil Parkinson and other Conservatives tried to attack the miners as victims of their former militancy, a portrait which owed more to myth than to reality.

The politics of Labourism again proved to be both a vehicle for protest but also a barrier to any radical challenge to parliamentary and economic orthodoxy. Miners' leaders in all coalfields argued for mass demonstrations and the involvement of diverse pressure groups within society to press for a change of energy policy. The Labour Party again became the focus of organization, and many MPs spoke at meetings in the coalfields attacking the policies of the Conservatives. Labourism thus presented itself as a forum for activism during the crisis and most miners still felt that the only hope of success in saving pits and securing a long-term future would be the election of a Labour government.

It was at the parliamentary level that the limitations of Labourism became most apparent. The PLP had a clear choice of opposing the closures and concentrating on events outside Westminster or it could collude with the government and endorse the position of the Select Committee to conduct an

---

[48] The concept of community became central in challenging closure decisions, utilizing the resources of the trade unions, voluntary groups and local authorities. These came together in the Coalfield Communities Campaign established in 1985 to represent the needs and interests of the coalfield population affected by industrial decline. See Coates and Brown, *Community under Attack*, p.52.

investigation into coal. Once the decision was taken to comply with the Select Committee, it was likely that some kind of compromise would emerge whereby limited concessions would be a stopgap, but would not lead to a long-term future.[49] The miners themselves were under no illusion as to what route would be taken, and accepted the fact that the industry would continue to decline as a result of the Select Committee report. Within each coalfield, the link between the NUM and the Labour Party was not diluted, and the pragmatism of the miners underlined the necessity of defeating the Conservatives electorally. The most active miners on the left of the Labour Party might not have fully endorsed the performance of the party in the House of Commons, but they felt that the only avenue of protest was through a powerful opposition leading to electoral success. In national terms the protest could be viewed as a victory for Labour, but locally protests were motivated by a 'rainbow coalition' of individuals and groups who came together to save the pits.[50]

THE BATTLE FOR POINT OF AYR

Before Michael Heseltine's announcement of thirty-one pit closures, the gloom cast over Point of Ayr was being lifted. In June 1992, British Coal claimed that, in the currently worked area, there was access to 29 million tonnes of reserves which could be extracted quickly by 'pillar and stall' methods.[51] Nonetheless, new technology also meant shedding more labour. The workforce in 1992 numbered 494, and British Coal stressed that due to the success of the 'continuous miner' system many more miners would be offered redundancy.[52] The environment underground had changed rapidly since the strike, and the men found that they were continually pushed harder to enhance production.

[49] Although many felt constrained by the prominence of the select committee system, as in the 1960s a number of MPs could have attacked the government in a more robust fashion in Parliament.

[50] In north Wales the threat to Point of Ayr brought together Plaid Cymru, Labour, Liberal Democrats and a host of politically diverse individuals to fight for the survival of the colliery.

[51] Management at the pit concluded that there were 25 million tonnes of coal reserves in the North District that was yet to be exploited, though this would require expensive drivages through 'hard rock'. In terms of output, 80 per cent of coal produced went to Fiddlers Ferry Power Station, which was only one hour away.

[52] British Coal Midlands and Wales Group Colliery Profile: Point of Ayr, June 1992: NUM, Wrexham.

This was having an effect on safety, and the management encouraged the non-reporting of minor accidents by offering those miners who were accident-free the chance to enter prize draws. The workforce was generally young, as many of the older miners who were close to retirement found it uncomfortable to work under roof bolts as the only means of support. Nonetheless, the atmosphere remained comradely and many felt that it was a preferable work environment compared with the factory, which was the only other option locally.

It was generally feared that, although Point of Ayr was a success, it would eventually close owing to the shrinking of its market for coal. In September a letter from Tim Sainsbury MP to Michael Portillo, the chief secretary of the Treasury, was leaked to the NUM; it clearly stated:

> It looks likely that British Coal will make the announcement of colliery closures in the second half of September. We are expecting them to announce all the closures in one go. As you know, many communities are likely to be seriously hit by the closures.[53]

In the previous August, Vic Roberts had reported to the AEC that British Coal had announced that the entire surface operations at Point of Ayr would be privatized and that existing employees would be offered new contracts under a different employer.[54] The men at the pit felt that this was probably a prelude to complete privatization, though they resigned themselves to the fact that even this would be preferable to closure. Production continued to improve, and then on 14 October the colliery manager, Peter Redford, announced that the pit would close in March 1993. Redford claimed that he was just as shocked as the union at the decision, especially in the light of the recent successes. Redundancy was now compulsory and would be applied to miners, supervisors and management.[55]

The AEC met and immediately announced that a campaign would be launched to save the pit, in conjunction with local

[53] Letter from Tim Sainsbury MP, minister for Industry, to Rt. Hon. Michael Portillo MP, chief secretary of HM Treasury, September 1992 (confidential). This letter was received by the NUM on 17 September 1992: Patrick Heesom collection.
[54] North Wales NUM minutes of AEC, 12 August 1992: NUM, Wrexham.
[55] Letter from Peter Redford, the Point of Ayr manager, to all workers, 14 October 1992: NUM, Wrexham.

communities and the county council.[56] The union wanted to integrate the local initiatives with the larger mobilization to secure the future of all thirty-one pits threatened with closure. The schism in the DCLP was temporarily put on hold as all branches close to Point of Ayr worked to defend the pit. Councillor Barbara Roberts wrote a number of letters to the local press expressing dismay at the closure announcement, since Point of Ayr had not been on the initial list of closures. The local Labour MP, David Hanson, argued that there should be an integrated energy policy and condemned the 'dash for gas'.[57] Over 200 miners, their families and supporters attended the massive rally organized by the NUM in London, and the north Wales coast began to buzz with political activity. However, a number of former strikers felt a level of animosity towards the new-found concern over pit closures expressed by those who had rejected the strike call in 1984. The majority of the twenty strikers who still worked at the colliery chose not to go to London and some of those who did travelled on a separate bus. Paul Parry, a strike activist, recalls that there were only two strikers on the main bus from the pit, and he left London with mixed emotions.

> Biting tongues was the order of the day, but of course that day we were fighting shoulder to shoulder . . . I actually felt sorry for some of them. If only they had known the comradeship of our brothers and sisters of 1984–85, of our wives on the picket line . . . I shed more of a tear or two that day, thinking how it could have been and of course, if it would have been, we wouldn't be here again, marching to save the pits.[58]

For the duration of the campaign, a fragile unity in north Wales was maintained, though some strikers resented the fact that a number of local union officials were promoting themselves as fighters for the union when they had previously undermined it eight years earlier by crossing picket lines. The mobilization for the London demonstration was successful in developing local initiatives, with petitions, marches and letters to the press keeping the issue of closure on the agenda. Seven hundred former

---

[56] North Wales NUM minutes of AEC, 26 November 1992: NUM, Wrexham.
[57] *Chester Chronicle*, 6 November 1992.
[58] *Red Kite: Newsletter for a Democratic Left in Wales*, 10 (November 1992).

and existing miners from Point of Ayr marched with their
supporters through Prestatyn, once the bastion of Conservative
support in Delyn, and received a warm reception. Ann Clwyd,
David Hanson and Les Kelly spoke on behalf of the Labour
Party and urged the people of north Wales to keep up the
pressure on the government. Other speakers claimed that there
was a feeling of anger and betrayal in the town and that the
miners were being victimized regardless of their success. Kelly
intimated that British Coal was already up to its 'dirty tricks',
which suggested that if the pit remained open there would have
to be another round of redundancies.[59]

The campaign to save Point of Ayr marked a dramatic shift in
pit closures in north Wales. Previously with the closure of Llay
Main, Hafod, Ifton, Gresford and Bersham, the economic arguments went largely unchallenged and attempts to mobilize public
support for the union were found wanting. On this occasion, the
national perception of the miners as a 'dying breed' managed to
touch even the most conservative areas of the coalfield.[60] No
coalfield was immune to closures, and the press could no longer
point a finger at the scare tactics of Scargill. From the outset,
Clwyd County Council pledged its support and called in the
mining experts, McCloskey Coal Information Services, to carry
out a viability study.[61] This was complemented by the strength of
public support in the country mobilized against the policies of an
increasingly unpopular government. In north Wales, as in other
areas, people with no previous interest in political activity were
turning up to meetings, signing petitions and arguing the case for
coal in different forums.

McCloskey Information Services compiled a comprehensive
report on Point of Ayr. This was submitted to the Select Committee on Trade and Industry. The report concluded that the
American mining techniques at the pit had been a success and
the coal was of high quality. The authors argued strongly that
under no circumstances should the colliery be closed, as Point of

---

[59] *Daily Post*, 2 November 1992.
[60] What emerged was a cross-class campaign that was to serve Tony Blair well in May
1997, when Wales became a Conservative-free zone as seats in the north fell to Labour.
[61] *Rhyl Journal*, 2 December 1992. Although the county council was under Labour
control, tensions within the constituency party over local planning proposals affected the
unity of the miners' natural allies.

Ayr was one of the 'crown jewels' of British Coal.[62] On 25 January 1993, it seemed probable that the pit would be saved but the workforce would continue to be cut. The Welsh secretary, David Hunt, indicated that the pit would continue to produce coal but the miners would have to wait another month to hear if it had a long-term future. Kelly welcomed the announcement and felt that the strength of the local campaign had been instrumental in forcing the government to change its mind on the continuation of coal mining in north Wales.

The engineers appointed by Heseltine, J. T. Boyds, also accepted the future viability of the pit as a mining laboratory for American methods of extraction that could eventually be applied to other British collieries. However, Boyds insisted that future success would only be forthcoming with the introduction of longer shifts, redundancies at all levels and the implementation of compulsory weekend working.[63] The pit might have had an extension of its life but miners continued to opt for redundancy, as many feared that privatization would lead to even more instability. The feeling of pessimism was compounded when the electricity industry regulator, Stephen Littlechild, gave the go-ahead for the regional electricity companies to sign a new five-year deal with coal producers. This would in effect cut the market by more than half within a year and even further in each of the following four years.[64]

The 1992 coal crisis had plunged north Wales once again into political activity whereby a coalition of pressure groups in and outside the industry made a significant impact on the government and prevented the closure of Point of Ayr. Nonetheless, the pit was changed for ever, as most of the 'old guard' of the union and the bulk of the faceworkers took up the offer of redundancy. Many of the older characters disappeared, and the young workforce that remained was solely concerned with maximizing wages in a period of pessimism and looming privatization. At a special meeting of the AEC on 6 April 1993, Vic Roberts announced that he would be leaving the industry. This symbolized

[62] McCloskey Coal Information Services Ltd, 'The case for Point of Ayr' (November 1992), paper submitted to the House of Commons Select Committee on Trade and Industry: Patrick Heesom collection.
[63] *Evening Leader*, 25 January 1993.
[64] *Guardian*, 24 February 1993.

the passing of the old order. Roberts had been a central figure on the lodge for many years and a stalwart of all the major strikes. He was respected by the men at Point of Ayr and was re-elected after the strike of 1984–5 even by those who had continued to work. Roberts did not, however, forget his links with the trade union movement, and on finding subsequent employment in a small factory, he was immediately elected as the union representative for the workforce. His popularity as a union official at Point of Ayr was due to the fact that, at all times, he remained close to the men at the point of production, having little time for political factionalism or the temptations of a full-time position. His last speech to the annual delegate conference in 1993 was a moving occasion, and he was thanked by all present for his contribution to the union in a period of crisis and decline.

Within four months of the initial closure announcement, 150 miners had opted to leave Point of Ayr, and the remaining workers numbered fewer than 300.[65] On the eve of privatization, the pit retained an NUM membership, though a rapidly declining one. Mark Begley replaced Vic Roberts as delegate, and Bernie Haniewicz, the lodge secretary, took the mantle of area president. British Coal and its pit managers were aware that the industry was in its dying days, and in readiness for privatization the company adopted an increasingly authoritarian attitude to the remaining miners at the pit. The lodge secretary complained to the AEC that the management was not allowing him sufficient time off for trade union duties and it was becoming increasingly difficult for the lodge to operate effectively.[66] By mid-summer 1994 manpower had been further reduced to around 200, and only two production units were in operation instead of the promised three. The surface was also completely privatized, leaving the total British Coal workforce at 155. Kelly reported to the delegate conference that the national workforce was now below 10,000, with only a handful of collieries remaining. The NUM in north Wales consisted of only about 100 full-paying members – and the spectre of non-unionism had also returned to

---

[65] North Wales NUM minutes of annual delegate conference, 24 April 1993: NUM, Wrexham.

[66] North Wales NUM minutes of special AEC, 19 July 1994: NUM, Wrexham.

the coalfield. He argued that the decision to fight to keep the pit open was a courageous one which he would continue:

> It has always been my policy to fight tooth and nail for the mineworker and his welfare, and I will continue to do so whilstever there is a breath left in me. My life has always been in mining, once a miner always a miner.[67]

The area secretary and the lodge were finding it harder to operate owing to the intransigence of British Coal and the lack of commitment on their part to traditional structures of consultation. The 'check-off' system of deducting union subscriptions from miners' wages had already been halted following the one-day strikes of 1993. Further, the management was working to force miners to sign up to a new 'package of employment' which would introduce flexible working patterns into the industry.[68] At national level, Arthur Scargill reported that union membership post-privatization would be approximately 9,000, both full and limited members.[69]

Point of Ayr might have been saved from the closure of 1992–3 but the environment underground had undergone rapid change. As British Coal continually pressed their advantage and became increasingly hostile to the union, some felt that a private company could be no worse in terms of industrial relations. What remained of the coal industry was to be once again in the hands of the coal owners, and almost fifty years of state ownership were about to come to an end as the industry languished in a state of distress. The NUM was rapidly approaching extinction as a political and industrial force, largely confined to the pages of labour history and symbolizing an industrial and political heritage that the main political parties wanted to forget.

PRIVATIZATION AND THE DEATH OF COAL

British Coal was sold off to the private sector in December 1994, with only twenty collieries remaining in production; there had

---

[67] NUM North Wales minutes of annual delegate conference, 30 June 1994: NUM, Wrexham.
[68] NUM North Wales minutes of AEC, 22 September 1994: NUM, Wrexham.
[69] NUM NEC report, 14 October 1994: David Howell collection.

been 958 in 1947 at the time of nationalization.[70] At Point of Ayr the privatization process had started earlier, with the number of private contractors almost equal to the number of British Coal employees in the last days of state control. What remained of the industry was to be sold off in five regional businesses based on Scotland, Wales, the north-east, the central coalfield and the numerous opencast sites.[71] North Wales was to be included in the central coalfield and was bought by RJB Mining, which already had a significant base at the colliery through the privatization of the surface.

The nature and progress of the privatization was to be monitored by the establishment of a Coal Authority which would take over the licensing functions of British Coal and issue licences to the successor companies. Clause 2 (1) (b) stressed that the duty of the authority was to secure, as far as practicable, 'that an economically viable coal mining industry in Great Britain is maintained and developed by the persons authorised by that party to carry on coal mining operations'.[72] This clause was to be rendered meaningless as RJB Mining soon found out: they were forced to close pits owing to the nature of the energy market and the continuation of the 'dash for gas'. The Conservatives had created a kind of 'Frankenstein's monster' with a privatization of energy that sealed the fate of what remained of the British coal industry. The market from the outset was stacked against coal from the day when the government allowed 'sweetheart' deals between the electricity generators and the owners of gas-fired power stations. As more gas-fired power stations were constructed, the market for coal shrank, despite the fact that it was a cheaper form of energy. In 1997, coal could still produce electricity at 1.6p per kilowatt-hour in contrast with the cost of gas at 2.2p per kilowatt-hour.[73]

North Wales provides a microcosm of national developments whereby the 'dash for gas' was helped by local Labour councils, leading to pit closures and job losses. During the Christmas

[70] Mahmud Nawaz, 'The coal industry: a quantitative analysis', Research Paper 94/8 (17 January 1994): (Patrick Heesom collection).
[71] Letter from David Hanson MP to Les Kelly re details of planned privatization of the coal industry, 30 September 1993: NUM, Wrexham.
[72] Christopher Barclay, *The Coal Industry Bill* [Bill 4 1993/94] (update), Research Paper 94/7 (17 January 1994): Patrick Heesom collection.
[73] *Guardian*, 19 August 1997.

period of 1994, union leaders in the coalfield met with officials of
RJB Mining to discuss the future of Point of Ayr under private
ownership. Les Kelly, for the NUM, claimed that morale was at
an all-time low owing to the general uncertainty in the industry,
and that the miners wanted assurances from the company on
union recognition and future investment. RJB Mining agreed
that a role for the union in the future of the pit would be
beneficial to both sides. The union was happy with this initial
optimism as the last days of British Coal were marred by an
increasingly bitter relationship between management and men.
From the outset, the private company aimed to expand industrial
markets for coal and was not at the moment concerned with the
implementation of flexible working, which British Coal had
previously planned.[74]

The workforce was at first apprehensive, though initially there
was little difference in terms of the working environment between public and private ownership. Miners still relied on extensive overtime to boost wages and were constantly pushed in terms
of production targets. Within six weeks of private ownership,
RJB Mining executives visited Point of Ayr and requested that
the union agree to the implementation of compulsory nine-hour
shifts to get the pit back into profit, as it had recently experienced
problems with roof instability in drivages underground. The
NUM remained opposed to the compulsory extension of shifts
and emphasized that any overtime must remain on a voluntary
basis. This was not a problem for the company as the bulk of the
workforce was happy to put in extra hours; many still feared that
closure could be announced at any time in the near future.

Throughout early 1995, the pit continued to experience
problems with the 'continuous miner' system. RJB announced
that the pit would be given until October 1995 to prove itself in
terms of profitability. However, there was some optimism as the
company announced that it planned to recruit a number of
apprentices and the check-off system of collecting union dues
would be reactivated.[75] The union, both nationally and locally,
was totally demoralized but was still able to represent the membership at each colliery. In a ballot over a substantial pay claim

[74] *Prestatyn Visitor*, 29 December 1994.
[75] North Wales NUM minutes of annual delegate conference, 7 June 1995: NUM,
Wrexham.

and negotiating rights, the miners voted in favour of a series of one-day strikes. The action was subsequently halted when RJB challenged the NUM in the High Court and won. The company claimed that the action was to start too late to comply with the legislation relating to the time between a ballot and the stoppage. Meanwhile, the miners at Point of Ayr continued to work hard, with each man putting in extra hours to boost productivity; but the pit continued to fail to reach targets set by the company.

At the annual delegate conference of the North Wales NUM in May 1996, Kelly attacked the previous management of British Coal and felt that it was to blame for the precarious position of the pit:

> The much heralded financial success of the RJB Company certainly should be raising very serious questions about the previous British Coal management at all levels, and the present Government. Contrary to all their protestations, there does, after all, appear to be a market for coal. The closing down of the Nationalised Coal Industry was more to do with political dogma than market forces.[76]

Kelly was right in one sense, as former pits that were to be closed were now showing promise, particularly Tower colliery in south Wales, which was run by the miners themselves. Nonetheless, RJB, which owned most of the pits, found itself in a similar position to that of British Coal in terms of the availability of markets. After initial optimism, the climate of despair returned to Point of Ayr and miners felt that their days were numbered. Furthermore, the company appeared to be reneging on its pledge to work closely with the union. Kelly complained that RJB seemed to be adopting an increasingly hostile attitude to the patterns of negotiation that had been agreed from the outset of privatization.[77]

The north Wales miners felt increasingly isolated; other RJB pits were some distance away in Yorkshire and Nottinghamshire. A number of men felt that in another crisis, like that of 1992, Point of Ayr would be the first to close because it was out on a limb. The earning of maximum wages was their sole concern

---

[76] North Wales NUM minutes of annual delegate conference, 18 May 1996: NUM, Wrexham.
[77] Interview with Les Kelly, May 1997.

and the added safety buffer of the British Coal redundancy scheme also comforted them. The NUM at this point was concentrated in a rump membership, and it was harder for the lodge to generate support for the union because of the economic climate and uncertainty about the future of the pit. Kelly still sat on the NEC, but felt that the national union was too concerned with its internal politics. He wanted it to be more resilient in maintaining pressure on the private company in order to secure a viable future for the membership. Each constituent area of the union was now merely concerned with its own survival. Both south Wales and Scotland, whose remaining pits were not owned by RJB, steadily played less of a role on the NEC.

Miners in north Wales continued to play a part in the politics of the DCLP, looking to a general election as the salvation of the local coal industry. Scargill hit the headlines with his much-publicized break with the Labour Party and the founding of his own Socialist Labour Party (SLP) in response to the abandonment of Clause 4 and the commitment to public ownership. Scargill merely wanted to construct a party that promoted the policies of Labourism, and the split from the Labour Party represented nothing new in terms of ideology.

The Labour Party under Tony Blair was rapidly undergoing an ideological transformation that was first started by Neil Kinnock, and this was taken up with gusto by the various north Wales branches. Miners retained their political pragmatism and felt that electoral victory meant everything to the future of the coal industry. They were soon to be disappointed: the party under Blair's leadership seriously undermined the identity of Labour as an organization committed to public ownership, the redistribution of wealth and opposition to draconian trade union legislation. Scargill was clearly opposed to what he saw as a Labour Party conversion to a mere 'social democratic' organization with little commitment to public ownership.

Scargill played a central role in the campaign to defend Clause 4 and maintained his criticism of Blair's leadership. The party held a special conference to debate the issue, and a massive majority voted to ditch the commitment to public ownership that had been part of the constitution of the Labour Party since 1918. In January 1996, Scargill announced that he was leaving the Labour Party and forming the SLP, with Clause 4 forming the cornerstone of its policies.[78] This was clearly an attempt to re-establish a movement committed to Labourism, and Scargill quickly stressed that Trotskyists would not be welcome. The policy documents of its founding conference in May 1996 committed the organization to nationalization, unilateral nuclear disarmament, full employment and the abolition of all anti-trade union laws introduced by the Conservatives.[79] Others on the left treated Scargill's party with derision, as did the majority of members of the NEC. The revolutionary left felt that it would be a diluted socialist party because of its commitment to electoral politics. Ken Livingstone, a former ally of the NUM president and a member of the Socialist Campaign Group of MPs, referred to the membership of the SLP as a 'small bunch of nutters'.[80]

The NEC of the NUM from the outset maintained that there would be no question of the political levy going to the SLP since the bulk of the membership still supported the Labour Party. Many felt that Scargill himself was doing Blair a favour by leaving, thus further weakening the left inside the party. In north Wales, no members of the NUM joined the SLP. However, Scargill's defection clearly illustrated his commitment to the policies of the Labour left and indicates that the politics of Scargill can best be explained as a commitment to Labourism and not as the politics of the revolutionary left.[81] Within the Labour Party, Blair pressed for further changes to the organization. As the 1997 election approached, the membership was asked to endorse a pre-manifesto programme. A new code of conduct devised to control dissent was formulated and the power of the NEC and the conference was greatly reduced.[82]

[78] *Sunday Times*, 14 January 1996. By the early 1990s, the NUM nationally was outside the debate over Labour Party policy due to its depleted membership, perceived archaic policies, and lack of influence in the TUC. Nonetheless, it retained significant power bases at the local level, though they too were rapidly declining.
[79] SLP policy documents of founding conference, 4 May 1996: unpublished, in possession of author.
[80] *The Times*, 15 January 1996.
[81] Scargill represented an 'old school' Labour nationalizer committed to the trade union movement and generally critical of the extreme left. The policy documents of the SLP show clearly an expression of the former baggage of 'old Labour' and its view of state-directed planning and gradualist socialism.
[82] For details of the Blair transformation from a left perspective, see Leo Panitch and Colin Leys, *The End of Parliamentary Socialism: From New Left to New Labour* (London, 1997), pp.233–4.

The emphatic victory of the Labour Party on 1 May 1997 with a majority of 179 seats was welcomed by all sections of the Labour movement. Yet how far had the party changed, and was it still committed to the politics of Labourism? Blair clearly represented a new kind of Labour leader. The fashionable comparison with Gaitskell appears surprising, since the latter was committed to public ownership in a pragmatic sense and seemed comfortable with the role that the trade union movement played in the party. By 1995, the party under Blair's direction had ditched its commitment to full employment, public ownership and progressive taxation, all basic policies of Labourism. Internally the membership of the party had continued to rise, though the sociology of this membership and routes of influence in the party were undergoing significant change.[83] The traditional conveyor belt of trade union activity was increasingly sidelined as the national party gained more control over the constituencies. Blair staffed his office with advisers who had been relatively inexperienced in the Labour movement, thereby further undermining the union/party link.[84] A survey of the newly elected Labour MPs also suggested that the number drawn from the 'traditional working class' had declined. The majority of the new MPs firmly committed to the Blair project were adding further legitimacy to the politics of New Labour.

The rhetoric of equality and redistribution was still used, but in terms of policy, albeit apart from constitutional reform, radicalism was difficult to detect in Blair's government. But what of the working-class perception of the Labour Party: did this signify a break with Labourism? Discussions with former miners in north Wales suggested the opposite. Most men and women interviewed felt that the party was still their party and that reforming measures would be implemented during the course of the Parliament. In essence, to the men and women of former mining communities in north Wales, the party was still clearly Labourist.[85] The problem for Labour was that people's perceptions had been susceptible to change in the past. In the 1960s

[83] For details of the changing composition of Labour Party membership up to 1992, consult Patrick Seyd and Paul Whitely, *Labour's Grass Roots: The Politics of Party Membership* (Oxford, 1992), pp.27–55.

[84] See Andy McSmith, *Faces of Labour: The Inside Story* (London, 1997).

[85] This view came out of discussions with recently retired coal miners, their wives and union activists, September 1997.

there had been hostility to the failures of Wilson in some coal-fields, though this was muted and loyalty was assured because of the values espoused by the party. Even though the party might have moved further to the right than ever before, there was still a strong identification between the aspirations of the working class and the rhetoric of a number of Labour MPs. British Labourism was thought by some to be in its death throes, but as Saville argued in the early 1970s, 'Labourism, as a theory and a practice, is deeply rooted in the social structures and organisations of the British working class . . . this side of economic and social catastrophe, it is likely to prove stubbornly resistant to change.'[86]

The election of a Labour government in 1997 came too late to prevent the death of the coal industry in north Wales. The announcement of the closure of Point of Ayr in August 1996 was a shock to some but came as no surprise to others in the communities roundabout. Dissidents in the DCLP had earlier argued that the development of the Hamilton Oil gas terminal close to the colliery was the beginning of the end. Others in the party supported the development, stressing that it would bring local employment and secure the future of industrial development on the north Wales coast. The extraction of gas had a negligible effect on employment, and tensions within the constituency Labour Party remained. DCLP councillors who had previously fought against the 'dash for gas' shifted policy when Hamilton Oil placed cash on the table for projects in particular wards.

The NUM was well aware at the time of privatization that the pit was merely being used as a testing ground for new mining methods once the 'long-wall' system of mining was phased out. Throughout 1996 the pit continued to lose money and had a run of bad luck in encountering geological difficulties. On 7 August, Bill Rowell, the managing director of RJB, visited the pit to hold crisis talks with the management and the various trade unions. After some discussion, Rowell stated that the heavy losses at the pit were no longer sustainable and closure was the only course of action available to the company. RJB was concerned that the

---

[86] John Saville, 'The ideology of labourism', in Robert Benewick, R. N. Berki and Bhikhu Parekh (eds.), *Knowledge and Belief in Politics: The Problem of Ideology* (London, 1973), pp.213–27.

financial burden of Point of Ayr was having a detrimental effect on the viability of its other operations in the central coalfield.

Both the local NUM and NACODS delegates were shocked at the apparent speed with which the company wished to pursue closure. The manager announced that production would cease on 12 August. This made it difficult for the remaining workforce to assess the situation and construct a reasoned response to the announcement. To RJB, the economic case was clear: since the company had acquired Point of Ayr in December 1994, total losses amounted to £5 million, of which £2.85 million had been incurred during 1995 and £2.15 million from January 1996. Saleable output for 1995 had been 312,672 tonnes, compared with a budget prediction of 450,000 tonnes. For 1996, up to August, the saleable output had been 176,406 tonnes compared with a budget prediction of 231,800 tonnes. In the same meeting, the director made it clear that the first compulsory redundancies would commence on 9 November. The BACM representative raised a question in relation to the colliery review procedure, which had been previously operated by British Coal. Rowell replied that no such system of review now existed. Due to the nature of the privatization process, RJB felt that it was no longer obliged to construct such a scheme of appeal to challenge closure decisions. Bernie Haniewicz, the lodge secretary, took a firm stand and stressed that the union would not co-operate with the management on the question of closure until he had taken legal advice on the way that the decision had been conveyed to his membership. He pleaded with the company to delay the commencement of the salvage operation so that the option of a workers' buy-out could be explored. Some miners were optimistic about this as Tower colliery in south Wales was doing well under the ownership of former British Coal employees. Once again, the company showed a level of impatience and claimed that if the salvage of certain materials was delayed it could have a detrimental effect on its other collieries. The equipment at Point of Ayr was desperately needed elsewhere, and the company was unsure about the granting of a delay in the proceedings to enable the union to gauge the opinions of the workforce.[87]

[87] RJB Mining minutes of meeting held at Point of Ayr, 7 August 1996: NUM, Wrexham.

The Point of Ayr miners were deeply shocked by the decision, but many felt that the closure had been a possibility since the end of the strike in 1985. They were at least comforted by the option of a transfer to another RJB mine, probably in Yorkshire. The NUM met with Clwyd County Council over the possibility of the workers' buy-out, and the company reluctantly agreed to delay the salvage operation for four to six weeks while avenues were explored. The company put an initial price on the pit of £1.2 million. Just under 200 employees remained at Point of Ayr, and all felt that they had given their all to the success of the pit since the coal crisis of 1992. This was acknowledged by RJB in a press release: 'The loss making results at Point of Ayr is poor reward for an experienced and skilled workforce whom we will be happy to assist with a move to more productive work elsewhere.'[88]

The prospect of moving to another coalfield had not concerned the north Wales miners in the past. From the 1950s onwards the pits in the area had received labour from elsewhere; this continued right through to the late 1980s when the last of the Lancashire miners made their way to Point of Ayr from Sutton Manor. Only fifty-eight miners expressed an interest in moving to another RJB mine, even though the company worked to make the transition as smooth as possible. Those showing an interest could visit a number of pits with accommodation and expenses provided, and would be given the option of a trial period before making a final decision on the transfer. During this one-month trial period the men would have their redundancy pay protected.[89]

The NUM remained critical of the company and felt that everything was moving too quickly. They were still concerned to explore the future viability of the pit if the men decided to invest in it. The lodge wanted the offer of transfer to be held back to concentrate on gauging opinion on a buy-out. Once the company had pushed the issue of a transfer it immediately affected the perceptions of the miners, with many feeling that a move to another pit would be less of a gamble than to invest their redundancy pay in an alien concept of financial speculation. The

---

[88] RJB Mining press release on the closure of Point of Ayr, 7 August 1996: NUM, Wrexham.
[89] RJB Mining minutes of meeting to discuss redundancy terms and transfer conditions at Point of Ayr, 21 August 1996: NUM, Wrexham.

local communities immediately expressed their sadness at the decision of RJB to close the pit. Point of Ayr had been part of the landscape of the north Wales coast for well over 100 years. The closure also marked the end of a tradition of coal mining in the area that went back to the fifteenth century and had coloured social and political developments in both Flintshire and Denbighshire.

The *Liverpool Daily Post* claimed that the closure would not have the same impact as a closure in one of the more 'archetypal' pit villages that were now almost totally extinct.[90] The newspaper underestimated the depth of feeling concerning the pit, especially within the local labour movement and the numerous villages that had traditionally supplied it. Although the colliery had had a chequered political history, many felt that the closure represented a loss to the trade union movement in north Wales. In the villages of Mostyn, Ffynnongroyw and Penyffordd which had been associated with the pit, a sombre mood could be detected in the local pubs which were frequented by retired and soon-to-be-redundant miners.[91]

Within two weeks of the meeting held to announce the closure, the unions had declared that a buy-out was not viable. The discussions that preceded the decision had been marked by tensions between NACODS and the NUM. Les Kelly had been critical of the role that NACODS had been playing in dictating the course of discussions leading to the viability study. It was also felt that, owing to the demoralization of the workforce, the bid would falter once the miners realized that they would have to invest their redundancy money. Most of the men who had left after the announced closure in 1992 had been successful in gaining employment, albeit of a less secure and lower-paid sort. In general, the area of north Wales close to the colliery did not become an unemployment black spot, as did colliery villages in south Wales and parts of northern England.

On 23 August, the union informed RJB Mining that they would not be making a bid for the pit and that they would advise their members to accept redundancy or the option of transfer. The management claimed that the marketability of the coal had

---

[90] *Daily Post*, 21 August 1996.
[91] Observation of the author when visiting the various villages in August/September 1996.

not been a major factor in the decision on closure. The power stations and industries still had orders and they would now be supplied from other collieries.[92] Nonetheless, local Labour activists argued that the 'dash for gas' was a major factor in determining the fate of Point of Ayr. Patrick Heesom, a local Labour county councillor, initiated his own research into the viability of Point of Ayr and from the time of the closure announcement argued that the pit might have a long-term future if given the chance. But on 24 August, Graham Baines was the last man to emerge from the pit on a normal shift. It was fitting that Baines should be pictured in the local press as an image of the 'last miner'; both his father and grandfather had worked at Gresford and he was able to represent the miners of Flintshire and Denbighshire as the last of a generation of miners in north Wales.

The lodge secretary, Bernie Haniewicz, reported to local journalists that 'the pit had been there 130 years and it looks like it has finally come to an end'. Heesom was still not persuaded by the negative reports concerning the colliery and railed against those in the local Labour Party who had earlier argued in favour of the Hamilton gas terminal. He felt that his vociferous opposition to that project had been completely justified. The local MP, David Hanson, had supported the calls for a buy-out and was saddened at the outcome but felt that the local councils, the miners and local communities had done their best in fighting for the future of the coal industry in north Wales. Once again Ted McKay appeared in the local press to reopen some of the old wounds caused by the strike of 1984–5. He paid tribute to the men who had stood by the result of strike ballots and claimed that 'a fitting tribute would be the recognition of those miners who were stalwarts of the 1972 and 1974 strikes called by the union through the democratic process'.[93] This was another attack on the role of Scargill and the north Wales strike activists during 1984–5.

Heesom kept up the pressure, arguing for the retention of deep mining in north Wales, and he had the support of a number of DCLP branches. He developed a comprehensive press release, which argued that most miners did not willingly

---

[92] RJB Mining PLC press release, 23 August 1996: Patrick Heesom collection.
[93] *Daily Post*, 24 August 1996.

accept closure, contrary to the reports of RJB Mining. The document stressed that the adoption of American mining methods
had been responsible for the pit going from profit to loss in a
short period. In his view, the future of the industry relied on bulk
production, and had RJB Mining been committed to this the pit
would have remained open.[94] His allies in the local Labour Party
also felt that the company had bought the pit merely to secure
markets and not for the development of a long-term strategy for
the continuation of mining locally. The lodge felt that RJB could
have done more in terms of development but were swayed from
further action by the results of the feasibility study.[95] As with
earlier closures in the coalfield, the union still found a strategy of
defence against closures difficult to construct. The 'dash for gas'
and the rigged energy market against coal had seriously affected
the economics of the situation. Ironically, the fight to save Point
of Ayr in 1992 and 1996 was a more concerted effort than that
provided by the union over the closures of the 1960s, and a wide-
ranging support team was mobilized to press the case for coal.

Heesom, the most vocal critic of both British Coal and RJB,
went on to praise the work of Clwyd County Council in supporting the initial proposals for a workers' buy-out and ensuring that
the colliery was not closed overnight. It was clear to Heesom and
others in the NUM and NACODS that both state and private
ownership had failed to develop or indeed recognize the
potential of the colliery. From the outset, the management of
British Coal refused to listen to the arguments against adopting
American mining methods as the sole means of extraction.[96] RJB
Mining stressed to the county council that the decision had not
been based on concern for the market and offered geological
difficulties as the main reason for closure. Heesom and others
felt that the undue haste of the company in wishing to close the
pit was deliberate, as part of a desire to undermine any
comprehensive plan to save Point of Ayr. Contrary to the views
of RJB Mining, the majority of the workers felt that the 'dash for
gas' had been the central reason why the pit was closed.[97]

[94] Press release by Labour councillor, Patrick Heesom, 27 August 1996: Patrick
Heesom collection.
[95] *Prestatyn Visitor*, 29 August 1996.
[96] Interview with Patrick Heesom and Les Kelly, September 1997.
[97] Fax message from Patrick Heesom to Diane Ashton of the *Rhyl Journal*, 11
September 1996: Patrick Heesom collection.

The North Wales NUM had to decide whether to wind up its organization now that the last pit in the area had closed, or to continue to represent the thousands of retired miners who remained in the coalfield between Rhyl and Wrexham.[98] A month after the announcement of the closure, the AEC decided to continue to function for at least another two years.[99] This decision was welcomed by the miners in the Wrexham district and the villages close to Point of Ayr, as there would still be an official who could deal with outstanding and future compensation claims. Les Kelly was pleased that a number of miners were keen to transfer elsewhere and was sure that they would fit in wherever they went: 'once a miner always a miner, irrespective of where they are working'.[100] The NUM retained a working membership at the pit until the summer of 1997; miners once used to the underground environment now patrolled the surface as security guards.

Once again, the attempts by the union and local pressure groups to oppose a pit closure through existing channels of protest proved to be futile. The powerlessness of the union to pursue a different strategy in a hostile economic environment suggests that the workers themselves had little control over the outcome once the company had made a decision on closure. This raised serious doubts about the pluralist nature of British society: a concerted effort by a number of pressure groups working in unison was not enough to overcome a state-directed energy policy which discriminated against coal. It also raised questions about the strategy of relying on traditional avenues of protest in challenging the decisions of employers and the government's industrial polices.

Within what remained of the NUM in north Wales, the area secretary and others played a crucial role in advising those men opting for redundancy. Kelly retained his position on the NEC, thus keeping alive the north Wales presence in the rapidly shrinking NUM. The fifty or so men who had expressed an interest in transferring to Yorkshire still felt unsure about moving their families to a strange environment. Some Point of Ayr miners decided to take up the offer of RJB Mining and transferred.

[98] North Wales NUM minutes of trustees' meeting, 10 June 1997: NUM, Wrexham.
[99] North Wales NUM minutes of special AEC, 10 September 1996: NUM, Wrexham.
[100] *Daily Post*, 18 November 1996.

Several of them settled at the Prince of Wales Colliery in Pontefract and soon adapted to the pattern of mining life in the Yorkshire coalfield.[101]

On 23 July 1997 the *Rhyl Journal* reported that a huge blast had signalled the closure of the last coal mine in north Wales. The NUM collected the final subscriptions from its few remaining members at the site, and a chapter of industrial and political history was concluded. The centrality of the community to the culture of mining had collapsed much earlier with the closure of Hafod. But Point of Ayr had still been an industrial and political landmark on the north Wales coast that raised emotions amongst the inhabitants of the coastal villages. An archetypal mining community might have been absent, but the notion of class consciousness was no weaker than in other areas. With the financial scandals that rocked the union in 1990, the coalfield instinctively defended the union leadership. In 1992, when it was announced that thirty-one pits would close, the level of political activity in defence of jobs was unprecedented in the history of the coalfield, with support exceeding that given in the strike of 1984–5.

Point of Ayr was the first pit to experience closure under private ownership and this signalled further uncertainty for the remaining fourteen pits owned by RJB Mining. A year later, the company announced that it was to close one of the newest pits in Britain, Asfordby colliery in Leicestershire. Industry and city experts maintained that more closures would follow and that it was possible that no pits would remain by the turn of the century. Colin Godfrey, the marketing director of RJB, claimed that the company would not produce coal that it could not sell, and the bias towards gas was placing coal at a huge disadvantage.[102]

---

[101] RJB Mining initially claimed that over fifty miners were interested in a future in the Yorkshire coalfield and they arranged a visit to a number of pits. The Prince of Wales in Pontefract was the preferred option as it was close to a conurbation. David Baldwin, a young electrician, was at first enthusiastic and took up the offer of a month's trial. Nonetheless, within a matter of weeks he felt that his family would suffer, as they would not be able to settle; he opted for redundancy and remained in Prestatyn. Once the trial period was over the number of miners opting to stay on at the Prince of Wales was whittled down to a hard core. In October 1997, only eighteen north Wales miners remained in Yorkshire. Several of those deciding to stay continued to reside in north Wales, returning home at weekends. The aversion of miners to moving from their own coalfield says much about the workers' commitment to place and the power of local identity. Discussion with David Baldwin and Michael Bellis, north Wales miners who transferred to Yorkshire, December 1996.

[102] *Guardian*, 19 August 18 and October 1997.

Privatization had not saved the industry and it was clear that what was needed was government intervention to create a 'level playing field' for coal to compete with gas and other sources of energy. The Labour Party had traditionally been the vehicle for articulating the demands of the trade unions in stressing the importance of such intervention. However, New Labour under Tony Blair was no longer responsive to organized labour or even to a corporatist model of economic and social policy. The view of the north Wales miners, in the last days of Point of Ayr, was that the Labour Party offered the only route to challenging a Conservative-directed energy policy. This pragmatic approach to economic problems on the part of the miners and their union representatives had been a feature of their political culture throughout the twentieth century. The party continued to command solid support in the old mining communities of Denbighshire and Flintshire. On 16 September 1997, Blair visited Wrexham to campaign for a positive response to the Welsh devolution question and was treated like a superstar. Simon Hoggart writing in the *Guardian* illustrated this:

> To-nee! Tonee! They shouted, not just the girls waving from above Marks and Spencers, but the young lads as well. Sometimes they chanted like a football crowd; other times they were more ragged. All the time the sound bounced off the walls and boomed around the shops. This is a new phenomenon in British politics: the Prime Minster as rock star.[103]

The visit of Blair once again exposed the strength of a Labourist identity that signified more of a cultural affiliation to politics than an ideological one. To the working class of Wrexham, a Labour leader was still seen as 'one of us'. This was surprising as Blair himself, and increasingly the party he led, appeared not to share the aspirations of the unemployed, the low-paid and the trade union activists who would have formed part of the crowd in Wrexham that greeted him. Direct involvement in policy-making took second place, as the negative vote in Wrexham and Flintshire opposing Welsh devolution illustrated, but the attachment of the miners to the Labour Party, as a relationship between them and an organization which was viewed as

---

[103] *Guardian*, 17 September 1997.

representing the interests of the working class, was still strong.[104] A month later, when it was announced that Wrexham Lager, the local brewery, was to close, the director, Erwin Elkin, put the blame on 'Thatcherism'. The decline in industries such as steel and mining had led to a fall in sales of local lager.[105] Wrexham remained a town closely identified with Labour politics.

The annual meeting of the North Wales Area of the NUM on 8 July 1997 was the last, though the office in Wrexham continued to function.[106] The miners of north Wales remain, however, as a social group, and a number of institutions sustain the legacy of the industry and promote the history of the area union. From Chirk on the English border to Wrexham and along the coast to Rhyl, the area retains a political identity that has been shaped by its industrial past. The miners' institutes at Ifton, Wrexham, Rhos and Llay are frequented by a large number of former miners who have retained their political affiliation to the Labour Party. Until recently, the Bee Folk Club in Rhyl still met on Friday nights, and songs remembering strikes and lock-outs were sung by members of the local trades council and activists from 1984–5. A number of choirs remain, with miners represented in those of both Flint and Trelawnyd. The Point of Ayr Colliery Band still wins awards, though it now only contains two former miners. In a number of pubs along the north Wales coast between Flint and Rhyl one can still encounter former coal miners prepared to recall their days in the industry, the volatile relationship between trade unions, employers and the state, and their contribution to the broader pattern of British history.

The closure of Point of Ayr represented the end of an era for coal mining in north Wales. As the first pit to be closed in the new era of privatization, it suggested that there was no future for deep-mined coal in Britain. It may also signify a developing fissure in the politics of Labourism, as the 'victims' of 'Thatcherism' and industrial decline are increasingly sidelined in the policies of New Labour. One thing is certain: the miners as an organized force will no longer provide a platform for input into

[104] To the Labour voters of north-east Wales the politics of devolution were clearly unrelated to what they perceived as 'old Labour' values. It was not going to bring jobs to the area or secure the welfare state. Wrexham voted 54 per cent against and Flintshire was more emphatic with a 61 per cent 'no' vote.

[105] *Guardian*, 11 October 1997.

[106] North Wales NUM minutes of trustees' meeting, 10 June 1997: NUM, Wrexham.

the affairs of the Labour Party. Yet the traditions and perceptions of coal communities remain as a reminder of the importance of a once great industry in shaping the politics of the British
labour movement.

CONCLUSION

The history of the north Wales miners was marked by moderation and autonomy. The isolation of the coalfield and the cultural and political forces within it produced a fragile unity. This unity was sufficient to enable the NUM and the Labour Party to consolidate its presence in Denbighshire and Flintshire. Within the federal structure of the NUM, the North Wales Area was able to maintain its position, surviving the factional disputes in the union for more than thirty years. In the late 1970s this fragile unity began to unravel as each British coalfield fell victim to the rapid rate of pit closures. A decade earlier the national union managed to suppress dissent regarding the closure issue, but the rise of the left in key coalfields ensured that it would not go away. The closure question intensified divisions within and between areas of the national union. The strike in 1984–5 destroyed the power of the NUM, hastening the decline of coal as an essential energy source and of the miners as providers of political leadership to the labour movement.

The focus on north Wales in the preceding chapters has outlined three crucial areas of working-class development: the importance of local identity in influencing the growth and politics of labour organizations; the centrality of the workplace in inhibiting and promoting forms of politics that led to challenges and accommodations in relations between capital and labour; and, perhaps most significantly, the importance of Labourism as an expression of occupational identity, class consciousness and a political practice that has been at once a vehicle for collective action and a basis for divisiveness in the post-war history of the British miner.

In terms of the history of Wales, the northern coalfield challenges the dominant assumptions implicit in existing labour histories of the Principality. The stereotypical images that spring from the pages of texts on the south Wales miners are absent from the history of coal in Denbighshire and Flintshire. Divisions were exposed in mining trade unionism and in the wider community of labour politics, revealing a complex picture of Welsh working-class experiences. The one feature shared by north Wales, south Wales and other coalfields was a commitment to the ideals of the Labour Party, but otherwise the pattern of trade union education, strike activity, leftist activism and solidarity was much more diverse.

The development of trade union organization in the coal industry in general, and in north Wales in particular, was marked by continuity in terms of the politics of coal miners from the 1920s onwards. Two world wars and the growth and influence of the Labour Party cemented the commitment of the MFGB and later the NUM to the ideology and practice of Labourism. This characteristic form of politics dominated all coalfields and remained unshaken by the Communist challenge and, in Wales, by the rise of nationalism. From the outset, the developing link between union, party and community grew out of relationships in the productive process. The support for Labour in Flintshire was concentrated in industry, especially in coal. The colliery provided a forum of politicization stemming from relations between managers and men underground and the more fragile unity of trade union organization. State control of the industry in the First World War and the findings of the Sankey Commission convinced miners of the capacity of the state to pursue beneficial economic and social change. The Labour Party provided the vehicle for such a change. Miners embraced Labourism as a practical approach to solving industrial relations problems at colliery level and as a means of providing a strategy for transforming the nature of the British state.

The politics of Labourism were an inclusive ideology and a mobilizing force that enabled it to defeat movements and ideas to its left and right.[1] This was often done with the help of Communists and others further to the left of mainstream Labour. From Arthur Horner and Will Paynter of the Communist Party to Arthur Scargill and Peter Heathfield of the Labour left, the dominant ethos was one of making nationalization work and securing a role for the trade union at all levels in the industry and the wider society. Class as a vehicle of social

[1] By the time of the formation of the CP in 1920–1, Labourism had already displaced Liberalism in the MFGB as the dominant form of politics that would remain unshaken for the rest of the century.

change was central, influenced by a political consciousness that was strengthened by management/worker antipathy from the 1890s onwards. This gave impetus to the break with Liberalism that was complete amongst the north Wales miners by the 1920s. Nonetheless, owing to its lack of flamboyance as an ideology, Labourism was acceptable to trade union officials like Edward Hughes and others as a 'common-sense' solution to the problems of the coal industry and the position of the working class in British society.

Contrary to the view of a number of Marxist writers, Labourism in north Wales did not reflect a level of 'false consciousness'. In Denbighshire and Flintshire this form of politics was dependent on the work of active individuals who worked as persuaders in a hostile political environment in order to garner support for labour representation within Liberalism and, later, in the Labour Party. From the rank and file through to the district leadership, miners applied their consciousness as a class to a form of politics that reflected, and sought to improve, their experience in the workplace. Nonetheless, Labourism proved both a strength and a weakness in the future political development of the north Wales miners. Between the wars, Labourism offered a solution to the problems of the industry through state ownership and a general commitment to improve the status of the working class through the redistribution of wealth. It provided a link between the miner, the workplace, the community, the union and national politics. It did not, however, secure a durable industrial solidarity in the North Wales Area of the NUM. The fragile unity that did emerge was unable to withstand the pressures of coal economics in the post-war period.

Because of the apparently amorphous nature of Labourism as an ideology, miners could justify their positions and actions in the union by various interpretations of what Labourism was. In the 1920s, miners who defied the policies of the union by returning to work before the end of strikes and lockouts could still maintain an allegiance to the Labour Party. Members of the POAIU in the 1930s could also use Labourism as rhetoric in order to attack the left in the MFGB and the claims of the CP.[2]

---

[2]   After the strike of 1984–5, UDM members remained committed to the politics of the Labour Party and found the transition from NUM to UDM merely a rational choice as to which union could best represent their interests. The ex-delegate of the UDM from

CONCLUSION   249

After the Second World War, this became more acute as the politics of the Cold War and the perceived success of Labour nationalizations further cemented the miners to the party and thereby reduced the likelihood of embracing strategies to the left of the 'parliamentary road to socialism'.[3] During the period of intense factionalism in the NUM throughout the 1970s, both left and right regarded themselves as custodians of traditional Labour values. The contrasting figures of Gormley and Scargill are the starkest examples of the ability of miners' leaders to contest the political terrain of working-class politics by using a similar discourse of struggle and solidarity.

The nationalization of the industry in 1947 was a crucial moment in the realization of Labourist politics. Public ownership was welcomed with great optimism at all pits in north Wales. Although little changed in terms of power relations at the point of production, miners' leaders now had an enhanced position in terms of collective bargaining, and some felt that they had direct access to the government because of the link between union and party. This had a twofold effect on the politics of the miners and the NUM leadership. First, the Attlee administration fastened the union to the rhetoric of the party, and this was complemented by a fear that victory for the Conservatives would mean a return to the poverty and the despondency of the 1920s and 1930s. Second, the union was left unwilling or unable to develop alternative strategies of protest once it became a victim of

Point of Ayr Colliery regarded himself as a loyal trade unionist and a persistent Labour voter. Nonetheless, in the 1987 general election in the Mansfield constituency, the Conservative vote increased, leaving a majority of fifty-six for Alan Meale, a Scargill sympathizer. Similarly, in the Sherwood constituency, which contained a number of Nottinghamshire miners, the Conservatives retained the seat with an increased majority. Frank Haynes, the former NUM official and between 1979 and 1992 Labour MP for Ashfield, worked to minimize divisions between NUM and UDM miners in Nottinghamshire. However, due to his support for UDM miners remaining in the Labour Party and his abstention in a vote against the Tory government's Coal Bill which recognized the UDM, his NUM sponsorship was withdrawn.

[3] Although the Cold War remained important in terms of the politics of the trade union movement in general, the NUM remained largely unaffected. Communists continued to win elections, often with the support of the right, as Watson of Durham supported the election of Paynter. Horner and Paynter were regarded as giants of the movement by both wings of the union. The role of Communists in the trade unions at the level of the rank and file can be found represented in Nina Fishman's essay, 'No home but the trade union movement: Communist activists and reformist leaders 1926–1956', in Geoff Andrews, Nina Fishman, and Kevin Morgan (eds.), *Opening the Books: Essays on the Social and Cultural History of the British Communist Party* (London, 1995), pp.102–23.

Labour's industrial policies in the 1960s. In a sense, the miners had become prisoners of a politics which they had played a central role in constructing.

The commitment to Labour's pragmatism was acute in the north Wales coalfield as the union increasingly struggled to protect the industry in Denbighshire. After the initiation of public ownership, the number of strikes fell rapidly and the absence of a coherent left suggested that the miners were relatively happy with the nationalization process.[4] However, the 1960s brought a wave of pit closures that almost decimated the coalfield and left it with only two pits by 1974. The timidity of the response of the north Wales leadership to the closures of Llay Main, Hafod and Ifton exposes the depth of the commitment to moderate Labour in the coalfield and the acceptance of economic orthodoxy advanced by the Wilson government. Alf Robens as NCB chairman and a number of moderate area officials were able to minimize the impact of closures by placing the blame elsewhere and by stressing the need for a modern coal industry that would deliver higher wages to those who remained employed.[5] In essence, the basis of the unity that the miners expressed was an amalgam of 'occupational identity' and a commitment to the politics of the Labour Party. This rested uneasily in a federated union that was increasingly becoming factionalized owing to the pressures on the industry in the late 1960s.

The radicalization of particular areas of the NUM in the late 1960s, leading to the surface strikes of 1969, stemmed from two events. First, the signing of the NPLA in 1966 was favoured by the left as a way of transcending area identities. Second, the heightened rate of pit closures initiated by the Wilson government was followed by the move to the left in Yorkshire. The closures affected each constituent area differently, so transforming the politics of the union nationally. The right of the NUM was weakened by the rate of closures in the traditionally moderate north-east coalfield. The left was strengthened by the

---

[4] For figures from nationalization through to 1966, see Roy Church and Quentin Outram, *Strikes and Solidarity: Coalfield Conflict in Britain, 1889–1966* (Cambridge, 1998), pp. 82–3, 88.

[5] The rhetoric of modernization took hold from the 1950s as miners enjoyed more leisure time and higher levels of disposable income. A number of miners had the opportunity to leave the industry at this time; many did but returned for higher wages and because of familiarity with work underground.

rise of Yorkshire to being the dominant power broker on the NUM NEC: the politics of the Yorkshire Area moved leftwards and it became numerically much more important. In north Wales, support for Labour remained largely unchallenged, and the impact of the NPLA was minimal in terms of the politics of the union. Relationships underground changed little irrespective of technological advances and the union showed continuity in terms of an established route to the leadership. The 1970s, however, witnessed a transformation in terms of strike action nationally and the politics of the union locally. This owed much to individual initiative and little to changes in the labour process or the broader politics of the labour movement.

The 1972 and 1974 miners' strikes had a dramatic impact on the union, the Labour Party and the Conservatives. After their fall from office, the Conservatives in opposition started to plan their later assault on the so-called trade union problem. Within the NUM, the impetus of the strikes raised optimism on the left that increased the level of factionalism within and between the federated areas. The Labour Party gained political capital out of the strikes, but here also the left was able to mobilize and press for increasingly radical policies. In north Wales the newly elected agent, Ted McKay, began to use the power of the area and its vote on the NEC to challenge the emergence of the left. Previously, the coalfield had played only a minor part in internal disputes but had generally promoted a programme of moderation. The role of McKay was to divide the union in 1984–5, again demonstrating the ability of union leaders to influence the pursuit of militant or moderate policies depending on the local balance of power.

North Wales experienced two waves of English in-migration before the strike, but the contingent of Lancashire miners had a minimal effect on the politics of the union. In terms of the culture of particular villages, the impact was more marked. Already from the 1950s, the nature of village life in Mostyn, Ffynnongroyw, and Penyffordd was being transformed due to economic and cultural change. For the first time access to the towns of Rhyl and Prestatyn became easier and young miners enjoyed a level of disposable income that allowed them to participate in a youth culture beyond the confines of the villages. Nonetheless, the localism of particular identities led to clashes with contract workers, foreign workers and the English from Lancashire. The Lancashire miners experienced both the liberating and constraining effects of community.[6] In Wrexham the miners had been exposed to the metropolitan influence of a large town and, from the 1920s, they moved from pit to pit, undermining the cohesiveness of the traditional colliery villages. From the 1950s onwards the coalfield underwent a period of industrial and cultural change, yet particular features proved extremely durable: patriarchy, deference and localism.

The strike of 1984–5 exposed the fragile weakness of the NUM both nationally and locally, but this does not suggest that the class consciousness of the miners had been diluted or that there was an uneven level of consciousness between particular coalfields. Striking and working miners justified their positions in the language of Labourism, claiming to represent the traditions of the union. Previous activism in the Labour Party and in the NUM was not a sure guide to those who would be most committed to the strike. In north Wales, the situation was made even more divisive by the failure of the agent to promote a definite policy of support for, or opposition to, the stoppage.

Both pits were affected by their geographical separation, and the wider political cultures of Denbighshire and Flintshire had an uneven effect on the strikers at Bersham and Point of Ayr. In Wrexham, Labour organization outside the mining villages had been secure for some time. At Point of Ayr, although there was almost total commitment to Labour amongst miners, the pit was in a Conservative rural enclave that generated little support for the miners once the strike was under way. The vacillation of the area agent and the absence of a national ballot compounded the situation and ensured that the strike would be weaker in Flintshire than in Wrexham, where there was total commitment for eight months.[7]

---

[6] The notion of the 'working-class community' has been romanticized by a number of authors, especially in accounts of the strike of 1984–5. See Raphael Samuel, Barbara Bloomfield and Guy Boanas (eds.), *The Enemy Within: Pit Villages and the Miners' Strike of 1984/85* (London, 1986).

[7] Leadership remained a crucial issue for Point of Ayr formally and informally. Union officials were not active community figures because the workforce was dispersed and the faceworkers who constituted an informal leadership underground largely ignored the strike call, thereby reducing the likelihood that the majority of miners would respect picket lines.

Once again the strike demonstrated the ability of Labourism to transcend the politics of left and right in the trade union movement. A number of miners who ignored the strike call remained active in the Labour Party, as did a small number who joined the breakaway UDM. The image of miners as a cohesive occupational group, rooted in traditional notions of working-class experience, remained. In north Wales, the re-election of Scargill to the national presidency in 1988 relied on miners who had ignored the strike call in 1984. After the strike, the union became concentrated at Point of Ayr, when Bersham's closure brought coal mining in Wrexham to an end. The autonomy of the area survived, with the union retaining its position on the NEC. Lodge officials and others continued to press the claims of the north Wales miners locally and nationally.

Les Kelly worked to minimize the divisions caused by McKay in the national union and was successful in preventing the growth of the UDM at Point of Ayr. The coal crisis of 1992 led to further demoralization when the pit was included on the original list of closures. Once again, the parameters of Labourism in offering an alternative to the economic orthodoxy of the government failed to produce a strategy; perhaps this was inevitable now that the union had lost much of its potency in terms of numbers and role in the generation of power. The response of the north Wales miners in the organizing of demonstrations and petitions was admirable, though the initial optimism was soon undermined by the 'stay of execution', the work of a select committee and the eventual closure of many of the pits on the original hit-list. The subsequent closure of Point of Ayr represented the end of an era for mining in north Wales and signalled that privatization was no solution to the problems of the British coal industry.[8]

The story of the north Wales miners sheds light on a region of Britain and an area of the NUM that has been neglected so far in the writing of labour history. Their experience exposes the complexity of the relationships between miners, unions and politics, rendering claims of miners as 'archetypal proletarians' simplistic.

---

[8] Conventional projections show the coal market broadly stable to 2005, but with European Union production falling by 40 per cent and imports from outside the EU rising by two-thirds. For more details of the state of the European coal market after the British coal crisis of 1992, consult Mike Parker, *The Politics of Coal's Decline: The Industry in Western Europe* (London, 1994).

A study of the north Wales coalfield presents a revisionist picture of the nature of solidarity amongst British coal miners. The 'class consciousness' of the miners was formed by their experiences in the workplace which eventually led them to support the Labour Party. The process of politicization was not a top-down experience; miners themselves actually contributed to the dominance of Labourism and were averse to socialist strategies operating outside the tradition of union politics. Further, although social structure was important in both Denbighshire and Flintshire in affecting the development of the union and the course of labour politics, the individual was an active agent in the construction of local identities.

The miners of north Wales saw themselves as members of a class, and this shaped their political affiliations. The identity of class transcended the politics of gender and ethnicity, but only supported a fragile unity that reached no further than an electoral commitment to the Labour Party. The organizational forms that this class consciousness took offer an insight into the world of the coal miner, his family and community. The shifting parameters of labour history and the fashionable trends of academe have sought to move away from the institutional perspective in seeking answers to complex questions.[9] As the preceding chapters have highlighted, a search through the debris of working-class organizations can tell us much about the experiences of men, women and children within and beyond the workplace.

The miners and their leaders were in no doubt that the trade union movement and the Labour Party could together provide a vehicle for social transformation, despite the challenges and defeats. As A. J. Cook proclaimed in the aftermath of the 1926 lockout, 'the Miners Federation would never be broken . . . they would begin the struggle again.'[10] The mines of north Wales may have disappeared from the landscape but the memory of the industry lives on. The monument of miners at work in Wrexham town centre is a symbolic image of a past built on coal and a future that will owe much to the trade union struggles of the twentieth century.

---

[9] For methodological debates in labour history, see Lenard R. Berlanstein (ed.), *Rethinking Labor History: Essays on Discourse and Class Analysis* (Chicago, 1993); and the numerous articles in two important journals, *Labour History Review* and *Labor History*.

[10] A. J. Cook, quoted in Paul Davies, *A. J. Cook* (Manchester, 1987), p.134.

BIBLIOGRAPHY

A. Manuscript sources
B. Interviews
C. Personal collections
D. Reports and miscellaneous documents
E. Theses, dissertations and broadcasts
F. Newspapers and periodicals
G. Articles published in books and journals
H. Books

A. Manuscript Sources

Flintshire County Record Office, Hawarden
The coalfield archive is housed in one collection, National Union of Mineworkers (N. Wales Area) MSS. The material was deposited by NUM area officials between 1982 and 1997 under the catalogue numbers D/NM/1–1696. The MFGB/NUM archive is wide-ranging, including an almost complete set of district/area executive minutes from 1890 to the 1980s. Papers relating to disputes and conciliation are also well represented from periods of private and public ownership. The collection of lodge minute books is incomplete, but Point of Ayr colliery provides a lucid account of lodge affairs from the 1890s to the present, although there is a gap for much of the 1960s. The papers of all the agents of the area, consisting of letters, diaries, speeches and reminiscences are deposited. Minutes of pit consultative meetings are represented, especially for Point of Ayr, Gresford and Bersham. The collection also contains NUM circulars, compensation claims, productivity reports, colliery papers, lodge accounts, safety and welfare papers, pamphlets and restricted material relating to the miners' strike of 1984–5.

The collection of NCB material is limited, but the NUM retained copies of public inquiries, Ministry of Labour documents and papers relating to output in the Western Area of the corporation. Papers relating to other areas of the NUM also form part of the archive, including documents on the Lancashire coalfield. Papers relating to the miners and the Labour and Communist parties are held but are largely sketchy and form only a small part of the collection. Material relating to the coal industry in north Wales can also be found outside the NUM catalogues. It has been deposited by individuals and is held separately. These items include unpublished manuscripts, plans of colliery developments, and papers relating to the local political parties. The most important catalogues apart from the main archive are listed below.

D/DM/1207/1–3 Deeside Trades Council and Labour Party minute book 1948, 1962
D/DM/340/57 Leaflets issued by Shotton Communist Party

D/DM/377/1–20 East Flintshire Constituency Labour Party papers 1955, 1976
D/DM/477/1 Papers on activities of the Liberal and Communist parties in north Wales 1972, 1975
D/GR/313 Miscellaneous Labour Party papers
D/JO/1–75 Tom Jones, T&GWU papers and correspondence
D/NM/1033–44 Communist Party leaflets
D/NM/1043 East Flintshire Labour Party minutes and papers 1964–74
D/NM/1469 Wrexham Divisional Labour Party and Trades Council minutes 1974/5, 1981/2, 1985
NT/789 Transcripts of interviews with former Clwyd coal miners

National Union of Mineworkers (North Wales Area), Grosvenor Road, Wrexham
The NUM offices in Wrexham contain a complete record of MFGB/NUM National Executive minutes and reports of all the national conferences. Material relating to Point of Ayr after 1986 and subsequent privatization is also deposited. Some of the material in the NUM offices is unavailable in the county record office in Hawarden, but there is some replication. Important documents relating to the strike of 1984–5 are housed in the Wrexham office. There are plans for the remaining documents in the office to be transferred to Hawarden in due course.

Denbighshire County Record Office, Ruthin
DD/DM/334/1–11 Records of Wrexham Trades Council and Divisional Labour Party including minutes, accounts and material on Wrexham Independent Labour Party
DD/DM/698/1–28 James Idwal Jones MP papers 1924, 1970
DD/LH/272 North Wales coal owners, papers and correspondence 1929
DD/W/422–7 Plaid Cymru circulars 1960, 1968

South Wales Coalfield Collection, University of Wales, Swansea
South Wales Miners Federation minutes and files
Miner (South Wales)

National Museum of Labour History, Manchester
Miscellaneous Labour Party material relating to Wales
Newspaper cuttings on Huw T. Edwards
Communist Party material relating to Wales

National Library of Wales, Aberystwyth
Huw T. Edwards papers
Labour Party Wales archive
Robert Richards papers

B. Interviews

Although this book is largely document-based, utilizing the extensive records of the North Wales NUM, the study was complemented by an oral history project. This consisted of formal interviews and informal discussions stretching over a five-year period and involving over sixty miners and their families. Between 1995 and 2000, the author met individuals in homes, public houses, clubs, cafés and Indian restaurants. Participant observation also played its role, as the author grew up in the coalfield and worked in one of the pits between 1985 and 1992. A successful attempt was made to interview miners and their families who had worked in the various pits in the coalfield from the 1920s onwards. Nonetheless, the bulk of oral evidence was drawn from the miners of pits that were nationalized after 1947: Llay Hall, Llay Main, Hafod, Ifton, Black Park, Bersham, Point of Ayr and Gresford. A number of interviews also took place with members of local Labour Party branches and members of miners' support groups. Labour Members of Parliament, local councillors and miners from other British coalfields also provided information. The interview methodology took a number of forms, including structured questionnaires, open discussions and telephone conversations.

C. PERSONAL COLLECTIONS

Bellis, Tony (North Wales NUM)
Beynon, Huw (Cardiff University)
Davies, Albert (North Wales NUM)
Heesom, Patrick (Clwyd County Council)
Hett, Ann (Bersham Miners' Support Group)
Hett, Kieth (North Wales NUM)
Howell, David (University of York)
Hughes, Albert (NACODS North Wales)
Jones, Keith (TGWU, Cardiff)
Kelly, Les (North Wales NUM)
Kemp, Steve (NUM Yorkshire)
Newell, Colin (North Wales NUM)
Parry, Heather (North Wales NUM)
Parry, Paul (North Wales NUM)
Read, Jack (North Wales NUM)
Walsh, John (NUM Yorkshire)
Williams, Jimmy (North Wales NUM)

D. REPORTS AND MISCELLANEOUS DOCUMENTS

Barclay, Christopher, *The Coal Industry Bill* [Bill 4 1993/4] (Update. This replaces 93/118) Research Paper 94/7 17, January 1994. Science and Research Environment Section, House of Commons Library (Patrick Heesom collection)
Colliery Official, a, 'Future of Britain's coalmines: nationalisation or not?' 1943 (NUM, Wrexham)
DTI Coal Review (November 1992) (Patrick Heesom collection)
Flint Divisional Labour Party Circulars (Patrick Heesom collection)
Nawaz, Mahmud, 'The Coal Industry: A Quantitative Analysis', Research Paper 94/98, 17 January 1994. Social and General Statistics Section, House of Commons Library (Patrick Heesom collection)
NCB Circular: 'News from the coal industry 1967' (NUM, Wrexham)
NUM information bulletins 1948–9 (NUM, Wrexham)
Rees, T. M. Haydn, 'The case for the redevelopment of the mining industry with particular reference to Gresford', Clwyd County Council, 1973 (NUM, Wrexham)

Robens, Lord, 'Nationalised coal policies: an address on the policies of a nationalised industry in relation to the government, trade unions, private enterprise, and the consumer', 1963 (NUM, Wrexham)

Robens, Lord, 'Address by Lord Robens to the Institute of Metals', 11 March 1969 (NUM, Wrexham)

Siddall, Norman, 'Winning horses', a paper given to NCB production staff conferences, autumn 1967 (NUM, Wrexham)

E. Theses, dissertations and broadcasts

BBC Wales, 'A rock and a hard place' (1993)

Gildart, Keith, 'The social and political development of the north Wales Miners 1945–96' (University of York, D.Phil. thesis, 1998)

Holloway, Frank, 'Industrial Flintshire in the interwar years' (University of Wales, Ph.D. thesis, 1979)

Hughes, Edward, 'My recollections at Point of Ayr colliery from 1887–1898', unpublished manuscript, 1924 (CRO Flintshire)

Hughes, Gwilym, 'My life at Point of Ayr colliery', unpublished manuscript, 1974 (in possession of author)

Northall, Helen, 'Point of Ayr Industrial Union, 1926–44' (University of Wales, BA Hons. Dissertation, 1979)

Venn, Sally, ' Labour politics in north east Wales: a study of the North Wales Miners Association, 1898–1947' (University of Wales, MA thesis, 1994)

Zweiniger-Bargielowska, Ina-Maria, 'Industrial relationships and nationalization in the south Wales coalmining industry' (University of Cambridge, Ph.D. thesis, 1989)

F. Newspapers and Periodicals

Bersham Star: for striking miners and supporters (CRO Flintshire)
Birmingham Mail
Chester Chronicle
Coal News
Colliery Guardian
Colliery Yearbook
Daily Mirror
Daily Post
Daily Telegraph
Evening Leader
Financial Times
Flintshire County Herald
Flintshire Observer
Guardian
Hansard
Independent
Labor History
Labour History Review
Liverpool Daily Post
Marxism Today

Miner
Miner (South Wales Miners' Federation) (Miner's Library, Swansea)
Mold, Deeside and Buckley Leader
Morning Star
New Statesman and Society
News Chronicle
News Line
North Wales Miners Magazine (CRO Flintshire)
Point of Ayr Half Yearly Magazine (CRO Flintshire)
Point of Ayr Pioneer (CRO Flintshire)
Prestatyn Visitor
Prestatyn Weekly
Rhos Herald
Rhyl and Prestatyn Gazette
Rhyl Journal
Shropshire Star
Socialist Worker
Sunday Times
Red Kite: Newsletter for a Democratic Left in Wales
The Times
Transport and General Workers Record
Western Mail
Wrexham Leader

G. ARTICLES PUBLISHED IN BOOKS AND JOURNALS

Anderson, Perry, 'Origins of the present crisis', *New Left Review*, 23 (1963), 26–53
Benson, John and Neville, Robert, 'A bibliography of the coal industry in Wales', *Llafur: Journal of the Society for the Study of Welsh Labour History*, 2, 4 (1979), 78–91
Beynon, Huw, 'The miners' strike at Easington', *New Left Review*, 148 (1984), 104–15
Brody, David, 'Labour relations in American coal mining: an industry perspective', in Gerald D. Feldman and Klaus Tenfelde (eds.), *Workers, Owners and Politics in Coal Mining: An International Comparison of Industrial Relations* (Oxford, 1990)
Broomfield, Stuart, 'The apprentice boys strikes of the Second World War', *Llafur: Journal of Welsh Labour History*, 3, 2 (1981), 53–67
Burge, Alun, 'The Mold riots of 1869', *Llafur: Journal of Welsh Labour History*, 3, 3 (1982), 42–57
Campbell, Alan, Fishman, Nina and McIlroy, John, 'The post-war comprehensive: mapping industrial politics, 1945–64', in Campbell, Fishman, McIlroy (eds.), *British Trade Unions and Industrial Politics: The Post-War Compromise, 1945–64* (Aldershot, 1999)
Church, Roy A., 'Employers, trade unions and the state, 1889–1987: the origins and decline of tripartism in the British coal industry', in Gerald D. Feldman and Klaus Tenfelde (eds.), *Workers, Owners and Politics in Coal Mining: An International Comparison of Industrial Relations* (Providence, RI, 1990), 12–73
——, Outram, Quentin and Smith, David, 'The militancy of British miners 1893–1986: interdisciplinary problems and perspectives', *Journal of Interdisciplinary History*, 22, 1 (1991), 49–66

Egan, David, 'The Unofficial Reform Committee and the *Miners' Next Step*', *Llafur: Journal of the Society for the Study of Welsh Labour History*, 2, 3 (1978), 64–80

Ellis, Tom, 'Death of a colliery', *Denbighshire Historical Transactions*, 21 (1972), 94–108

Evans, Neil and Jones, Dot, ' "To help forward the great work of humanity": women in the Labour Party in Wales', in Tanner, Williams and Hopkin (eds.), *The Labour Party in Wales, 1900–2000* (Cardiff, 2000)

Fishman, Nina, 'No home but the trade union movement: Communist activists and reformist leaders 1926–1956', in Geoff Andrews, Nina Fishman and Kevin Morgan (eds.), *Opening the Books: Essays on the Social and Cultural History of the British Communist Party* (London, 1995).

Francis, Hywel, 'Emlyn Williams (1921–1995)', *Llafur: Journal of Welsh Labour History*, 7, 1 (1996), 5–7

Gildart, Keith, 'Men of coal: miners' leaders in north-east Wales, 1890–1961, *Llafur: Journal of Welsh Labour History*, 8, 1 (2000), 111–29

——, 'Militancy, moderation and the struggle against company unionism in the North Wales Coalfield 1926–44', *Welsh History Review*, 20, 3 (2001), 532–64

Harries, P. H. G., 'Cwmllynfell colliery: an early attempt to form a workers' co-operative', *Llafur: Journal of Welsh Labour History*, 7, 2 (1997), 41–51

Howell, David, 'The 1984/85 miners' strike in north Wales', *Contemporary Wales*, 4 (1991), 67–98

——, 'Wilson and history: 1966 and all that', *Twentieth Century British History*, 4, 2 (1993), 174–87

Hughes, Edward, 'My recollections at Point of Ayr Colliery, 1887–1890', *Llafur: Journal of Welsh Labour History*, 2, 4 (1979), 38–53

Hyman, Richard, 'Reflections on the mining strike', *Socialist Register* (1985/6), 330–54

Jones, Bill, Roberts, Brian and Williams, Chris, ' Going from darkness to light: south Wales miners' attitudes towards nationalisation', *Llafur: Journal of Welsh Labour History*, 7, 1 (1996), 96–110

Jones, Melvyn, 'Long-distance migrants and cultural identity: the example of a Welsh colony in south Yorkshire', *Journal of the British Association for Local History*, 26, 4 (1996), 223–36

Jones, R. Merfyn, 'A note on 1926 in north Wales', *Llafur: Journal of Welsh Labour History*, 2, 2 (1977), 59–64

——, 'Notes from the margin: class and society in nineteenth century Gwynedd', in D. Smith (ed.), *A People and a Proletariat: Essays in the History of Wales, 1780–1980* (London, 1980)

Jones-Evans, P., 'Evan Pan Jones – land reformer', *Welsh History Review*, 4 No. 2 (1968), 143–60

Laidlaw, Roger, 'The Gresford disaster in popular memory', *Llafur: Journal of Welsh Labour History*, 6, 4 (1995), 123–39

Lockwood, D. 'Sources of variation in working class images of society', *Sociological Review*, 14, 3 (1966), 249–67

McAllister, Ian, 'The Labour Party in Wales: the dynamics of one-partyism', *Llafur: Journal of Welsh Labour History*, 3, 2 (1981), 79–89

McIlroy, John and Campbell, Alan, 'Still setting the pace? Labour history, industrial relations and the history of post-war trade unionism', *Labour History Review*, 64, 2 (1999), 179–99

McLean, Iain, 'On moles and the habits of birds: the unpolitics of Aberfan', *Twentieth Century British History*, 8, 3 (1997), 285–309

Nairn, Tom, 'The English working class', *New Left Review*, 27 (1964), 43–57

Pryce, W. T. R., 'Language areas in north-east Wales, *c.*1800–1911', in Jenkins (ed.), *A Social History of the Welsh Language: Language and Community in the Nineteenth Century* (Cardiff, 1998)

Pye, Sylvia, 'The great British miners' strike of 1985–86', in Marat Moore (ed.), *Women in the Mines: Stories of the Life and Work* (New York, 1996)

Rimlinger, G., 'International difference in the strike propensity of coal miners: experience in four countries', *Industrial and Labour Relations Review*, 12, 3 (1959), 389–405

Rogers, Emlyn, 'The history of trade unionism in the coal mining industry of north Wales to 1914' (unpublished University of Wales MA thesis, 1928)

——, 'Labour struggles in Flintshire, 1830–1850', *Transactions of the Denbighshire Historical Society*, 5 (1953), 14–15

——, 'The development of trade unionism in the north Wales coalfield to 1914', *Transactions of the Denbighshire Historical Society*, 12–23 (1963–74): vol. 12, 110–35; vol. 13, 219–40; vol. 14, 209–34; vol. 15, 132–57; vol. 16, 100–27; vol. 17, 147–76; vol. 18, 113–35; vol.19, 188–216; vol. 20, 184–204; vol. 21, 74–93; vol. 22, 236–46; vol. 23, 238–63

——, 'The Union Society of the miners of Rhosllanerchrugog and its neighbourhood, 1876–1901', *Transactions of the Denbighshire Historical Society*, 22 (1973), 236–46

Samuel, Raphael, and Stedman Jones, Gareth, 'The Labour Party and social democracy', in Samuel and Jones (eds.), *Culture, Ideology, Politics: Essays for Eric Hobsbawm* (London, 1982)

Saville, John, 'An open conspiracy: Conservative politics and the miners' strike 1984/85', *Socialist Register* (1985/6), 295–329

——, 'Labourism and the Labour government', *Socialist Register* (1967), 43–71

——, 'Britain: prospects for the 1970s', *Socialist Register* (1970), 203–15

——, 'The ideology of labourism', in Benewick, Berki and Parekh (eds.), *Knowledge and Belief in Politics: The Problem of Ideology* (London, 1973)

Scargill, Arthur, 'The new unionism', *New Left Review*, 92 (1975), 3–33

Thompson, E. P., 'The peculiarities of the English', *Socialist Register* (1965), 311–62

Williams, Chris, 'The South Wales Miners' Federation', *Llafur: Journal of Welsh Labour History*, 5, 3 (1990), 45–56

Williams, David Lee, 'A healthy place to be? The Wrexham coalfield in the interwar period', *Llafur: Journal of Welsh Labour History*, 7, 1 (1996), 87–95

Zweiniger-Bargielowska, Ina-Maria, 'South Wales miners' attitudes towards nationalisation: an essay in oral history', *Llafur: Journal of Welsh Labour History*, 6, 3 (1994), 70–84

——, 'Miners' militancy: a study of four south Wales collieries during the middle of the twentieth century', *Welsh History Review*, 16, 3 (1993), 356–83

H. BOOKS

Addison, Paul, *The Road to 1945* (London, 1975)

Adeney, Martin and Lloyd, John, *The Miners' Strike of 1984/85: Loss without Limit* (London, 1986)

Allen, Vic, *Trade Union Leadership: Based on a Study of Arthur Deakin* (London, 1957)

Idem, The Militancy of British Miners (Shipley, 1981)

Anderson, Perry, *English Questions* (London, 1992)

Andrews, Geoff, Fishman, Nina and Morgan, Kevin (eds.), *Opening the Books: Essays on the Social and Cultural History of the British Communist Party* (London, 1995)

Arble, Meade *A Coal Miners Journal* (New York, 1976)

Arnison, Jim *The Shrewsbury Three: Strikers, Pickets and 'Conspiracy'* (London, 1974)

Arnot, Robin Page, *The Miners* (London, 1949)

——, *The Miners: Years of Struggle* (London, 1953)

——, *The Miners: In Crisis and War* (London, 1961)

——, *The Miners: One Union, One Industry* (London, 1979)

Austin, Tim (ed.), *The Times Guide to the House of Commons 1997* (London, 1997)

Baylies, Carolyn, *The Yorkshire Miners: The History of the Yorkshire Miners, 1881–1918* (London, 1993)

Beaton, Lynn, *Shifting Horizons* (London, 1985)

Beckett, Francis, *The Enemy Within: The Rise and Fall of the British Communist Party* (London, 1995)

Bellamy, Joyce M. and Saville, John (eds.), *Dictionary of Labour Biography*, vol.1 (London, 1972)

—— (eds.), *Dictionary of Labour Biography*, vol.2 (London, 1974)

Benewick, Richard, Berki, R. N. and Parekh, Bhikhu (eds.), *Knowledge and Belief in Politics: The Problem of Ideology* (London, 1973)

Berlanstein, Lenard R. (ed.), *Rethinking Labor History: Essays on Discourse and Class Analysis* (Illinois, 1993)

Beynon, Huw (ed.), *Digging Deeper: Issues in the Miners' Strike* (London, 1985)

Beynon, Huw and Austrin, Terry, *Masters and Servants: Class and Patronage in the Making of a Labour Organisation, the Durham Miners and the English Political Tradition* (London, 1994)

Brophy, John, *A Miner's Life* (Madison, 1964)

Brown, Colin, *Fighting Talk: The Biography of John Prescott* (London, 1997)

Bulmer, Martin, *Mining and Social Change: Durham County in the Twentieth Century* (London, 1978)

Callinicos, Alex, *Theories and Narratives: Reflections on the Philosophy of History* (Cambridge, 1995)

Callinicos, Alex and Simons, Mike, *The Great Strike: The Miners' Strike of 1984/85 and its Lessons* (London, 1985)

Campbell, Alan, Fishman, Nina and Howell, David (eds.), *Miners, Unions and Politics, 1910–1947* (Aldershot, 1996)

Campbell, Alan, Fishman, Nina and McIlroy, John (eds.), *British Trade Unions and Industrial Politics: The Post-War Compromise, 1945–64* (Aldershot, 1999)

——, (eds.) *British Trade Unions and Industrial Politics: The High Tide of Trade Unionism, 1964–79* (Aldershot, 1999)

Campbell, Beatrix, *Wigan Pier Revisited: Poverty and Politics in the Eighties* (London, 1984)

Campbell, John, *Edward Heath: A Biography* (London, 1993)

Challinor, Raymond, *The Lancashire and Cheshire Miners* (Newcastle, 1972)

Church, Roy and Outram, Quentin, *Strikes and Solidarity: Coalfield Conflict in Britain, 1889–1996* (Cambridge, 1998)

Cliff, Tony and Gluckstein, Donny, *The Labour Party: A Marxist History* (London, 1988)

Coates, Ken and Brown, Michael Barratt, *The Blair Revelation: Deliverance for Whom?* (Nottingham, 1996)

——, *Community under Attack: The Struggle for Survival in the Coalfield Communities of Britain* (Nottingham, 1997)

Cohen, G. A., *Karl Marx's Theory of History: A Defence* (Oxford, 1978)

Conway, Alan (ed.), *The Welsh in America: Letters from Immigrants* (Cardiff, 1961)

Coombes, B. L., *These Poor Hands: The Autobiography of a Miner Working in South Wales* (London, 1939)

Crewe, Ivor and King, Anthony, *SDP: The Birth, Life and Death of the Social Democratic Party* (Oxford, 1997)

Crick, Michael, *Scargill and the Miners* (Harmondsworth, 1985)

——, *The March of Militant* (London, 1986)

Curtis, Tony (ed.), *Coal: An Anthology of Mining* (Bridgend, 1997)

Davies, A. J., *To Build a New Jerusalem: The British Labour Party from Keir Hardie to Tony Blair* (London, 1996)

Davies, Paul, *A. J. Cook* (Manchester, 1987)

Dennis, Norman, Henriques, Fernando and Slaughter, Clifford, *Coal is Our Life: An Analysis of a Yorkshire Mining Community* (London, 1956)

Derickson, Alan, *Workers' Health, Workers' Democracy: The Western Miners' Struggle, 1891–1925* (Ithaca, 1988)

Dodd A. H. (ed.), *A History of Wrexham* (Wrexham, 1989)

Dodd A. H. (ed.), *The Industrial Revolution in North Wales* (Wrexham, 1990)

Dorey, Peter, *The Conservative Party and the Trade Unions* (London, 1995)

Douglass, David John, *Pit Sense versus the State: A History of the Militant Miners in the Doncaster Area* (London, 1994)

Dubofsky, Melvyn and Van Tine, Warren, *John L. Lewis: A Biography* (Chicago, 1986)

Edwards, Huw T., *It Was My Privilege* (Denbigh, 1957)

——, *Hewn from the Rock* (Cardiff, 1967)

Eliot, Gregory, *Labourism and the English Genius: The Strange Death of Labour England* (London, 1993)

Ellis, Tom, *Miners and Men: Mining Engineering* (London, 1971)

Evans, E. W., *Mabon (William Abraham, 1842–1922): A Study in Trade Union Leadership* (Cardiff, 1959)

Evans, Richard J., *In Defence of History* (London, 1997)

Fagge, Roger, *Power, Culture and Conflict in the Coalfields: West Virginia and South Wales, 1900 –22* (Manchester, 1996)

Farman, Christopher, *The General Strike: May 1926 Britain's Aborted Revolution?* (London, 1974)

Feldman, Gerald and Tenfelde, Klaus (eds.), *Workers, Owners and Politics in Coal Mining: An International Comparison of Industrial Relations* (Oxford, 1990)

Fevre, Ralph and Thompson, Andrew (eds.), *Nation, Identity and Social Theory: Perspectives from Wales* (Cardiff, 1999)

Fielding, Steve, Thompson, Peter and Tiratsoo, Nick, *England Arise: The Labour Party and Popular Politics in 1940s Britain* (Manchester, 1995)

Fine, Ben, *The Coal Question: Political Economy and Industrial Change from the Nineteenth Century to the Present Day* (London, 1990)

Fine, Bob and Millar, Robert (eds.), *Policing the Miners' Strike* (London, 1985)

Foot, Michael, *Aneurin Bevan, 1897–1945* (London, 1982)

Foote, Geoffrey, *The Labour Party's Political Thought: A History* (London, 1985)

Francis, Hywel, *Miners Against Fascism: Wales and the Spanish Civil War* (London, 1984)

Francis, Hywel and Smith, David, *The Fed: A History of the South Wales Miners in the Twentieth Century* (London, 1980; new edition: Cardiff, 1998)

Galloway, Robert, *Annals of Coal Mining and the Coal Trade*, vol.2 (England, 1971)

Gamble, Andrew, *The Free Economy and the Strong State: The Politics of Thatcherism* (Oxford, 1989)

Garside, W. R. *The Durham Miners, 1919–1960* (London, 1971)

Gibbs, Colin, *Clatter of Clogs* (Bersham, 1990)

Gilbert, David, *Class, Community and Collective Action: Social Change in Two British Coalfields, 1850–1926* (Oxford, 1992)

Goodman, Geoffrey, *The Miners' Strike* (London, 1985)

Gormley, Joe, *Battered Cherub* (London, 1982)

Gramsci, Antonio, *The Prison Notebooks* (London, 1981)

Green, Penny, *The Enemy Without: Policing and Class Consciousness in the Miners' Strike* (London, 1990)

Gregory, Roy, *The Miners in British Politics, 1906–1914* (Oxford, 1968)

Griffin, Colin, *The Leicestershire Miners, 1914 –1988* (London, 1989)

Griffiths, James, *Pages from Memory* (London, 1969)

Griffiths, Robert, *S. O. Davies: A Socialist Faith* (Llandysul, 1983)

Harrison, Royden (ed.), *Independent Collier: The Coal Miner as Archetypal Proletarian Reconsidered* (Brighton, 1978)

Haslam, Dave, *Manchester England: The Story of the Pop Cult City* (London, 1999)

Heffer, Eric, *Labour's Future: Socialist or SDP Mk 2* (London, 1986)

Idem, Never a Yes Man: The Life and Politics of an Adopted Liverpudlian (London, 1993)

Hennessy, Peter, *Never Again: Britain, 1945–51* (London, 1992)

Hett, Keith, *Bersham Pit Bottom and Other Poems* (private publication, 1986)

Hinton, James, *Labour and Socialism: A History of the British Labour Movement, 1867–1974* (Brighton, 1983)

Hobsbawm, Eric, *The Forward March of Labour Halted* (London, 1981)

——, *On History* (London, 1998)

Hodges, Frank, *My Adventures as a Labour Leader* (London, 1925)

Holland, John, *The History and Description of Fossil Fuel: The Collieries, and Coal Trade of Great Britain* (London, 1968)

Horner, Arthur, *Incorrigible Rebel* (London, 1960)

Howell, David, *British Social Democracy: A Study in Development and Decay* (London, 1976)

——, *British Workers and the Independent Labour Party, 1888–1906* (Manchester, 1983)

——, *A Lost Left: Three Studies in Socialism and Nationalism* (Manchester, 1986)

——, *The Politics of the NUM: A Lancashire View* (Manchester, 1989)

——, *The British Coal Crisis, 1992–93* (York Papers in Politics and Policy, no. 2)

Hughes, John and Moore, Roy (eds.), *A Special Case? Social Justice and the Miners* (Harmondsworth, 1972)

Hutton, Will, *The State We're In* (London, 1995)

Irving, Terry (ed.), *Challenges to Labour History* (Australia, 1994)

James, Arnold J and Thomas, E., *Wales at Westminster: A History of the Parliamentary Representation of Wales, 1800–1979* (Llandysul, 1981)

Jenkins, Geraint H. (ed.), *A Social History of the Welsh Language: Language and Community in the Nineteenth Century* (Cardiff, 1998)

Jenkins, Keith, *The Postmodern History Reader* (London, 1997)

Jenkins, Roy, *A Life at the Centre* (New York, 1991)

Jevons, Stanley, *The British Coal Trade* (London, 1915)

Jones, Bill and Williams, Chris, *B. L. Coombes* (Cardiff, 1999)

——, (eds.), *With Dust Still in His Throat: A B. L. Coombes Anthology* (Cardiff, 1999)

Jones, Gareth Stedman, *Languages of Class: Studies in English Working Class History, 1832–1982* (Cambridge, 1983)

Jones, Lewis, *Cwmardy: The Story of a Welsh Mining Valley* (London, 1937)

Jones, Lewis, *We Live: The Story of a Welsh Mining Valley* (London, 1939)

Jones, Mervyn, *A Radical Life: The Biography of Megan Lloyd George* (London, 1991)

Jones, R. Merfyn, The *North Wales Quarrymen, 1874–1922* (Cardiff, 1982)

Jones, Thomas, *A Diary with Letters, 1931–1950* (London, 1969)

Jones, William D., *Wales in America: Scranton and the Welsh, 1860–1920* (Cardiff, 1993)

Kavanagh, D. and Seldon, A. (eds.), *The Thatcher Effect* (Oxford, 1990)

Kaye, Harvey J., *The British Marxist Historians* (Oxford, 1984)

Kaye, Harvey J. and McClelland, Keith (eds.), *E. P. Thompson: Critical Perspectives* (Cambridge, 1990)

Kirby, M. W., *The British Coalmining Industry, 1870–1946* (London, 1977)

Kogan, David and Kogan, Maurice, *The Battle for the Labour Party* (Glasgow, 1982)

Kornhauser, Arthur, Dubin, Robert and Ross, Arthur, M., *Industrial Conflict* (New York, 1954)

Lawson, Jack, *A Man's Life* (London, 1932)

——, *Peter Lee* (London, 1936)

——, *The Man in the Cloth Cap: The Life of Herbert Smith* (London, 1941)

Lerry, G. G., *The Collieries of Denbighshire: Past and Present* (Wrexham, 1968)

Lightman, Gavin, *The Lightman Report* (London, 1989)

Livingstone, Ken, *If Voting Changed Anything They'd Abolish It* (London, 1987)

MacFarlane, L. J., *The British Communist Party: Its Origins and Development until 1929* (London, 1966)

MacGregor, Ian with Rodney Tyler, *The Enemies Within: The Story of the Miners' Strike, 1984/85* (Glasgow, 1986)

Macintyre, Stuart, *Little Moscows: Communism and Working Class Militancy in Interwar Britain* (London, 1980)

Mandelson, Peter and Liddle, Roger, *The Blair Revelation: Can New Labour Deliver?* (London, 1996)

Marriott, John, *The Culture of Labourism: The East End between the Wars* (Edinburgh, 1991)

Marwick, Arthur *The Sixties: Cultural Revolution in Britain, France, Italy and the United States, c. 1958–c. 1974* (Oxford, 1998)

Masterman, Len, *Television Mythologies: Stars, Shows and Signs* (London, 1984)

McKibbin, Ross, *Ideologies of Class: Social Relations in Britain, 1880–1950* (Oxford, 1986)

McSmith, Andy, *John Smith: Playing the Long Game* (London, 1993)

——, *Faces of Labour: The Inside Story* (London, 1997)

Meyer, Anthony, *Stand Up and Be Counted* (London, 1990)

Miliband, Ralph, *Parliamentary Socialism: A Study in the Politics of Labour* (London, 1973)

Miller, Jill, *You Can't Kill the Spirit: Women in a Welsh Mining Valley* (London, 1986)

Milne, Seamus, *The Enemy Within: The Secret War against the Miners* (London, 1994)

Minkin, Lewis, *The Contentious Alliance: Trade Unions and the Labour Party* (Edinburgh, 1971)

——, *The Labour Party Conference: A Study in Intra-Party Democracy* (Manchester, 1980)

Moffat, Abe, *My Life with the Miners* (London, 1965)

Moore, Marat (ed.), *Women in the Mines: Stories of Life and Work* (New York, 1996)

Moore, Robert, *Pit-Men, Preachers and Politics* (Cambridge, 1974)

Morgan, K. O., *Rebirth of a Nation: Wales, 1880–1980* (Oxford and Cardiff, 1981)

——, *Labour in Power, 1945–1951* (Oxford, 1984)

——, *Labour People: Leaders and Lieutenants, Hardie to Kinnock* (Oxford, 1992)

——, *Callaghan: A Life* (Oxford, 1998)

Morgan, Kevin, *Against Fascism and War: Ruptures and Continuities in British Communist Politics, 1935–41* (Manchester, 1989)

Morgan, W. John and Coates, Ken, *The Nottinghamshire Coalfield and the British Miners' Strike, 1984/85* (Derby, n.d.)

Morris, Margaret, *The General Strike* (London, 1976)

Neuman, Andrew Martin, *Economic Organisation of the British Coal Industry* (London, 1934)

Noel, Gerard, *The Great Lock-Out of 1926* (London, 1976)

Osmond, John, *Creative Conflict: The Politics of Welsh Devolution* (Llandysul, 1977)

—— (ed.), *The National Question Again: Welsh Political Identity in the 1980s* (Llandysul, 1985)

Ottey, Roy, *The Strike: An Insider's Story* (London, 1985)

Panitch, Leo and Leys, Colin, *The End of Parliamentary Socialism: From New Left to New Labour* (London, 1997)

Parker, Mike, *The Politics of Coal's Decline: The Industry in Western Europe* (London, 1994)

Parker, Tony, *Red Hill: A Mining Community* (London, 1986)

Parry, Cyril, *The Radical Tradition in Welsh Politics: A Study of Liberal and Labour Politics in Gwynedd, 1900–1920* (Hull, 1970)

Paynter, Will, *My Generation* (London, 1972)

Pelling, Henry, *The Origins of the Labour Party, 1880–1900* (Oxford, 1966)

Pimlott, Ben, *Harold Wilson* (London, 1992)

Pitt, Malcolm, *The World on Our Backs: The Kent Miners and the 1972 Miners' Strike* (London, 1979)

Political and Economic Planning Group, *Report on the British Coal Industry: A Survey of the Current Problems of the British Coal Industry and the Distribution of Coal, with Proposals for Reorganisation* (London, 1936)

Powell, David, *The Power Game: The Struggle for Coal* (London, 1993)

——, *What's Left: Labour Britain and the Socialist Tradition* (London, 1998)

Pretty, David A., *The Rural Revolt That Failed: Farm Workers' Trade Unions in Wales, 1889–1950* (Cardiff, 1989)

Pugh, Jane, *A Most Expensive Prisoner: Tom Jones Rhosllannerchrugog's Biography* (Wales, 1988)

Reed, David and Adamson, Olivia, *Miners Strike, 1984/85: People versus State* (London, 1985)

Reid, Jimmy, *Reflections of a Clyde Built Man* (London, 1976)

Richards, Andrew J., *Miners on Strike: Class Solidarity and Division in Britain* (Oxford, 1997)

Robens, Lord, *Ten Year Stint* (London, 1972)

Routledge, Paul, *Scargill: The Unauthorised Biography* (London, 1994)

Samuel, Raphael, Bloomfield, Barbara and Boanas, Guy (eds.), *The Enemy Within: Pit Villages and the Miners' Strike of 1984/85* (London, 1986)

Samuel, Raphael and Jones, Gareth Stedman (eds.), *Culture, Ideology, Politics: Essays for Eric Hobsbawm* (London, 1982)

Saunders, Jonathan, *Across Frontiers: International Support for the Miners' Strike, 1984/85* (London, 1989)

Saville, John, *The Labour Movement in Britain* (London, 1988)

Scott, W. H., Mumford, Enid, McGivering, F. C. and Kirby, J. M., *Coal and Conflict: A Study of Industrial Relations at Collieries* (Liverpool, 1963)

Seddon, Vicky (ed.), *The Cutting Edge: Women and the Pit Strike* (London, 1986)

Seifert, Roger and Unwin, John, *Struggle without End: The 1984/85 Miners' Strike in North Staffordshire* (Newcastle under Lyme, 1988)

Seyd, Patrick and Whiteley, Paul, *Labour's Grass Roots: The Politics of Party Membership* (Oxford, 1992)

Shaw, Eric, *Discipline and Discord in the Labour Party* (Manchester, 1988)

Shepherd, Robert, *Enoch Powell: A Biography* (London, 1996)

Sirs, Bill, *Hard Labour* (London, 1985)

Skidelsky, R., *Thatcherism* (London, 1988)

Smith, David (ed.), *A People and a Proletariat: Essays in the History of Wales, 1780–1980* (London, 1980)

Smith, Ned, *The 1984 Miners' Strike: The Actual Account* (Kent, 1997)

Sopel, Jon, *Tony Blair: The Moderniser* (London, 1995)

Stead, Jean, *Never the Same Again: Women and the Miners' Strike* (London, 1987)

Sutcliffe, Lesley and Hall, Brian, *Let Them Eat Coal: The Political Use of Social Security during the Miners' Strike* (London, 1985)

Tanner, Duncan, Williams, Chris and Hopkin, Deian (eds.), *The Labour Party in Wales, 1900–2000* (Cardiff, 2000)

Taylor, Andrew, *The Politics of the Yorkshire Miners* (London, 1984)

Thomas, W. Gerwyn, *Welsh Coal Mines* (Cardiff, 1976)

Thompson, E. P., *The Making of the English Working Class* (London, 1963)

Thompson, Willie, *The Good Old Cause: British Communism, 1920–1991* (London, 1992)

Thurcroft, The People of, *Thurcroft: A Village and the Miners' Strike – An Oral History* (Nottingham, 1986)

Waddington, David, Jones, Karen and Critcher, Chas, *Flashpoints: Studies in Public Disorder* (London, 1989)

Walker, Peter, *Trust the People* (London, 1987)

Waller, Robert, *The Dukeries Transformed: The Social and Political Development of a Twentieth Century Coalfield* (Oxford, 1983)

Watkins, Harold M., *Coal and Men: An Economic and Social Study of the British and American Coalfields* (London, 1934)

Widgery, David (ed.), *The Left in Britain, 1956–68* (London, 1976)

Wiffen, John S. *Gresford's Bevin Boys: A Wartime Miner's Experiences Underground in North Wales* (Corwen, 1991)

Williams, Chris, *Democratic Rhondda: Politics and Society, 1885–1951* (Cardiff, 1996)

———, *Capitalism, Community and Conflict: The South Wales Coalfield, 1898–1947* (Cardiff, 1998)

Williams, E. J., *The Derbyshire Miners* (London, 1962)

Williams, Emlyn, *George: An Early Autobiography* (London, 1961)

Williams, Gwyn, *When Was Wales? A History of the Welsh* (London, 1985)

Williams, Philip M. (ed.) *The Diary of Hugh Gaitskell, 1945–56* (London, 1983)

Williamson, Stanley, *Gresford: The Anatomy of a Disaster* (Liverpool, 1999)

Winterton, Jonathan and Winterton, Ruth, *Coal, Crisis and Conflict: The 1984/85 Miners' Strike in Yorkshire* (Manchester, 1989)

Wood, Leslie W. *A Union to Build: The Story of UCATT* (London, 1979)

Young, Hugo, *One of Us: A Biography of Margaret Thatcher* (London, 1989)
Zweig, F., *Men in the Pits* (London, 1949)

INDEX

Aberfan, 72–3
Aberystwyth, 40
Abraham, William (Mabon), 1, 2, 102
Acrefair, 124
Alders, Frederick, 85
Allen, Vic, 54, 71, 77, 79–80, 117, 142
Alyn and Deeside, 183
Anglesey, 46
Asfordby, 204, 242
Associated Society of Engineers and
    Firemen (ASLEF), 168, 170
Attlee, Clement, 20, 35, 36, 82, 249

Bagillt, 12, 14, 183
Baines, Graham, 239
Barnsley, 175
Barnsley West and Penistone, 214
Barron, Kevin, 212
Begley, Mark, 227
Bell, Trevor, 148, 149–50, 151, 197
Bellis, Tony, 80
Benn, Tony, 142, 206
Bersham, 26, 27, 28, 44, 45, 50, 52, 53,
    58, 59, 61, 62, 66, 73, 74, 76, 77, 84,
    87, 89, 93, 101, 102, 113, 116, 117,
    121, 124, 125, 127, 128–9, 130–1,
    137–8, 141, 143, 144, 148, 149, 155,
    157, 159, 163, 164, 165, 168, 169,
    172, 173–80, 182, 185, 186, 188,
    191, 194–5, 196, 225, 252, 253
Bersham Star, 176
Bettisfield, 7, 14, 16, 31
Bevan, Aneurin, 1, 33, 34, 36, 200
Bevanites, 33, 36
Bevin boys, 48–9
British Insulated Calendar's Cables
    (BICC), 86
Bickershaw, 104
Birch, Nigel, 32, 35, 36–7, 38, 82, 84, 114
Birmingham, 115
Black Lane, 27
Black Park, 9, 26, 29, 43, 44, 48, 54, 56–8,
    82, 96, 99
Blair, Tony, 232, 233, 234, 243
Bolton, 193
Boyds, 218, 226

Boyds Report, 218–19
Bradford, 102, 104, 105, 106
British Association of Colliery
    Management (BACM), 96, 123, 236
British Celanese, 114
British Coal, 196, 197, 198, 202, 203,
    204–5, 209, 210, 214, 215, 216, 217,
    222, 223, 225, 227, 228–9, 230, 231,
    232, 236, 240
Brussels, 185
Brymbo, 7, 124, 126
Brynkinallt, 9, 12
Brynmally, 18
Buckton, Ray, 168
Burnley, 89, 155, 166, 180

Caernarfon, 46
Callaghan, James, 146, 152, 153
Cambrian Combine strike (1910–11), 33
Campaign for Nuclear Disarmament
    (CND), 36
Cardiff, 200
Caribbean, 46
Carr, Robert, 115
Chadburn, Ray, 148, 151
Cheetham, Lynne, 185
Chester, 7, 19, 40, 42, 78, 101, 176, 188
Chester Chronicle, 134
Chirk, 7, 9, 29, 56, 58, 99, 101, 103, 194,
    244
Chirk Green, 99
Churchill, Winston, 36–7
Citrine, Walter, 29
Clapham, Mick, 214, 218
Clarke, John Alfred, 97
Clwyd, Ann, 225
Clwyd County Council, 225, 237, 240
Coal Authority, 229
Coal Industry Bill, 84
Coal News, 138, 204, 215
Cokemen's Union, 200
Cold War, 21, 36, 41, 43, 69, 249
Communism, 2, 27, 33, 38–9, 48, 49, 71,
    84, 127, 133, 135, 147
Communist Party (CP), 21, 36, 37, 38,
    39–43, 49, 64, 69, 71, 74, 102–3,